101 Best Resumes

101 Best Resumes

JAY A. BLOCK
MICHAEL BETRUS

McGraw-Hill
New York San Francisco Washington, D.C. Auckland Bogotá
Caracas Lisbon London Madrid Mexico City Milan
Montreal New Delhi San Juan Singapore
Sydney Tokyo Toronto

Library of Congress Cataloging-in-Publication Data

Block, Jay A.
101 best resumes / Jay A. Block, Michael Betrus.
p. cm.
Includes index.
ISBN 0-07-032893-5 (pbk.)
1. Résumés (Employment) I. Betrus, Michael. II. Title.
HF5383.B534 1997
808′.06665—dc21 96-49936
CIP

McGraw-Hill

A Division of The ***McGraw-Hill*** *Companies*

1 2 3 4 5 6 7 8 9 0 AGM/AGM 9 0 0 9 8 7 6 5

ISBN 0-07-032893-5 (pbk.)

The sponsoring editor for this book was Betsy Brown, the editing supervisor was Fred Dahl, and the production supervisor was Suzanne W. B. Rapcavage. It was set in New Century Schoolbook by Inkwell Publishing Services.

Printed and bound by Quebecor / Martinsburg.

Contents

Alphabetical Listing of Resumes*

**Editor's Note:* We acknowledge that most, but not all, of the resumes in the book are in alphabetical order. Therefore, the preceding list is provided as a quick reference to finding the resume you need.

Introduction

The new realities of securing employment in today's changing world require a new belief. That belief is that searching for a job is a thing of the past. Designing your career and taking a proactive, self-directed approach is the success formula for today and tomorrow.

You would be surprised at how many competent professionals fail to regard a resume as a critical success factor. They will "throw something together" to get it over with and then hope for an interview. *A resume is critical to your success!* It is the only way for a prospective employer to initially evaluate you, just as a large corporation weeds out college graduates by their grade point averages. It may be unfair, but that is how the game is played. The employment screening process is so subjective that you will need any edge you can gain on your competition. There are still far too many poorly designed resumes. This book will help ensure that yours is not one of them.

Research shows that most people don't like the word "search." When they think of the word "search," they think of *searching* for the proverbial needle in the haystack. How do you feel when you lose your wallet and have to *search* for it? How do you feel when you're *searching* for misplaced car keys and you're running late for an important appointment? The answer: not very good. You feel panicked, hysterical, and completely out of control. The same feelings hold true for more of us who *search* for a job.

On the other hand, when we *design* our future, chart a course, and take responsibility for securing a satisfying job, we feel "in control." And, to be sure, personal control is the name of the career design game. In today's competitive world, it isn't smart to wait for the perfect job to be posted in the classified section of the newspaper and then compete for it with thousands of other candidates, or wait, with fingers crossed, for an employment recruiter or headhunter to call. Nor is it advisable to sit idly by the phone and hope employers will respond to a mass mailing of 500 or even 5,000 resumes. Instead what you want to do is strategically plan, orchestrate, and implement a well-conceived career design campaign that meets your specific needs.

So from this point on, "job search" is out and "career design" is in, and your dynamic resume must reflect your career aspirations. The resume is a critical part of your career design. Although no one gets hired solely on the basis of a resume, many job seekers miss even the interviewing opportunity because of an inadequate resume. Through careful planning you can make your resume the most important part of your career design.

101 Best Resumes offers you the best resumes from *the* top experts—the people who write resumes every day for a living. The top resume writers in the country have pooled their expertise to create 101 of the absolute best resumes available anywhere. Written by members of the Professional Association of Resume Writers, this book offers street-smart tips and cutting-edge techniques on resume writing, as well as insider advice on how to create resumes and cover letters that will help you land the job you want!

Jay A. Block
Michael Betrus

Acknowledgments

A very special thanks to Frank X. Fox, Founder and Executive Director of the Professional Association of Resume Writers. Without his vision and commitment to the resume writing industry in particular, and to the employment industry in general, this book and the wealth of knowledge that is contained in this book, would not have been possible.

I would like to acknowledge and thank the following certified members of PARW for their contributions to this publication. Collectively, 26 professionals produced 69 resumes to complement the author's 32 documents. In this way, the reader is introduced to a wide selection of resumes produced by certified professionals, nationwide.

	Pages That Resumes Appear on
1. Baskin, Beverly, MA, NCC, CPRW Baskin Business and Career Services Woodbridge, Princeton, and Marlboro, NJ (800) 300-4079	62, 72, 94, 123, 130, 153
2. Benedict, Alesia, CPRW Career Objectives Rochelle Park, NJ (800) 206-5353	67, 85, 86, 96, 126
3. Berkowitz, Mark D., NCCC, CPRW Career Development Resources Yorktown Heights, NY (914) 962-1548	148
4. Blahnik, Sheila M., CPRW Business World Norcross, GA (770) 279-5400	176
5. Culp, Carla L., CPRW Best Impression Resume Writing & Design Edwardsville, IL (618) 692-4090	78
6. Dallmann, Barbie, CPRW Happy Fingers Word Processing & Resume Service Charleston, WV (304) 345-4495	66, 137
7. Davis, Becky J., PLS, CPRW Connections Secretarial Services Waterville, ME (207) 872-5999	128
8. Deihl, Darby, CPRW D'Scribe Resumes Irving, TX (972) 556-1945	82, 138, 165, 177
9. Dib, Deborah W., CPRW Advantage Resumes of New York Medford, NY (516) 475-8513	56, 70, 116, 155, 160, 169
10. Driesslein, Marta L., CPRW Cambridge Career Services Knoxville, TN (423) 539-9538	49, 80, 150
11. Evans, Jonathan, CPRW Career Support Services Amherst, MA (413) 253-5700	118, 172

Pages That Resumes Appear on

12. Enelow, Wendy S., CPRW — 52, 88, 90, 100, 124
The Advantage, Inc.
Lynchburg, VA
(804) 384-4600

13. Franke, Julianne S., MS, CPRW — 171
Career Development & Resume Center
Lilburn, GA
(770) 381-9407

14. Harvey, Beverly, CPRW — 46, 71
Beverly Harvey Secretarial Services
Orange City, FL
(904) 775-0916

15. Higgins, Susan, CPRW — 108, 135
Q Resume Service
Plain City, OH
(614) 873-3123

16. Karvonen, Nancy, CPRW — 99
A Better Word & Resume
Willits, CA
(707) 459-4066

17. Kasler, Melissa L., CPRW — 51
Resume Impressions
Athens, OH
(614) 592-3993

18. Klint, Ann, CPRW — 64, 156
Ann's Professional Resume Service
Tyler, TX
(903) 509-8333

19. Kursmark, Louise, CPRW — 139
Best Impression
Cincinnati, OH
(513) 792-0030

20. Saburn, Sandy A., CPRW — 161
Coastal Resume Writers
Wilmington, NC
(910) 395-5500

21. Schuette, Walt, CPRW — 104, 136, 144
The Village WordSmith
Fallbrook, CA
(800) 200-1884

22. Schuster, Deborah L., CPRW — 54, 59, 68, 134, 158, 167
The Lettersmith Writing & Design
Newport, MI
(313) 586-3335

23. Siwatu, Makini, CPRW — 120
Accent on Words
Belmont, CA
(415) 595-2514

24. Suarez, John A., CPRW — 77, 110, 115, 145, 175
The Resume Center
O'Fallon, IL
(618) 624-0707

25. Whitcomb, Susan Britton, CPRW — 83, 111, 122, 178
Alpha Omega Resume Services
Fresno, CA
(209) 222-7474

26. Youngquist, Matthew B., CPRW — 114, 117, 159
Moore & Associates
Seattle, WA
(206) 224-7612

1

How to Use This Guide

This guide offers a variety of tools for you. We will review the different sections and components of a resume. We will review different resume formats, and which to use for various occasions. The largest portion of the book is dedicated to showcasing the best resumes that members of the Professional Association of Resume Writers have created for their clients. Every resume has been produced by a Certified Professional Resume Writer and was actually used by a client.

We have done enough research on this subject to know that most people buy a book like this for the sampling it provides, and the instruction that accompanies it may or may not be read. So, if you choose not to read the guidelines we have set forth, please consider the following tips in using the book:

- Even if a particular sample resume is not in your area of expertise, we feel you will benefit by looking it over anyway. It may include an appealing format or approach you may like. For example, many different headlines and title styles are sampled.
- Take a good look at the box of hints for a given resume. We've tried to make it easy for you to see the strategy the Certified Professional Resume Writer used in designing that resume.
- Notice the relaxed writing style in the cover letters. Try not to write in too stiff or formal a manner.
- Really look over "Tips to Get You Hired" starting on page 181. They will provide you with savvy tips you won't find anywhere else.

Again, look at the many sample resumes provided by the Certified Professional Resume Writers. Whatever you do for a living, you should still look at the formats of *all* the resumes for ideas on layouts, different ways of writing, and the impact of including graphics and clip art in your resume. The resumes also exemplify a variety of different ways that people have utilized the "5 P's" you will learn about in Chapter 6.

2

Finding Job Openings

There are several primary sources of job leads:

- Networking
- Contacting companies directly
- Classified advertisements
- Executive recruiters and employment agencies
- Online services

Other sources include trade journals, job fairs, college placement offices, and state employment offices. One of the most difficult tasks in life is securing work and planning a career. A career is important to everyone, so you must create a plan of action utilizing more than one of the career design strategies at the same time.

NETWORKING

The buzzword of the 80s and 90s has been networking—connecting with people. Networking *is* people-connecting and when you connect with people you begin to assemble your network. Once your network is in place, you will continue to make new contacts and communicate with established members. People in your network will provide advice, information, and support in helping you to achieve your career goals and aspirations.

Networking accounts for up to 70% of the new opportunities uncovered. So what is networking? Many people assume they should call all the people they know, personally and professionally, and ask if they know of any companies that are hiring. A successful networker's approach is different.

A successful networker starts by listing as many names as possible on a sheet of paper. These can include family, relatives, friends, coworkers and managers (past and present), other industry contacts, and anyone else you know. The next step is to formulate a networking presentation. Keep in mind it need not address potential openings. In networking the aim is to call your contacts asking for career or industry advice. The point is, you're now positioning yourself not as a desperate job hunter, but as a *researcher.*

It is unrealistic that you will go far asking people for advice like this:

> *John, thanks for taking some time to talk with me. My company is likely to lay people off next month and I was wondering if your company had any openings or if you know of any?*

This person hasn't told John what he does, has experience in or wants to do. John is likely to respond with a *"No, but I'll keep you in mind should I hear of anything."* What do you think the odds are John will contact this person again?

A better approach is to ask for personal or industry advice and work on developing the networking web:

> *John, Amanda Mancini at BMI suggested I give you a call. She and I have worked together for some time, and she mentioned you work in finance and are the controller of Allied Sensors. I work in cost accounting and feel you'd likely be able to offer some good career advice. I'd really appreciate some time. Could we get together for lunch some time in the next week or so?*

You have now asked for advice, not a job. People will be much more willing to help someone who has made them feel good about themselves or who appears to genuinely appreciate their help. This strategy can be approached in many ways. You can ask for: job search advice (including resume or cover letter advice); overall career advice (as shown above); industry advice; key contacts they may know; information about various companies/people/industries; other people they may know. It is important that the person you network through likes you. When someone gives you a reference, it is a reflection of that person. They will not put themselves at personal or professional risk if they aren't confident you will be a good reflection on them. Finally, send each person you speak with a thank-you letter. That courtesy will be remembered for future contacts.

CONTACTING COMPANIES DIRECTLY

Aren't there one or two companies you've always been interested in working for? Ideally you may know someone who will introduce you to key contacts there or inform you of future openings. The best way to get introduced to a targeted company is to have a current employee personally introduce you or make an introductory phone call for you. You could make the introduction and reference the employee you know. We'll get into this later, but if you don't know anyone at a targeted company, a recruiter may be a good source of contact for you, even if it involves no job order for them.

You could send an unsolicited resume, but the likelihood of this materializing is low. Most large profile companies receive thousands of resumes a year, and few are acted on. Corporate recruiters Jackie Larson and Cheri Comstock, authors of *The New Rules of the Job Search Game,* don't regard mass mailed resumes very seriously. Part of the problem is that too many resumes are written as past job descriptions and are not *customized* toward a targeted position.

Conrad Lee, a retained Boca Raton recruiter, believes "information is the most important thing in contacting companies directly. Don't call just one person in the company and feel that is sufficient. That person may have their own job insecurities or be on a performance improvement plan. You should contact five to ten people and only then can you say you contacted that company directly." New job search strategies all suggest targeting a select few smaller companies (under 750 employees, as larger companies are still downsizing) intensely rather than blanketing a thousand generically. Contacting the head of your functional specialty in that company is a good start. Is it hard? Of course. You're facing rejection, probably feeling like you're bothering busy people, begging or maybe even feeling inferior. Would you feel inferior if you were calling hotels and ticket agencies for Super Bowl information? Of course not. What if some can't help you? You just get back on the phone until you achieve your goal. These contacts should be approached the same way. You have a great product to sell—yourself. Position yourself as someone of value and as a product that can contribute to the target company.

The key is to position yourself for individual situations. This requires specialized letters, resumes, and strategies tailored for each situation.

CLASSIFIED ADVERTISING

When you depend on classified advertisements to locate job openings you limit yourself to only 7–10%, or less, of all available jobs, plus you are competing with thousands of job hunters who are reading the same ads. Keep in mind that the majority of these ads are for lower-wage positions. Do not disregard the classifieds, but at the same time, don't limit your options by relying too heavily on them. Answering ads is more effective at lower levels than higher. An entry-level position or administrative support position is more likely to be found using this method than a director's position. But it is easy to review advertisements. Check the local paper listings on Sunday, the paper of the largest metropolitan area near where you live, and even a few national papers like the *Wall Street Journal* (or their advertisement summary, *The National Business Employment Weekly*) or the *New York Times.*

You may gain company insight by looking at the ads that don't necessarily match your background. You may see an ad that says "Due to our expansion in the Northeast we are looking for ..." You have just learned of an expanding company that may need you. Review papers that have good display ads like the *Los Angeles Times, The Chicago Tribune,* or any other major Sunday edition.

EXECUTIVE RECRUITERS AND EMPLOYMENT AGENCIES

Employment agencies and executive recruiters work for the hiring companies, not for you. There are thousands of employment agencies and executive recruiters nationwide. Employment agencies generally place candidates in positions with a salary range under $40,000. Executive recruiters place candidates from temporary service at the administrative or executive level to permanent senior-level management. Recruiters can be a great source of hidden jobs, even if they do not have a position suitable for you at a given time.

Recruiters and agencies will have a greater chance of successfully locating a position for you if your professional discipline is of a technical or specific nature, such as accounting, engineering, or sales. The most comprehensive listing of executive recruiters is McGraw-Hill's *Guide to Executive Recruiters* by Michael Betrus.

ONLINE SERVICES

Information technology is changing the way job seekers locate employment opportunities. Job hunters are now connecting with hiring authorities electronically. Thousands of astute individuals have already tapped into these powerful new technologies (databases, electronic bulletin boards on the Internet, and other online employment services) to help them achieve their career goals.

One of the most comprehensive publications on this subject is *The Online Job Search Companion* by James Gonyea (McGraw-Hill). In general, though, the sources for job leads online are the Career Center in America Online, the classifieds in Compuserve, and the various newsgroups on the Internet (keywords are "jobs" or "employment"). You will notice that the great majority of the job leads seen are very technical in orientation (engineering, programming, etc.). However, they are inexpensive to access and you may identify a lead through E-mail contact with hiring managers or other job seekers.

All of the above methods are excellent and necessary in your career design.

3

Taking an Inventory of Your Skills

Have you ever known a highly successful sales professional who didn't have a firm grasp and knowledge of his or her product? Ask any experienced salesperson what the secret to success is and they'll say that it's knowing the product, knowing the customer, and matching the benefits of the product to the needs of the customer. This is a powerful success formula.

The job search is a sales and marketing endeavor. There is simply no way around this: *You* are the product, *you* are the salesperson, and *you* must define your customers and promote yourself to them. So, like the highly successful salesperson, the key to your success is to know your product (you) inside and out, and match the benefits of the product to the needs of your potential customers (prospective employers). In sales, we call this selling features and benefits. You must know the features of the product, known as *marketable skills,* and determine what specific benefits result from those features that would interest a prospective employer. In other words, the only reason for someone to hire you is for the benefit you offer that person or company. If an interviewer were to ask you what your strengths are, what skills you bring to the table, or what contributions you feel you could make to the company, he is actually asking you to identify your features and the benefit that the company would realize by hiring you.

In order to effectively communicate the features and benefits of the product, namely you, you must first take an inventory of your skills. In the simplest of terms, there are three categories of skills:

- Job-related skills
- Transferable skills
- Self-management skills

JOB-RELATED SKILLS

There are four categories of job-related skills: 1) working with people, 2) working with data and information, 3) working with things, and 4) working with ideas. Though most of us work with all four categories at one time or another, we tend to be attracted to one or two areas in particular. Successful teachers, customer service representatives, and salespeople must be particularly skilled at working with people. Financial controllers, weathermen, and statistical forecasters possess outstanding skills in working with data and information. Engineers, mechanics, and computer technicians enjoy using their skills to work with things, and inventors, writers, and advertising professionals must have solid creativity and idea skills.

Which category do you tend toward? *You need to determine which job-related skills you are strongest in and which you enjoy the most. Then write a brief paragraph stating why you feel you are skilled and qualified to work with the category you selected.*

TRANSFERABLE SKILLS

Transferable skills are just that—transferable from one environment to another. If you enjoy working with people, your specific transferable skills might include leadership, training, entertainment, mentoring, mediation, persuasion, public speaking, conflict resolution, or problem-solving skills. If you enjoy working with data and information, your specific transferable skills might include research, analysis, proofreading, editing, arranging, budgeting, assessing, measuring, evaluating, surveying, or pricing. If you enjoy working with things, your specific transferable skills might include knowledge of equipment, repair, maintenance, installation, set-up, troubleshooting, or building. And finally, if you enjoy working with ideas, your specific transferable skills might include creating, developing, reengineering, restructuring, painting, writing, problem solving, planning, or brainstorming.

So take fifteen minutes, sit down with a pen and paper and write down all the skills and abilities you possess *that have value to another company.* Transferable skills are marketable and tangible qualifications that will have value to many organizations. An accountant, human resources manager, or logistics manager at General Motors has tangible transferable skills that are of value to many companies both in and out of the automotive industry.

SELF-MANAGEMENT SKILLS

Self-management skills are skills that are personality and value oriented. Self-management skills are those that describe your attitude and work ethic. They include creativity, energy, enthusiasm, logic, resourcefulness, productive competence, persistence, adaptability, and self-confidence. One cautionary note, however: *Try not to be too general in describing your self-management skills.* When you identify a specific skill, always be prepared to explain how that skill will benefit a prospective employer. For example, if you're analytical, how does that make you better prepared for a position you have designed for yourself?

When you identify and recognize your skills, you begin to know your product. If you know your product inside and out, you will never be caught off guard in an interview. In fact, you will be able to reinforce your value by emphasizing specific accomplishments you've achieved in the past, using those specific skills.

In summary, writing a powerful resume requires that you identify your marketable skills because they represent the heart of the resume. Your ability to confidently sell yourself in an interview despite stiff competition depends on knowing your skills and communicating the benefits of those skills to the interviewer. Strategic resume preparation begins with identifying what you have to offer based on where you plan to market yourself. It is the foundation for developing a powerful resume, and will be the foundation of successful interviewing as well.

4
What Is a Resume?

The resume is the driving force behind career design. Ironically, it's not the resume itself that is critical; it's the energy, planning, strategy, and commitment behind the resume. For a professional athlete or actor it's the preparation that makes or breaks the performance. In career design, the effort that goes into the preparation of your resume will play a major role in the outcome of your campaign. If you invest quality time and energy in developing a comprehensive and focused resume, you'll get quality results! On the other hand, if you put your resume together without much thought or reason, simply writing down your life's story and distributing it to potential employers, chances are you'll experience less than impressive results. In fact, you'll probably end up in the unenviable position of joining the 80% club—those who are dissatisfied with their jobs.

The resume is the driving force of career design if it is constructed in a strategic and methodical manner. With this in mind, let's define resume. Webster defines it as "a statement of a job applicant's previous employment experience, education, etc." This definition is hardly adequate, so let us offer you a clear and concise definition.

> *A resume is a formal written communication, used for employment purposes, notifying a potential employer that you have the skills, aptitude, qualifications, and credentials to meet specific job requirements. A successful resume is a marketing tool that demonstrates to a prospective employer that you can solve his problems or meet her specific needs, and thus, warrant an employment interview in anticipation of being hired.*

In order to demonstrate that you can meet the needs of employers, you must have specific goals and objectives. Too many job seekers have vague, ambiguous, or uncertain career goals. They say, "I want a good paying job with a progressive organization," or "I'm open to most anything." Forget that approach! You wouldn't say to a travel agent, "I'd like to go on a vacation somewhere interesting," or "I'm open to most anything." The age-old question applies: "If we don't know where we're going, how will we ever get there, or know when we've arrived?" There is no doubt that the quality of your career—the quality of your life—is a matter of choice and not a matter of chance *only if a choice is made.*

How does all this tie into writing resumes? There are only two types of resumes that have proven to be effective in career design, and most people use neither type. If you took every resume in circulation today and put them end to end, they would circle the earth over 26 times. That amounts to about 650,000 miles of resumes. And here is a statistic that is truly astonishing: Approximately 98% of all resumes being circulated today don't do justice to the candidates they describe. In other words, most of the resumes are autobiographical in nature, describing just the background and experience of a candidate. The problem with autobiographical resumes is that they simply don't work.

Hiring managers and personnel professionals don't read resumes for education or entertainment. The bottom line is this: If you can identify an employer's needs or problems and *explicitly* demonstrate that you can fill those needs or effectively solve those problems, you'll be interviewed and eventually hired. It's logical and makes good common sense. In Chapter 5 we'll explain which resumes work, and why.

5

Successful Styles and Formats for Resumes

Here are the two types of resumes that are powerful and that work:

- The Targeted Resume
- The Inventory Resume

If you know the job classification and/or the industry or environment in which you want to work, you are a candidate for a **targeted resume.** In essence, you can identify (target) what you want to do either by job title, by industry, or both.

If you are a generalist, open to a number of options or unable to clearly identify what you want to do but able to identify your marketable skills, you are a candidate for an **inventory resume.** An inventory resume promotes one's marketable skills to a diversified audience.

TARGETED RESUME

If you know your target audience, you must create a resume that emphasizes your skills, abilities, and qualifications that *match* the needs of your target. Position the text on your resume to match the job requirements as closely as possible. For example, if you're seeking a sales position but are not fussy about what industry you sell in, you would identify the key assets and value that you bring to the table. Five such assets might be:

1. Possessing exceptional closing skills.
2. Having an active network in place that would be especially enticing to a future employer who is looking for a candidate to ignite a sudden surge of new business.
3. Having been trained by a reputable company so a new learning curve is literally nonexistent.
4. A proven and verifiable track record of specific sales accomplishments.
5. The ability to turn around a flat and phlegmatic territory into a flourishing one.

The problem with most resumes, according to hiring authorities, is that people simply list responsibilities. You will seldom be hired based on past responsibilities, but *you have an excellent chance of being hired based on former accomplishments*.

INVENTORY RESUME

If you cannot clearly identify your target, then your resume should highlight your accomplishments and skills in a more generic manner. What benefits will a prospective employer receive in return for employing you? What skills do you bring to the table that will enhance and contribute to his or her organization?

Let's take the example of a branch manager of a bank who is making a career change. He might have five specific skills that he can market to any number of industries, so he would develop an inventory resume with a portfolio of inventory assets that might include the following:

1. Solid sales and marketing skills.
2. Excellent financial and budgeting skills.
3. Training and development abilities.
4. Seasoned operations management skills.
5. Strong computer aptitude.

After advertising these specific skills on the resume, the balance of the document would focus on specific achievements in these five areas.

Regardless of which resume type you choose, you must incorporate pertinent information that addresses the needs, concerns, and expectations of the prospective employer or industry. Samples of both resume types are included in this book.

COMMUNICATING CRITICAL MESSAGES

A resume must communicate *critical messages*. What are critical messages? A resume is a 30-second advertisement. Understanding that, critical messages are likened to "hot buttons," using marketing terminology. Critical messages are messages that the reader of your resume needs to read. They ignite enthusiasm and eventual action—which is an interview.

Career design is an exercise in self-marketing, and it's okay to be creative and to get excited about your future. When it comes to marketing yourself, there is just one ironclad rule for resume writing, and here it is:

There can be no spelling or typographical errors, and the resume must be well organized and professionally presented, consistent with the industry you are pursuing.

That's it! Yes, brief is better, 1 to 2 pages unless you have a very unique situation. And today, many successful career designers are incorporating graphics in their resumes, packaging them in a vibrant, exciting, and professional manner. For the first time, career designers are getting enthusiastic and excited about their resumes. After all, if *you* can't get excited about your resume, how do you expect anyone else to get excited about it?

So to this end, there are two main objectives to a resume. The obvious one is that the resume is a hook and line, luring a prospective employer to take the bait and invite you to an interview. And the second objective of the resume is to get you pumped up, and prepare you for the interview and the process of securing a job.

RESUME FORMATS

Chronological Format

The chronological format is considered by many employment professionals and hiring authorities to be the resume format of choice because it demonstrates continuous and upward career growth. It does this by emphasizing employment history. A chronological format lists the positions held in a progressive sequence, beginning with the most recent and working back. The one feature that distinguishes the chronological format from the others is that under each job listing, you communicate your 1) responsibilities, 2) skills needed to do the job, and, most importantly, 3) specific achievements. *The focus is on time, job continuity, growth and advancement, and accomplishments.*

Functional Format

A functional format emphasizes skills, abilities, credentials, qualifications, or accomplishments at the beginning of the document, but does not correlate these characteristics to any specific employer. Titles, dates of employment, and employment track record are deemphasized in order to highlight qualifications. *The focus is squarely on what you did, not when or where you did it.*

The challenge of the functional format is that some hiring managers don't like it. The consensus seems to be that this format is used by problem career designers: job hoppers, older workers, career changers, people with employment gaps or academic skill-level deficiencies, or those with limited experience. Some employment professionals feel that if you can't list your employment history in a chronological fashion, there must be a reason and that reason deserves close scrutiny.

Combination Format

This format offers the best of all worlds—*a quick synopsis of your market value (the functional style), followed by your employment chronology (the chronological format).* This powerful presentation first addresses the criteria for a hire—promoting your assets, key credentials, and qualifications, supported by specific highlights of your career that *match* a potential industry or employer's needs. The employment section follows with precise information pertaining to each job. *The employment section directly supports the functional section.*

The combination format is very well received by hiring authorities. The combination format actually enhances the chronological format while reducing the potential stigma attached to functional formats. This happens when the information contained in the functional section is substantive, rich with relevant material that the reader wants to see, and is later supported by a strong employment section.

Curriculum Vitae (CV)

A curriculum vitae (CV) is a resume used mostly by those professions and vocations in which a mere *listing of credentials* describes the value of the candidate. A doctor, for instance, would be a perfect candidate for a CV. The CV is void of anything but a listing of credentials such as medical schools, residencies performed, internships, fellowships, hospitals worked in, public speaking engagements, and publications. In other words, *credentials do the talking.*

The Resumap

The resumap is a new format that clearly breaks with tradition. The writing of the resume is a left-brain exercise where thoughts occur in a rational, analytical, logical, and traditional manner. By engaging the right brain in this endeavor (the creative, imaginative, and stimulating side of the brain), the resume becomes a more dynamic document. Examples of the resumap are found on pages 58, 109 and 110.

HOW TO SELECT THE CORRECT FORMAT

Consider using a chronological format if you have an impeccable work history and your future ties to your past. Contemplate using a combination format if you have few deficiencies in experience, education, or achievements. Consider a functional format if you are a student, returning to the workforce after an extended absence, changing careers, have worked many jobs in a short period of time, have had employment breaks, or have any other history that would make using a chronological or combination format challenging. Feel free to use a CV if your credentials speak for themselves and no further information is required of you until the interview. Use a resumap when you want to be different and make a statement.

In the end, exercise common sense and design a resume that best promotes *you.* There are no rules, only results. Select the format that will afford you the best chance of success.

6

The 5 P's of Resume Writing

Now it's time to review the 5 P's of an explosive resume:

- Packaging
- Positioning (of information)
- Punch, or Power Information
- Personality
- Professionalism

PACKAGING

Packaging is a vital component to sales success. Most people wouldn't think of purchasing something from a store if the packaging was slightly broken. Paper stock, graphics, desktop publishing, font variations, and imaginative presentations and ideas are part of the packaging process. Most resumes are prepared on white, ivory, or gray paper. Conforming may be a recipe for disaster, so make your resume "professionally" stand out from the crowd. You'll want to remain professional and, in some cases, on the conservative side. There are various paper styles and presentation folders that are professional but unique, and provide a competitive edge. Office supply stores or your local printer will be a good source of different paperstocks.

POSITIONING OF INFORMATION

Positioning means organization. Organize the data on your resume so that it's easily accessible to the reader and the reader is able to quickly grasp significant information. You need to create a section of the resume (the Introduction, as we'll discuss later) where the key information will be displayed. In other words, by creating a highly visible section within the resume, you manipulate the reader's eyes to hone in on information that you deem essential to getting an interview. By doing this you make the best use of the hiring authority's ten to twenty seconds of review time.

You can have the best credentials in the world, backed by a powerful personality, complemented by the strongest references, but these career-making credentials are useless if your resume is sloppy, poorly organized, and difficult to read. No matter how superior you are to your competition, the prospective employer will almost never read a poorly presented document.

PUNCH OR POWER INFO

This "P" is by far the most important. When you deliver the Punch, you deliver the information that the hiring manager wants to see. It means that you are supplying the reader with *Power Info*. Power Info is information that *matches a career designer's skills, abilities, and qualifications to a prospective employer's needs.* Quite simply, Power Info is delivering the knockout Punch, indicating to a prospective employer that you meet the criteria for hire.

The employer's task is to locate candidates whose overall credentials and background meet his or her needs. Your task is to demonstrate, in your resume and later during an interview, that you have what he or she is looking for. So the starting point of all career design resumes is projecting and anticipating hiring criteria. You need to be aware of the types of people who will be reviewing your resume. Furthermore, you must determine what kind of information he or she seeks that will provide you with a clear competitive advantage and spark enough interest to warrant an interview.

The challenge for so many people writing resumes is to directly address the concerns of hiring authorities. The challenge is to get into the hiring person's head. What is he or she thinking? What does he or she want? What can you show him or her that will make him or her react? In many instances, it's specific, quantifiable achievements.

This is a good time to emphasize the importance of noting specific accomplishments on your resume. The fact that you were responsible for doing something in a past job in no way assures anyone that you were successful! If your resume is full of generalities, responsibilities, and job descriptions, and lacks specific successes and achievements, how do you expect a prospective employer to differentiate your resume from the other 650,000 miles of documents? The majority of attention should be placed on your accomplishments and achievements. Responsibilities don't sell. Benefits, results and success sell. What you were responsible for in the past has little impact on your future. *What you specifically accomplished highlights your past and determines your hireability.*

PERSONALITY

Hiring managers want to hire people with pleasing personalities. Your resume can have its own personality. Packaging can convey a unique personality and so can words. We are suggesting that by the use of sumptuous vocabulary, you can turn a rather dull sentence into a more lavish and opulent one. Substitute the word "ignited" for "increased." Change the term "top producer" to "peak performer." Instead of "being responsible for something," show that you were "a catalyst for major improvements in...."

Remember, words are power. Make use of the more than 750,000 available to you in the English language. A resume does not have to be a lackluster instrument. Lighten up and let your resume dance a bit, sing a little, and entertain the reader. By displaying a personality, you display emotion. And more than any other single element, emotion sells!

PROFESSIONALISM

Countless hiring managers believe that how a person presents himself or herself professionally will determine how professionally one will represent their company. We purchase expensive clothing, practice good hygiene, and make sure we look our very best when going to an interview because we want to make a good, lasting, and professional first impression. The resume must do the same. Once again, you are the product and you are the salesperson. Your resume is your brochure. Would you hire yourself, based on the professionalism of your resume?

What is professionalism? Well, would you ...

- Send your resume out without a cover letter, or would you enclose a personal cover letter addressed specifically to a targeted individual on matching stationery?
- Fold your resume into thirds and stuff it in a business envelope, or would you send the resume out in an attractive flat envelope without folding it at all?
- Send the resume by regular mail, or use overnight or two-day air to make a more powerful entry into the organization of destination?
- Expect the prospective employer to call you after receiving your resume (reactive responsibility), or would you make it clear that you will telephone him or her within a week to arrange an interview?

Think about these questions for just a moment. What would seem more professional to you? There is a tremendous shortage of professionalism out there. Embrace professionalism and you'll discover that you'll be invited to more and more interviews. That means more opportunities.

7

Anatomy of a Career Design Resume

Regardless of the resume type you choose or the format you decide upon, there are six primary sections that make up a successful career design resume, along with numerous subsections that can also be incorporated. The five primary sections are:

1. Heading
2. Introduction
3. Employment Section
4. Education
5. Miscellaneous Sections

THE HEADING

The heading, also referred to as your *personal directory,* consists of your name, address (with full zip code), and phone number (with area code). If you carry a portable phone or pager or have a fax machine, you can include these phone numbers in your heading. We do not recommend that you include a work number. Many hiring managers do not look favorably upon furnishing a work number. They may conclude that if you use your present company's phone and resources to launch a job search campaign on company time, you might do the same while working for them.

There are two basic methods for setting up your heading: the traditional and creative methods. The traditional method is the centered heading. This is effective for any resume, including those that will be scanned by a computer. The creative style consists of any heading that is not centered. Look at some of the many different examples of headings in the sample resumes. For style and layout ideas, look at resumes even if they do not represent your profession.

THE INTRODUCTION

An effective, power-packed introduction consists of *two or three sections*. The introduction sets the tone of the resume and swiftly connects your area(s) of expertise with the prospective employer's needs. It must answer the initial query, "What do you want to do?" or "What value can you provide my company?"

The first section of the introduction identifies who you are and what you have to offer. It is delivered in one of the following three forms:

- Title
- Objective
- Summary

For target resumes, consider using a title or an objective. An objective should not be used if it limits your scope. For example, if you work in operations, an objective might exclude opportunities that you don't even know exist. However, if you work as a nurse or accountant, your objective may be clearly defined. When developing an inventory resume, you should incorporate a summary to kick off your introduction. The purpose of the summary is to convey the scope of your experience and background and to indicate to the reader your key strengths and areas of expertise. *The first section of the introduction must ignite initial interest and make the reader want to continue.*

THE EMPLOYMENT SECTION

The employment section is, in the majority of cases, the most important section of your resume. (Resumes of recent college graduates are among the exceptions, when academic achievements and extracurricular activities are given more weight than employment experience.)

The employment section will have the most influence on a prospective employer in determining if you get an interview, and ultimately, a job offer. This section highlights your professional career and emphasizes experience, qualifications, and achievements. The employment module normally begins with your most recent position and works backwards (allocate the most space to the most recent positions and less space as you go back in time). If you have a sensible and strategic reason to deviate from this guideline, and it enhances your document, go for it. Otherwise reference the following information for each employer:

1. Name of company or organization
2. City/town and state where you worked
3. Dates of employment
4. Titles or positions held

How far back do you have to go? That's entirely up to you. You do not have to go back more than 10 to 12 years unless you have a good reason to do so. For instance, if you want to get back into teaching, something you did 18 years ago, but stopped to raise your children, you'll want to go back 18 years. But the rule of thumb is 10 to 12 years. For the most part, what we did 15 years ago is of little consequence to an employer today.

Experience is not limited to paying jobs. If applicable and advantageous, include volunteer work if it enhances your candidacy. Do not include salary, reasons for leaving, or supervisor's name unless you have a very specific reason for doing so. Salary history and requirements, if requested, should be addressed in the cover letter.

HOW THE EMPLOYMENT SECTION SHOULD LOOK

When using a chronological or combination format, provide specific information for each employer you worked for and for each job you performed. Include three pieces of information for each employer/job:

1. **Basic responsibilities and industry- or company-specific information**
2. **Special skills required to perform those responsibilities**
3. **Specific accomplishments**

The listing of your job responsibilities should read like a condensed job description. Bring out only the highlights, not the obvious. Finally, use positive and energy-oriented words. The words you choose should reflect your energy level, motivation, charisma, education level, and professionalism. Emotion and action sell; use action and power words.

Briefly describe any special skills you used in carrying out past responsibilities. These skills might include computers that you operated, special equipment used, and bilingual capabilities. Other examples of skills that you might have employed include problem-solving, communications, organizational, or technical mastery. Review your daily tasks and you'll be surprise at the skills you use every day but take entirely for granted.

The major focus of the employment/experience section should be on your specific accomplishments, achievements, and contributions. What you did in terms of day-to-day functions has little impact. *What you accomplished through those functions determines hireability.* Achievements vary from profession to profession. You need to consider:

- Revenue increases
- Reengineering successes
- Awards and recognitions
- New technology introduction
- Mergers and acquisitions
- Problems identified and resolved
- Profit improvements
- Productivity improvements
- New policies and procedures
- Startups and turnarounds
- Inventory reductions
- Contributions made
- Expense savings
- Systems enhancements
- Quality improvements
- Reducing employee turnover
- Adding value to the company

When using a functional format, simply list the information—company name, city/state, dates of employment, and titles—and leave it at that.

EMPLOYMENT (OTHER)

Quite possibly, your employment history will go back 20 years or more. Focus the majority of your resume on the most recent 10 to 12 years, and provide a brief synopsis of the rest. You are not obligated to account for every minute of your life, so use this section to summarize activities performed many years ago if it will round out your employment background.

THE EDUCATION SECTION

The education section, as any other section, should position your credentials in the very best light without being misleading. List your highest degree first and work back. If you have attended six different colleges but have no degree, you might think that these efforts indicate that you are a lifelong learner. But it could also be interpreted as *project incompletion,* and work against you. Think carefully, strategize, and do what's right for you.

Generally, the education section appears at the beginning of your resume if you have limited work experience. A recent high school, technical school, or college graduate will, in most cases, fall into this category. As your portfolio of experience and achievements gains momentum, the education section will drop toward the end of the resume as newly formed experiences, skills, and accomplishments begin to outweigh educational experience in the eyes of a prospective employer. Finally, if your educational credentials are seen as critical, or are superior to those of competing candidates, you'll want to introduce this section early in the resume.

If you have a post-high school degree, you need not list high school credentials on the resume. A job seeker with no post-high school degree should include high school graduation on the resume. Particular details you might want to address under the heading of education include:

- Grade point average (GPA), if 3.0 or higher
- Class ranking
- Honors and awards
- Scholarships
- Intramural or varsity sports
- Clubs and special classes
- Relevant course work if directly related to your target profession (mostly for recent graduates)
- Special theses or dissertations
- Internships
- Research projects
- Extracurricular activities (tutoring, volunteer work, student activities/politics, working on school newspaper)
- Career-related jobs and activities while attending school

This is a good place to talk about hiding information. There are some very imaginative methods of trying to hide weaknesses, and without exception, they all fail. But that doesn't mean you should accentuate any flaws in brilliant colors for all to see. The best way to overcome a weakness is to identify a corresponding strength that will more than make up for the weakness. If you have an associate's degree in business when a bachelor's degree is required, what can you do? Pinpoint areas of experience where you've proven yourself, especially where practical experience and a proven track record stands out. Demonstrate high energy and enthusiasm and stress your commitment to give 200 percent. Also, enroll in a community school and begin earning your bachelor's degree and state this in your resume and/or cover letter.

You need to honestly address your weakness by demonstrating powerful strengths and assets. Even if you are successful in initially fooling a hiring authority, you can be sure that the interview will be quite uncomfortable. If questions are asked that you can't answer satisfactorily, you're in for an embarrassing, defensive, and unproductive meeting. You will come across as conniving and unethical.

MISCELLANEOUS SECTIONS

Military

If you served your country and received an honorable discharge, it is fine to briefly mention this in your resume. Unless your experience in the military is directly related to the profession you are pursuing (e.g., U.S. Navy aircraft mechanic applying for a job as a mechanic with an airline), then keep it very short, one to two lines at most. The more your military background supports your future career goals, the more emphasis you should give it. Underscore key skills and achievements.

Finally, and this is very important, translate military jargon into English. Many civilian employers were not in the military and can't relate to or understand military vernacular. If you are not sure of the proper equivalent civilian terminology when translating military verbiage to business terminology, seek out assistance. After going through the painstaking effort of getting a hiring or personnel manager to read your resume, you want to be absolutely certain she can easily understand the messages you are sending.

Interests

Interests are inserted to add a human element to the resume; after all, companies hire people, not robots. This is a section that should be kept brief, tasteful, and provocative insofar as the interviewer can use this information as an "ice breaker," and to set the tone of the interview. It helps to build rapport.

Obviously you will want to use an interest section when your interests match job requirements, skills, or related activities that enhance your chances of getting an interview, and a job offer. A country club manager may want to include tennis, golf, and swimming as hobbies. A computer teacher may want to list reading, attending motivational workshops, and surfing the Internet as hobbies. A salesperson may want to include competitive sports because many sales managers view strong competitive skills as a valuable asset in the highly competitive sales arena.

Provide one line (no more unless you have a compelling reason to do so) of information to show the reader your diversification of interests. You might try two or three athletic interests, two to three hobbies and/or two to three cultural interests. This gives the prospective employer a good profile of who you are outside of work.

Community Service, Special Projects, and Volunteer Work

Many organizations place a high degree of importance on community service. They value fundraising efforts, volunteering time to charities, and contributing to community improvement. In many cases it is good P.R. and enhances a company's image in the eyes of the public. Organizations that value these activities believe in the adage that "what we get back is in direct proportion to what we give." If you feel that supporting community activities, the arts, and other such causes will enhance your overall credentials, then by all means, include them on your resume.

Professional and Board Affiliations

Memberships and active participation in professional and trade associations demonstrate to a prospective employer that you 1) are a contributing member of your profession, 2) desire to advance your own knowledge and improve your skills, and 3) are committed to the future of your vocation. Pertinent affiliations should appear in your resume.

If you sit on Boards of Directors, this also indicates that you are well respected in your community and that you give of your time to other organizations, be they profit or non-profit entities. These distinguishing credits should be included in your resume.

Awards, Honors, and Recognitions

No doubt these are critical to your resume because they represent your achievements in a powerful and convincing manner. It's one thing to boast about your accomplishments—and that's good. But flaunt your accomplishments *supported by specific awards and recognitions,* and that will often be the one thing that separates you from your competition.

You can illustrate your honors and recognitions:

1. In the introduction section of your resume.
2. Under professional experience.
3. As a separate section.

Technical Expertise/Computer Skills

Incorporating a section describing your specific technical and computer skills may be an effective way to quickly introduce your skills to the reader. In a high-tech, ever-changing business environment, employers are looking for people with specific skills and, even more important, for people who have the ability to learn, adapt, and embrace new technologies.

In this section, consider using short bullets so the information is easily accessible. Information and data tend to get lost and confused when lumped together in long sentences and paragraphs.

Teaching Assignments

If you have conducted, facilitated, or taught any courses, seminars, workshops, or classes, include this on your resume, whether you were paid for it or not. Teaching, training, and educating are *in-demand* skills. They exhibit confidence, leadership, and the ability to communicate. If you have experience in this area, consider stating it on your resume.

Licenses, Accreditation, and Certifications

You may choose to include a section exclusively for listing licenses, accreditation, and certifications. Consider using bullets as an effective way to quickly and effectively communicate your significant qualifications.

Languages

We live and work in a global economy where fluency in multiple languages is an asset in great demand. Be sure to list your language skills at the beginning of the resume if you determine that these skills are critical to being considered for the position. Otherwise clearly note them toward the end.

Personal

Personal data consists of information such as date of birth, marital status, social security number, height, weight, and sex (if your name is not gender-specific), health, number of dependents, citizenship, travel and relocation preferences, and employment availability.

Employers, by law, cannot discriminate by reason of age, race, religion, creed, sex, or color of your skin. For this reason, many job seekers leave personal information off the resume. Unless you have a specific reason to include it, it's probably a good idea to limit or eliminate most personal information. For example, if you are applying for a civil service position, a social security number might be appropriate to include on the resume. Or, if you are applying for a position as a preschool teacher and have raised six children of your own, you may want to include this information on the resume.

Here's a good test for determining whether or not to include personal information on a resume: Ask yourself, "Will this information dramatically improve my chances for getting an interview?" If the answer is yes, include it. If the answer is no, or I don't know, omit it.

8

Cover Letters

You must include a cover letter when sending your resume to anyone. Resumes are impersonal documents that contain information about your skills, abilities, and qualifications backed by supporting documentation. In most cases, you'll send the same resume to a host of potential employers. A resume is a rather rigid instrument, and unless you customize each document for a specific audience, the resume is, for the most part, inflexible.

Phoebe Taylor, in her 1974 publication, *How to Succeed in the Business of Finding a Job,* provides advice on cover letters that, after 20 years, still holds true:

> *If you stop to think about it for a moment, all resumes have basic similarities. Librarians' resumes are look-alikes; accountants' resumes have much in common; and so on. To get the employer to single out the "paper you," you'll have to demonstrate some ingenuity to separate yourself from the crowd.*
>
> *The cover letter provides additional pertinent information and reemphasizes your qualifications consistent with the employer's needs. As your "personal messenger," it shows your uniqueness and your ability to express yourself on paper and gives a glimpse of your personality. Addressed to a real person, "Dear Mr. Johnson" or "Dear Ms. Winters," it becomes a personal communiqué. It proves to the reader that you made the effort and used your resourcefulness to find out his or her name and title.*

A cover letter allows you to get more personal with the reader. It is the closest you can get to building rapport without meeting in person. It is a critical component in getting an interview and, eventually, the job.

Cover letters should be brief, energetic, and interesting. A polished cover letter answers the following questions concisely and instantaneously:

1. Why are you writing to me and why should I consider your candidacy?
2. What qualifications or value do you have that I could benefit from?
3. What are you prepared to do to further sell yourself?

Cover letters work best when they are addressed to an individual by name and title. They should be written using industry-specific language and terminology. And finally, you must initiate some future action. Specifically, you want to let the reader know that you will be contacting them for the purpose of arranging an interview or whatever the next step will be. Be proactive! Don't expect them to call you; when possible, you should launch the next step and do so with confidence and an optimistic expectation.

Anatomy of a Cover Letter

What follows is the skeletal structure for a successful cover letter:

1. Your heading and the date
2. Person's name and title
3. Company
4. Address
5. Salutation
6. 1st paragraph: Power opening—talk about the organization, not you
7. 2nd paragraph: Purpose of this correspondence and brief background
8. 3rd paragraph: Punch the "hot button(s)"—what precisely can *you* do for *them*?
9. 4th paragraph: Closing and call to action (initiate your next move)
10. Sign-off

Consider the following quotation:

> *I would be lying if I told you that I read every resume that crossed my desk. But I have almost never not looked at a resume that was accompanied by a solid, well-written cover letter. The lesson here is that you must learn how to write a strong letter. A cover letter should do more than serve as wrapping paper for your resume. It should set you apart from other candidates.*

This quote comes from Max Messmer, CEO of Robert Half International, Inc., one of the world's largest staffing firms. Messmer suggests that most cover letters emphasize what candidates are looking for and not enough about the contributions a candidate can make to an organization. Therefore, when you are composing your letters, avoid overusing the pronoun "I," and focus instead on the contributions you will make to the company. Don't rehash what you deliver in the resume. Whenever possible, mention information that reflects your knowledge of the organization you are writing to or the industry as a whole. Bring current news or events into the letter that will show the reader you are up to date and current with industry trends.

The Broadcast Letter

There are times when a career designer is gainfully employed, content with the job, but restless enough to want to explore alternatives. Maybe you're bored, not earning what you feel you deserve, foresee trouble ahead, or just want a career change to try something different. *The challenge in this situation is that you don't want to take the chance of your current employer finding out that you're looking for other work.* That could cause really big trouble. The day you send out your first resume, you risk exposure. You can never be 100 percent sure where your resume will end up. Consequently, the moment you broadcast to anyone that you are exploring employment opportunities, you run the risk of exposing this to your present employer. The broadcast letter is a means to protect you to a certain degree, though even the broadcast letter is not foolproof.

The broadcast letter can also be used by those who have had 16 jobs in the past three years, who take time off from work on occasion or who are returning to the workplace following an extended absence. The broadcast letter becomes half cover letter, half resume. Though you'll need a resume sometime down the road, a broadcast letter is a technique used to attract initial attention without providing extensive detail or exposing information you'd rather not divulge at this time. Some career designers use this letter format because they feel people are more apt to read it than a resume. Secretaries, for instance, who screen incoming mail may not screen out broadcast letters as quickly as they do resumes.

Broadcast letters provide an effective means for discreetly communicating your employment intentions to executive recruiters or employment agencies or for informing key people in your network of your goals and objectives. The broadcast letter, by definition, *broadcasts your strengths and abilities in more depth than a cover letter but in less detail than a resume.* There are many advantages to sending out a broadcast letter. With them, you can:

- Avoid chronology of employment
- Provide a partial listing of former employers
- Communicate that you are presently employed and are, therefore, uncomfortable in advertising your present employer until there is interest in you as a viable candidate
- Speak about your strong employment record and accompanying assets without mentioning educational credentials that may be viewed by others as weak
- Overcome a challenging past, including alcohol or substance abuse difficulties, time spent in jail, physical or emotional encounters, or other similar obstacles.

A broadcast letter can be an effective way to introduce yourself and spark interest in your candidacy. You must be prepared, however, to address any challenges in subsequent communications with employers who show an interest in you after having reviewed the broadcast letter.

Chapter 9 includes ten sample cover letters for you to review. Look at each one and notice how many are written less formally than you might expect and allows the writer more creativity than a resume might. Try not to write the cover letter in too formal a style. Many entry-level candidates tend to write very stiff "professional" letters that prevent the reader from getting to know them.

OTHER COLLATERAL MATERIALS

Personal Calling Cards

It may not be practical to carry your resume everywhere you go or to every meeting or event you attend. But everywhere you go and at every meeting or event you do attend you should be networking. If you connect with an individual who might be of some assistance to your career design efforts, you must be prepared to leave a calling card. We highly recommend that you have 500 to 1,000 personal calling cards printed (they are not expensive), and make it a point to hand out 100 to 150 a week for starters! Include just the basic information including name, address, phone number and the career objective or short summary of qualifications.

Thank-You Notes

You should send thank-you notes to every person who makes even the most infinitesimal impact on your career design. Stock up on some stylish, classy notecards because even a small item like a thank-you note can make a huge difference in the outcome of your labors.

9
10 Action-Oriented Cover Letters

UNSOLICITED LETTER

STEVE DUDASH

504 Orange Circle, Crystal, MN 55428 (612) 555-8978

March 4, 1996

Mr. Arthur C. Bates, Executive Director
Palm Beach Visitors and Convention Bureau
122 Convention Plaza
West Palm Beach, FL 33408

Dear Mr. Bates:

Palm Beach County, according to reliable publications, is one of the fastest-growing counties in the United States. I applaud the tremendous work you are doing at the Palm Beach Visitors and Convention Bureau to attract major events, further improving the economic climate of our thriving area. Your achievements, showcased as the cover story in the latest *Convention Center, International,* are impressive, and I for one would like to be a contributing sales member of your professional team.

I understand from the article that you are looking to become the number one convention center in Florida, and I feel my sales skills and abilities can help tip the scales from Orlando to Palm Beach! I offer you:

* **9 years of proven experience in convention/event sales**
* **A verifiable track record for closing major national events**
* **Strong market analysis and strategic planning skills**
* **A personable, team-spirited professional with a strong network (national) in place**

I will be in West Palm Beach next month. If possible, I would like to visit and personally meet with you to introduce myself and my qualifications. I will take the liberty of calling you next week to arrange such a meeting.

Thank you for your time and consideration. I look forward to speaking and meeting with you soon.

Sincerely,

Steve Dudash

COLLEGE STUDENT RESPONDING TO CLASSIFIED AD

NIKA NIKSIRAT
215 Hartman Drive
Portsmouth, NH 03801
(603) 555-4606

January 26, 1996

Mr. Howard Speller, General Sales Manager
Speller Automobiles, Ltd.
325 Rolling Woods Highway
Dover, NH 03723

Dear Mr. Speller:

I am a recent college graduate with a **B.A. Degree in Automotive Marketing & Management.** I have also been part of a family-owned automobile distributorship for nearly all my life, so cars are my life!

I noticed your advertisement for *Automotive Sales and Marketing Assistant* in the June 14th edition of the *Dover Star,* and have submitted my resume for your consideration.

You mentioned in the advertisement that the successful candidate must have:

1) A Bachelor of Arts degree — **I do**
2) Excellent communications skills — **I do**
3) Ability to work well with people at all levels — **I do**
4) Eagerness to learn and "pay my dues" — **I am and I will**

This is a job that I believe was made for me. I am familiar with your operation, as I am originally from this area. I am available immediately, and offer you competence, dedication, and a good work ethic. If you don't mind, I will call you next week to see if a personal interview can be scheduled.

Thank you for your consideration and I look forward to speaking with you next week.

Sincerely,

Nika Niksirat

REFERRAL FROM A THIRD PARTY

BEN CHANG

125 Torrey Pines Drive
Del Mar, CA 92103
(310) 555-5330

September 21, 1996

Ms. Darleen Henley, Sales Coordinator
TJ Cellular Corp.
2300 La Jolla Blvd., Suite 400
La Jolla, CA 92164

Dear Ms. Henley:

A mutual acquaintance, Mr. Roger Smith, recommended that I contact you regarding a possible sales opportunity with TJ Cellular Corp. I have taken the liberty of enclosing my résumé for your review. Thank you in advance for your consideration.

I now realize that I have been missing "my calling." *I love sales, but have not been selling the products and services that I love.* I am a strong sales professional with solid technical skills, but have not been selling technical products. As Sales Manager for PDC (please refer to resume), I must have sent two dozen people to your company to purchase cellular phones (and they bought!), after they saw the slick phone I use that I purchased from you!

Now here's the irony—I get more excited promoting your phones than I have ever gotten from promoting anything I've ever sold—and I've been successful in all my sales endeavors! This is why I would like to pursue a sales position with TJ Cellular.

I have over 20 years of successful sales experience. I offer you the following:

⇒ **A strong closer; excellent cold-canvassing and market development skills**
⇒ **A professional demeanor**
⇒ **A strong network of contacts in place**
⇒ **Enthusiasm and high energy**

Though my résumé is quite detailed, it cannot fully profile the manner in which I have been successful. This can only be accomplished in a face-to-face meeting where we can exchange information and examine whether there might be mutual interest. I will call you in the coming week to arrange an interview. Again, I thank you for your time and review, and look forward to meeting with you soon.

Sincerely,

Ben Chang

RESPONDING TO CLASSIFIED AD USING T-BAR FORMAT

PATRICIA CAPIZZI
1031 Rainbow Lane
Irvine, CA 92720
(714) 555-1791

January 15, 1996

Marianne Cox, Director of Human Resources
Medical Products, Inc.
124 Grant Avenue
Irvine, CA 92720

Dear Ms. Cox:

I noticed your advertisement for Sales Manager in the June edition of the Medical Messenger. I am very interested in pursuing this opportunity and have enclosed my resume for your review.

YOUR REQUIREMENTS	MY QUALIFICATIONS
1. Minimum of 5 years' management experience in medical sales.	1. I have 8 years experience in medical sales.
2. Extensive training & coaching experience.	2. Received "Trainer of the Year" award, Bristol, Inc., 1994-95.
3. Proven ability to adapt sales programs to meet environmental and economic changes.	3. Increased territorial market share 32% per year over past 8 years.
4. A solid professional who is respected industry-wide.	4. Member & Past President, CA Medical Sales Association.

I recently read in a local newspaper that Medical Products, Inc. is streamlining its operations and is positioning itself to expand into the international arena. In addition to meeting the criteria you outlined in the above-mentioned ad, I speak four languages fluently and can be an asset in the area of international sales.

I will take the liberty of calling you early next week to discuss the possibility of arranging a face-to-face meeting to explore a number of ways I feel I can contribute to Medical Products, Inc. Have a great day and I look forward to speaking with you next week. Thank you.

Sincerely,

Patricia Capizzi

Encl: Resume

RETURN TO WORKFORCE

CYNTHIA REID-HERRING

1117 Aaron Lane, Reidsville, GA 30453 (912) 555-4337

March 9, 1996

Ms. Andrea Kazen, RN, Head Nurse
Thompson Medical Complex
230 Medical Way
Reidsville, GA 30453

Dear Ms. Kazen:

I have returned home! After 25 years of living in Florida, I have returned home to spend the second half of my life where it all began. I am presently exploring nursing positions at Thompson Medical Complex and have enclosed my updated resume for your review.

I worked here in the 1960s. I left on great terms, have outstanding references, and would love to come back and conclude my career where I started.

As you see from my resume, I have not formally worked in the past 24 months. I have spent time with my children and grandchildren, traveled a bit with my semi-retired husband, and have taken advantage of my free time to take a number of continuing education courses to improve my skills for 21st-century America—including computer courses, Advanced Nursing Techniques (JFK Medical Center), and other personal development-related workshops and seminars.

Now back in Georgia, I am seeking part-time employment. I am flexible as to the shifts and days I can work, and would like to find a position that would allow me to work about 24 hours per week. I can work three 8-hour shifts or two 12-hour ones. I have excellent letters of reference from my years in Florida, in addition to the fine reputation I left behind when I left Georgia some 25 years ago.

I will stop by your office next Tuesday between 2PM and 3PM to fill out your formal application. If you can take a few moments to see me at that time, I would be very grateful. I will call you on Monday to see if this can be arranged.

Thank you for your attention. I am excited about the possibility of returning to Thompson Medical Complex.

Sincerely,

Cynthia Reid-Herring, RN

BROADCAST LETTER—CURRENTLY EMPLOYED

JAMES BARESSI

125 Meadowlark Drive
Palm Beach, FL 33407
(407) 555-9102

May 6, 1996

Mr. Grant D. Powers, CEO
Golden Bear International
Golden Bear Plaza
11712 U.S. Highway 1
North Palm Beach, FL 33412

Dear Mr. Powers:

Your Controller, Mr. Gerald Haverhill, informed me that you are presently interviewing candidates for the position of MIS Manager. I would be very interested in pursuing this opportunity and would like to schedule a meeting to discuss it.

I have worked for a major entertainment company headquartered in the Southeast for the past 8 years as Director of MIS. Like Golden Bear International, my present employer has multiple divisions (14), employees located around the globe, and a worldwide reputation for excellence. Our company relies heavily on solid MIS management for our comprehensive data processing needs. I am proud to say that our department has remained "one step ahead of the company's growth," so we have consistently been in the enviable position to plan our future, rather than react to it. I am specifically responsible for developing MIS programs to address:

Tax Accounting	Budget & Reporting
Cash Management	Payroll (1,800 people)
Government Reporting	Audit Management
Inter-Company P&L's	Foreign Country Reporting
Purchasing & Inventory Control	Sales Forecasting
Management Reporting	Research & Development

Though I have been fortunate to have a myriad of bottom-line accomplishments, three in particular come to mind:

1) **Saved the corporation $1.3 million/year in research funds by convening and leading a "think tank" (9-person team) to study methods for reducing new product development (NPD) time through computertronics. Within 6 months, the group developed a method to reduce NPD by 67% through enhanced computertronics using a sophisticated software program. The results led to yearly savings of $1.3 million while concurrently enhancing product quality.**

James Baressi
Page 2.

2) **Saved the corporation $1.2 million per year by consolidating Data Processing departments of 4 new acquisitions. We improved DP and electronic reporting times by a near-impossible 50%, while reducing worldwide staffing requirements some 62% through consolidation.**

3) **Worked closely with programmers to create an innovative taxation reporting program that tracked 8 individual taxable categories for 11 countries. Results of this 9-month project were threefold: 1) Reduced tax penalties (late filings) 95% (From $187,000/year to less than $10,000); 2) decreased regulatory audits by nearly 85%; and 3) reduced duty and tax fees paid by over $203,000 a year.**

This is just a sampling of what our MIS department has contributed to the bottom line. I must admit that my ability to anticipate and strategically plan for growth is the key to success. Goal setting, organization, time management, accountability, and teamwork are at the foundation of my management philosophy. We love what we do and are proud of our accomplishments.

Mr. Powers, I enjoy my work very much and am challenged by it. As anticipatory as I am, I now foresee a possible merger with a Fortune 50 firm in the next 12 to 18 months. If this takes place, I would be asked to transfer out of South Florida. At this time, I would resist such a move and am exploring alternative employment opportunities. However, in the event I have not made a decision to accept new employment, I will be forced to relocate, thus the overly protective nature of this letter in not broadcasting to you, or anyone else, my current employer or employment history. I am sure you can appreciate that confidentiality is critical for me at this time.

If, after reviewing this letter, you feel as I do that I would be a valuable addition to your management team, I will gladly furnish you with a comprehensive resume.

Please expect my telephone call in the coming week. Quite possibly we could arrange a personal interview where I can further demonstrate my work ethic, history, and specific contributions.

Thank you for your time and consideration. I look forward to speaking with you next week.

Sincerely,

James Baressi

FOLLOW-UP TO INTERVIEW

Joe Saracino
1497 Dale Mabry Boulevard • Tampa, Florida 33587 • (813) 555-6684

February 8, 1996

Mr. Mike Cline
Director Sales and Marketing, PCS Wireless
3333 Westwood One
Tampa, FL 33587

Dear Mr. Cline:

I would like to thank you for meeting with me last week to discuss PCS Wireless and the possibility of my joining your team. I've been working in the wireless industry with Bell Atlantic since college, and becoming part of a startup operation is a very exciting prospect.

I have learned a great deal about the wireless industry over the last two years. Between the cellular incumbents, the new PCS licensees, resellers, and future C-Band entrants, your market is sure to be very competitive. Obviously pricing will become more competitive, but to become the market leader will require positioning beyond price.

PCS Wireless has the opportunity to change this local market, one of the largest in the country. With new services and a better quality product, you have a great opportunity to make your operation the new standard in Central Florida. Mike, I am very interested in becoming part of this team and building this customer base.

The marketing role I have at Bell Atlantic is a great foundation for working in a business development capacity with you. I have had to conduct market research, target market segmentation analysis, and competitive analysis, and prepared various business planning presentations. This kind of market research and wireless experience would be a key added value to your staff.

Thanks again for staying in touch over this. There are few opportunities one gets to work in a dynamic organization, and I'd like to be a part of this one. I would like to be involved in the sales or promotions part of your team, where I can be of the greatest value. I will talk to you more as you near your launch.

Sincerely,

Joe Saracino

LETTER TO EXECUTIVE RECRUITER

Kirby Hughes 1477 SW 40th Court, Coral Springs, Florida (954) 555-6583

September 12, 1996

Ms. Lori Harding
Robert Half International, Inc.
1450 E. Las Olas
Fort Lauderdale, FL 33444

Dear Ms. Harding:

If you are in search of a senior-level engineering manager for one of your executive searches, you may want to give serious consideration to my background.

Highlights of my experience are:

- M.S. Mechanical Engineering, University of Florida
  B.S. Electrical Engineering, Georgia Tech

- 16 years Engineering and Management experience with:

  —Pratt & Whitney; V.P. Engineering (aircraft division), 4 years
  —IBM; Director of Project Engineering (software interface), 7 years
  —Boeing Corporation; Project Engineer, 5 years

In my current capacity as Vice President for Pratt & Whitney I manage an engineering group of 450 responsible for aircraft motor design in three facilities in the country. This includes engineering design through to process design of manufacturing.

I have established a strong reputation for the quality and quantity of capital project work completed in my department. I have a solid reputation as a demanding and fair leader. The work performed under my direction has come in at or below budget, and we always meet project deadlines.

I have chosen to leave Pratt for personal reasons; they are unaware of my decision. My current compensation is about $130,000. Should you be interested, please contact me at home at (954) 555-6583.

Sincerely,

Kirby Hughes

LETTER TO EXECUTIVE RECRUITER

Christopher Gladden
846 Blue Ridge Circle
Miami, FL 33335
(305) 555-7893

June 3, 1996

Mr. John Loureiro
TTS Personnel
420 Lexington Avenue
New York, NY 10170

Dear Mr. Loureiro:

Several of my associates in the communications industry here in South Florida have mentioned you as someone experienced with similar firms in the New York area. We should talk soon.

My experience with sales and distribution of wireless communications products in this market is certainly one of success:

- After I became Regional Sales Manager for Pactel in 1988, we improved our sales by 55% in one year. The sales staff was demoralized, and we improved their training and replaced other staff members. Our market share is up to 22% in just three years.

- We created a selling program locally that resulted in an 18% higher closing rate, and that program was taken on the road to train all other Pactel sales reps.

Unfortunately, all this hard work has caused the company to be acquired. The new brass have indicated a desire to sell off the division I manage. This is a great opportunity for me to return to New York. I will call you next week to discuss possible opportunities in the "Big Apple."

Sincerely,

Christopher Gladden

LETTER FROM RECENT COLLEGE GRADUATE

Roberta Alexander
222 Highway 18, Scarsdale, NY 10001
(914) 555-8699

June 3, 1997

Mr. Bill Smith
Blockbuster Entertainment Corporation
100 Blockbuster Way
Fort Lauderdale, FL 33310

Dear Mr. Smith:

I really enjoyed meeting with you yesterday. It was interesting hearing all of Blockbuster's exciting new plans, and I was particularly excited about how this position fits into the big picture.

My skills would be a real advantage for Blockbuster at this time. I relish opportunities to be creative and solve problems, and it was great to see that Blockbuster hasn't lost its innovative spirit as it's grown. I agree you need someone who is flexible and comfortable working under pressure and time constraints, and I believe that someone could be me!

I'm sure many of the candidates you interviewed have the technical skills to function as a Field Support Representative. You stressed the importance of decision making in this position. That is one aspect that separates me from other candidates. I believe in problem solving and making decisions, and showing my supervisor the desired end result, not a half-finished product. Please follow up with my previous employer as we discussed.

I hope to hear from you soon. If you have any questions please call me at home or work.

Sincerely,

Roberta Alexander

10

101 Career Design Resumes That Will Get You Hired

ACCOUNTANT

LAWRENCE CROWE, C.P.A.

(904) 555-7654 • 1770 Arron Road • De

Excellent portfolio of skills at beginning
Strong chronology of employment
Solid and quantifiable achievements

CAREER PROFILE

CERTIFIED PUBLIC ACCOUNTANT / CHIEF FINANCIAL OFFICER with 18 years' experience in corporate accounting and 10 years' experience in multi-corporation accounting operations in the medical field. Areas of expertise include:

- Financial Administration/Reporting
- Operations Management
- Telecommunications Integration
- Multi-Corporation/Partnership Taxes
- Acquisitions/Joint Ventures
- Credit Lines/Administration
- Accounting Systems Design/Implementation
- Financial Planning/Analysis
- Acquisition Negotiations
- Premium Rate Strategies
- Equipment Leasing/Portfolio
- Multi-Site Retail Purchasing/Negotiations
- Strategic Planning/Budgeting
- Central Accounting Administration

PROFESSIONAL EXPERIENCE

Chief Financial Officer 1991 - Present
FOREST HOME MEDICAL CENTER, Orlando, Florida

Florida-based group of affiliated Home Health Care and Pharmacy Companies headquartered in Orlando, Florida.

- Design, implement, and manage all centralized accounting, management information systems, and internal control policies and procedures for 11 corporations.
- Manage accounting department consisting of controller and accounting staff.
- Prepare all Federal and State tax requirements including corporate, partnership, payroll, and property tax returns.
- Formulate appraisals and negotiate purchases of all group and company acquisitions.
- Negotiate contracts and purchasing commitments with manufacturers for buying group.
- Coordinate all financing and external reporting with financial institutions for the group.
- Spearhead groups to assess value of potential acquisition targets: observe and critique operations, determine feasibility and asset valuations.
- Instrumental in the negotiation and acquisition of $3 million home care and retail pharmacy stores; negotiated a $14 million contract for pharmaceuticals resulting in a savings of 1.5-3% on cost of goods for each retail store.
- Prepare and administer operating and cash budgets for each retail profit center.

Achievements:

- Instrumental in the research and coordination to integrate voice, data, and fax over data lines which will save $100-200k in long distance charges annually.
- Installed and manage a 10-node Novell Netware LAN, Solomon Accounting software, MicroSoft Office, and Excel.
- Instrumental in instituting MestaMed billing software resulting in a reduction of workforce and savings of $189k annually.
- Centralized subsidiary's previously subcontracted accounting functions to headquarters saving $89-90k annually.
- Increased credit lines from $1.5 million to $2.9 million in credit in 3 years resulting in a savings of .5 point on interest or $14k per year.
- Saved $87k in annual corporate management salaries through comprehensive management of the financial programs and credit administration of the group.
- Negotiated the purchase of an acquisition holding a market value of $2-3 million for less than $1.1 million.

Lawrence Crowe, C.P.A., Albany, Georgia 1990 - 1991

Sole practitioner.

- Management advisory services to home health care companies in the southeast concerning areas of management, financial, and tax consulting.
- Prepared clients' taxes including individual, corporate, and partnership filings.
- Formulated appraisals, prepared forecasts, and negotiated acquisitions of home health care companies for clients.
- Prepared "Compiled and Reviewed Financial Reporting" for clients including interim tax reporting requirements.
- Negotiated lines of credit with financial institutions for clients.

Chief Operating Officer 1985 - 1990
BEST MEDICAL RENTAL SUPPLY INC., Albany, Georgia

A Georgia-based Home Health Care company.

- Managed daily operations in conjunction with Regional Managers.
- Negotiated contracts and purchasing commitments with manufacturers for buying group consisting of 34 retail locations.
- Managed accounting department consisting of controller, billing auditor, and accounting staff.
- Prepared all Federal and state tax requirements including corporate, partnership, individual, and pension plan returns.
- Formulated appraisals and negotiated purchase of all acquisitions.
- Prepared and administered operating budgets for all retail locations.
- Received, secured, and disbursed all corporate funds concerning company operation in conjunction with the President and CEO.

Achievements:
- Designed, implemented, and managed all accounting and management reporting systems.

Partner / C.P.A. 1976 - 1985
MARTIN AND MARTIN COMPANY, P.C., Albany, Georgia

A six-partner public accounting firm.

- Coordinated and managed the firm's automated write-up practices which interfaced between accounting, data processing, and financial reporting functions.
- Prepared client's tax requirements.
- Assisted with certified audits of municipalities, banks, construction and retail clients.

EDUCATION

Certified Public Accountant—Florida State Board of Accountancy—1991

Certified Public Accountant—Georgia State Board of Accountancy—1983

Bachelor of Science Degree in Business Administration—1979
Valdosta State College, Valdosta, Georgia

PROFESSIONAL AFFILIATIONS

American Institute of Certified Public Accountants
Georgia Society of Certified Public Accountants
Florida Institute of Certified Public Accountants
Rotary Club—Board Member
Chamber of Commerce—Steering Committee

ACCOUNTANT

CHARLES CAREY

2223 August Square Road
Barrington, IL 60193

(708) 555-3174

Subtle title to open the resume just below heading
Strong chronology of employment
Solid and quantifiable achievements

ACCOUNTING MANAGER

PROFILE:

- More than 14 years in accounting, including responsibility for department procedures, budgets, and computer operations.
- Train and direct staff in accounting activities and in the use of Lotus 1-2-3, Supercalc 5, and AccountPro. Expert in full system conversions.
- Plan and conduct audits and variance analyses, process payroll and payroll tax reports and filings, and maintain/update accurate inventories.

EMPLOYMENT:

12/92 - Present

Scarpendous Displays, Inc., An Exhibit Set-Up and Service Firm
Senior Accounting Manager Chicago, IL
Responsible for the accurate and timely processing of accounts payable/receivable, payroll (48 employees), insurance and union reports, and sales tax/payroll tax reporting for this $2.1 million firm. Perform job costing, account analysis, and general ledger management using Lotus 1-2-3 and Excel.

- Freed up $32,000 by reducing A/R aging from 77 to 38 days
- Successfully directed conversion from an IBM System to a Novell Network
- Reduced accounting payroll costs 41% through automation

1/87 - 11/92

Lancer Systems, Manufacturing—Electrical Piping
Accounting Manager Chicago, IL
Trained and directed six employees in accounting department. Analyzed and interpreted forecasts, capital expenditures, and financial data for $3.2 million manufacturer. Directly involved in budget preparation and cash flow.

- Successfully negotiated a $650,000 credit line with major bank
- Detected costing problem that eventually saved the company $124,000/year
- Active participant in the successful implementation of just-in-time program

6/82 - 1/87

Coopers & Lybrand, Public Accounting
Senior Accountant Chicago, IL
Performed detailed financial audits for clients and recommended improvements in system procedures, documentation, and internal controls. Conducted reviews and compilations. Prepared corporate and individual income tax returns, and payroll/sales tax returns.

6/81 - 6/82

U.S. Riley Corporation, Manufacturing—Custom Furniture
Cost Accountant Chicago, IL
Assisted in budget forecasting, right out of college. Developed standard cost data and variance analyses. Reviewed capital expenditures and coordinated/reconciled physical inventories.

EDUCATION:

Ridgetown College, Santa Fe, New Mexico
Bachelor of Science: Accounting

REFERENCES:

Furnished Upon Request.

ACCOUNTANT

RUSTY WILLIAM CATES

78 Addington Place, #12, Calcu, Missouri 54321
(564) 555-3456

PROFILE

- **Academic training and interest in Accounting. Willing to travel or relocate. Well-versed in, and acquired hands-on experience (through college projects) of:**
  - financial statements & analysis
  - asset, liabilities, & stockholders' equity
  - cost & managerial accounting
  - accounting information systems
  - 10 K report & financial investors' analysis
  - revenue & expenses
  - pensions & leases
  - tax accounting
  - auditing
  - consolidations
- **Computers:** IBM / Macintosh platforms - DOS - MS Word - WordPerfect - Lotus -Excel - dBase - FoxPro - Power Point - most online services - Internet.

EDUCATION

- **Bachelor of Science - Accounting,** 1995
  University of Missouri, Currency, Missouri GPA: 3.6 / 4.0
  ACADEMIC FOCUS: FINANCIAL & COST ACCOUNTING & AUDITING ACTIVITIES
  - **Elected to leadership role and served on Finance and Social Committees** of Delta Omega Pi fraternity.
  - **Volunteered time and resources to the Boy's and Girl's Club of Lancaster** on a variety of projects.
  - **Participated in intramural college sports:** basketball, football, softball.
- **Currently enrolled at Calcu College of Finance**
  - Twelve-hour pre-CPA Examination coursework.

HIGHLIGHTS OF EXPERIENCE

WALLACE MANUFACTURING

- **Acquired first-hand knowledge of how a business runs,** both from an operational aspect and staffing requirements.
- **Learned the importance of completing work projects on time** - accepting personal responsibility for work quality - and contributing as a productive team member to accomplish an assignment.

Recent graduate, with education highlighted at the top
Strong portfolio of skills at the beginning
Solid computer skills in the profile section

RO'S DEPARTMENT STORE

- **Sold men's clothing and accessories** in high-volume retail environment. Determined customer needs and suggested items to complete wardrobe (and increase sales total).
- **Ensured complete customer satisfaction by providing attentive, personalized service** which resulted in building long-term customer relationships and repeat business.

ROX CORPORATION

- **Supplied manual labor** to several company cafeterias and the plastic packaging and shipping department.
- **Maintained a positive attitude while performing routine or menial functions.**

CITY OF CALCU

- **Planned, coordinated, and administered beginning and intermediate swimming classes for children.** Oversaw all operational and safety aspects of pool facility.
- **Obtained professional certifications** to perform duties as a Lifeguard and Swimming Instructor and motivated students to overcome their fear of water.

WORK HISTORY (during college)

- WALLACE MANUFACTURING, Calcu, Missouri
  Machine Operator: Plastic Molding (9/94-10/95)
- SPIRO'S DEPARTMENT STORE, Mile High, Colorado
  Sales Associate (10/93-10/94)
- XEROX CORPORATION, Johnson, Missouri
  Food Services & Tenite Plastic Departments (summers 1992, 1993)
- CITY OF CALCU, Calcu, Missouri
  Lifeguard & Swimming Instructor (summers 1987-1991)

ACCOUNTS PAYABLE

Strong, focused, two-line title
Solid portfolio of skills, including computers
Key accomplishments under employment

SHERRI BUCKNER

636 Cashiers Drive
West Palm Beach, FL 33413
(407) 555-2639

CREDIT & COLLECTIONS

- Combining Solid Negotiating & Interpersonal Skills -

OVERVIEW:

A highly motivated Credit, A/R, A/P, and Collections professional with a *verifiable* record of accomplishment spanning four years. Highly creative, recognized as a results-oriented and solution-focused individual. Areas of strength include:

- **Accounts Payable**
- **Problem Collections**
- **Organizational Skills**
- **Highly Computer Literate**
- **Work as Team Player**
- **Accounts Receivable**
- **Legal Aspects of Collections**
- **Solid Communication Skills**
- **Time Management Skills**
- **Research Abilities**

EDUCATION:

Clark Atlanta University, Atlanta, GA
Associate of Arts Degree: Mathematics & Accounting, 1992
GPA: 3.325 (Cum Laude)
- **Member:** Pi Mu Epsilon Professional Mathematics Society (1990-91)

COMPUTER SKILLS:

IBM and Mac Literate
WordPerfect, M/S Word, AmiPro
Lotus 1-2-3, M/S Excel, EasySpread II
Peachtree Accounting, Quicken, DacEasy, LedgerRight
EasyDun IV, Collector Jr.

PROFESSIONAL EMPLOYMENT:

PCS Prime Co., Boca Raton, FL — 1992 - 1996
Accounts Receivable/Payable Clerk
(Wireless communications carrier with 135,000+ customers and 340+ vendors)

- Full charge processing of all accounts receivable and payable
- Manage all petty cash and office supply expense accounts
- Reconcile bank balances; record general ledger entries
- Establish customer credit lines and set up credit accounts with vendors

Accomplishments

Reduced A/R aging from an average of 87 days to 63 days in less than 7 months
Established new credit criteria for new accounts, significantly reducing bad debt
Wrote credit policy and procedure manual for department

SPECIAL INTERESTS:

Aerobics	Roller Blading	Classical Music
Interneting	Gourmet Cooking	Karate

REFERENCES:

Promptly furnished upon request.

Personal information (height, weight, etc.) is fine for actors

"Listing" of experience—this represents his value

Will probably be accompanied by film clips and photos

ACTOR

Alex Kasler

Actor

1 North Lancaster
Athens, Ohio 45701
(614) 555-3993

Height: 6'0" • Weight: 175
Age: 27
Hair: Brown • Eyes: Green

SELECTED ACTING EXPERIENCE

1996	Evans	*Terra Nova*
1995	Senator Marshall/Judge	*America's Women* (nationally broadcast on PBS radio)
1995	Bob	*Athens Online* (Feature Film; Rajko Grlic, Exec. Producer)
1995	Taylor	*K2*
1995	Harry	*The Seahorse*
1995	Tommy (barman)	*The Plough and the Stars*
1995	Yefir	*Uncle Vanya*
1994	Priest/SS-Man	*Private Lives of the Master Race*
1994	Glenn Cooper	*Rumors*
1994	Jack	*Boy's Life*
1994	Moss	*Glengarry Glen Ross*
1994	Stage Hand	*Six Characters in Search of an Author*
1993	George	*Sorry, Wrong Number*

Voice-Over Work (Class Projects)

1995	Major George Swift	*The Twinkling Ornaments of the Night*
1995	Harry Rhyne	*Harry Rhyne, Hollywood Detective ("The Real McCoy")*
1995	Uncle Ted/Derek	*Bobby's World ("Bobby's Tooth or Dare")*

RELATED EXPERIENCE

Assistant Director - Monomoy Theatre Company

1993	*The King and I*	Directed by Alan Rust
1993	*Blithe Spirit*	Directed by Michael John McGann
1993	*A Lesson from Aldes*	Directed by Peter Hackett
1993	*The Matchmaker*	Directed by Isreal Hicks
1993	*Sorry*	Directed by David Jaffe

Stage Management

Production Manager, Ridges Auditorium, Athens, Ohio - 1992-present
Stage Manager, *Every Woman Loves a Fascist* - 1993

EDUCATION & TRAINING

OHIO UNIVERSITY, Athens, Ohio - 1996
Candidate for Bachelor of Fine Arts Degree - Major in Acting

Private Voice Lessons, Matthew Griffin (instructor) - 1994-present
Text and Voice, Independent Study, Kathy Devecka (instructor) - 1994-present

---

References and Additional Experience Provided Upon Request

ABIGAIL ANDERSON
119 Old Stable Road
Lynchburg, Virginia 24503
(804) 555-4600

Easily accessible skills and qualifications
Strong chronology of employment
Solid and quantifiable achievements

PROFESSIONAL QUALIFICATIONS:

Over 15 years experience in the planning and management of large-scale Office Services, Facilities Management Services, Purchasing and Administrative Support Functions for a Fortune 100 corporation. Consistently effective in streamlining and upgrading operations, improving productivity, and reducing annual operating costs. Qualifications include:

- Mail & Messenger Services
- Contract Negotiations
- Inventory & Materials Management
- Equipment Leasing & Acquisition
- Staff Training & Supervision
- Property Management
- Fleet Administration
- Insurance Administration
- Purchasing Management
- Budget Administration

PROFESSIONAL EXPERIENCE:

COMMUNICATIONS, INC., Lynchburg, Virginia 1987 to Present

($4 billion diversified entertainment conglomerate. Holdings include movie and publishing companies, entertainment/sports arena, baseball and basketball teams, and theme parks throughout the U.S.)

Senior Manager - Office Services

Plan, staff, budget, and direct the daily business operations of the Office Services Department, a support function servicing over 1,200 employees located at corporate headquarters in Lynchburg. Scope of responsibility includes all mail and shipping services, a large contracted messenger operation, and office support services throughout both facilities.

Hold concurrent responsibility for the management of Transportation Department operations for executive staff. Administer departmental policy, negotiate the purchase and sale of all vehicles, and manage related insurance programs. Currently control a 30-car corporate fleet.

Formulate and administer a $3.5 million annual operating budget. Train and supervise a staff of 26 Office Services and Facilities Management employees. Coordinate all related purchasing, materials management, vendor sourcing/selection, contract negotiations, and inventory planning/management functions. In addition, manage production of monthly promotional mailings of 5,000 to 50,000 pieces.

Achievements:

- Launched a complete reorganization of the Office Services department and cut annual operating expenses by 25%. Reduced staffing requirements, eliminated overtime, and restructured messenger service programs.
- Integrated several independent operating departments into one Office Services organization for an annual savings of more than $75,000.
- Sourced vendors, prepared bid packages, and negotiated cost-effective contracts for the outsourcing of mailroom and messenger services. Resulted in a substantial improvement in service delivery while reducing net operating costs by more than 25%.
- Introduced the use of presort mail, international mail, and bulk mail services into the corporation for a substantial reduction in annual postage and handling costs.

COMMUNICATIONS, INC. *(Continued):*

- Negotiated favorable equipment leases and facilities contracts to expand in-house operating capabilities and support to 1,200 employees.

- Coordinated transportation services for high-profile special events including Annual Stockholders meetings, Board of Directors meetings, and a series of national fundraising events.

RICHARDSON REALTY, New York, New York 1974 to 1987

Real Estate Assistant (1983 to 1987)

Fast-paced operations support position coordinating commercial, industrial, and residential real estate projects for the corporation. Reported directly to the President.

- Orchestrated a national employee relocation program for the transfer of personnel throughout various company locations. Negotiated the resale of homes in cooperation with local real estate brokers, coordinated home purchases, and expedited physical relocations.

- Negotiated with management of company leased buildings throughout the U.S. to monitor daily operations, resolve tenant problems, evaluate rental costs and contracts, and coordinate service delivery.

- Assisted with the planning and implementation of plant closure programs. Reviewed consultant contracts and negotiated vendor, utility, and contractor agreements. Monitored costs, maintained ledgers, and identified/resolved cost overrides.

Executive Secretary (1974 to 1983)

Promoted through a series of increasingly responsible secretarial and administrative support positions working directly with the executive management team.

EDUCATION:

UNIVERSITY OF VIRGINIA, Lynchburg, Virginia 1985 to 1988
Coursework in Business Administration, Planning & Communications

Licensed Real Estate Sales Associate, State of Virginia, 1984

PROFESSIONAL AFFILIATIONS:

National Association of Fleet Administrators
Mail Systems Management Association
Postal Customers Council

ADMINISTRATIVE ASSISTANT

Samantha K. Dunn

312 Northwest Avenue • Taylor, Michigan 48000 (313) 555-0537

Effective and simple resume
Good portfolio of skills
Easy-to-read format

Objective: A secretarial position in a fast-paced environment.

Skills:

- Excellent Organizational Skills
- Strong Customer Relations Skills
- Computer Proficiency
- Data Entry
- Telephone Answering, 12-Line System
- Word Processing & Typing
- 10-Key Calculator
- Filing

Computer: Lotus 1-2-3, WordPerfect 5.1, Microsoft Word, Alpha IV Data Base, DOS.

Experience:

Secretary 1990 to Present
ABC COMPUTER SERVICE, INC. Taylor, Michigan

Handled all word processing and typing. Entered data for reports, production items, shipping, and inventory. Maintained computerized inventory of all parts, supplies, and products. Helped plan and organize company functions. Answered the telephone and represented the company in a professional and businesslike manner.

Accomplishments:
- Researched and set up a voice mail answering system. Result: Saves time for both the receptionist and the customers.
- Created, organized, and set up an information center for manuals and schematics. Result: Better access to needed information, and less time searching for it.
- Employee of the Month, July, 1993.

Sales Clerk 1989 - 1990
THE GAP Taylor, Michigan

Education:

Word Processing/Data Processing 1987 - 1989
WAYNE COUNTY COMMUNITY COLLEGE Taylor, Michigan

Diploma 1987
MONROE HIGH SCHOOL Monroe, Michigan

References:

Furnished on request.

ADMINISTRATIVE ASSISTANT

Effective and stylish industry-specific graphic
Good portfolio of skills
Easy-to-read format

TRACEY A. TESTA
2281 Greenview Drive
Lake Worth, Florida 33489
(407) 555-9282

ADMINISTRATIVE SUPPORT

OVERVIEW: An administrative support professional recognized for taking a leadership role in support of top management. A proven and *verifiable* record for utilizing strong technical and interpersonal skills to enhance organizational efficiencies and profits.

STRENGTHS:

Computer

* Word Perfect 5.1/6.0	* Samna & Mortracs	* Windows Applications
* Microsoft Word	* Excel	* Quattro Pro
* Lotus 1-2-3	* Flow Charting	* Super Writer

Personal

* Work well (and competently) under stress while taking the pressure off superiors
* Present a highly professional demeanor and impeccable corporate image
* Work in harmony with all staff; a team-spirited professional
* High energy, motivated, and dependable. A good sense of humor
* Excellent communication skills; patient and resourceful in solving problems
* Trustworthy, ethical. Recognized for high degree of integrity

PROFESSIONAL EXPERIENCE:

Ocwen Financial, West Palm Beach, Florida — 1989 - Present
ADMINISTRATIVE ASSISTANT TO VICE PRESIDENT(S)

(1993 - Present) Prepare spreadsheets, correspondence, and various reports for V.P. Loan Operations. Handle shipping, post closings of mortgage loans, develop and prepare procedure manuals, and arrange all travel itineraries. Cross-train to accomplish other responsibilities to further assist the Vice President.

(1989 - 1993) Assisted Senior V.P., CFO and his managers. Interfaced with all Bank personnel within the corporate office and 16 branch locations. Prepared reports for Quarterly Board Meetings and other reports/financial documents.

State of Maryland/ — 1980 - 1989
Anne Arundel County Health Department, Arnold, Maryland
PERSONNEL ASSOCIATE

Performed specialized administrative assistant work assisting the Personnel Officer. Aided in the administration of State Merit System Rules and Regulations requiring interpretation, judgement, and explanations relative to the System.

Successfully interacted with the public, staff personnel, and intergovernmental agencies. Planned, assigned, and reviewed personnel actions and coordinated/directed the following benefit programs including: Retirement; Health Care; Credit Union; Out-Service Training.

EDUCATION: Anne Arundel College, Arnold, Maryland
Business Administration

INTERESTS: Enjoy: Exercise, Reading, and Outdoor Activities

- References & Supporting Documentation Furnished Upon Request -

David R. Fuery

454 East 79th Street
New York, NY 10021
Phone/Fax
(212) 555-6226

Author's favorite
Creative method for showcasing accounts in left margin
Functional format with expertise and achievements on first page
Strong chronological work history to complement the functional first page

Career Profile

Fashion and entertainment industry Advertising Production Specialist. Extensive credentials in key account sales, marketing, and management.

- Produce, cast, negotiate, and budget photo shoots for multimillion dollar domestic and international accounts.
- Extensive international exposure and contacts.
- World traveled, Paris educated, working knowledge of Italian.

Representative Accounts
L'Oréal
Faberge
Lord and Taylor
Saks
Spiegel
Neiman Marcus
Victoria's Secret
American Express
Condé Nast
Otto Versand

Expertise and Achievements

Production

- Coordinate and execute worldwide photo shoots.
- Direct twenty to forty international production teams.
- Engineer and maintain high-profile fashion photographers.
- Cast, book, and schedule leading models and performers.
- Supervise departmental staff of fifteen.

Sales and Marketing

- Open and retain million dollar accounts.
- Research domestic and international industry trends, develop new contacts.
- Develop sophisticated proposals; submit bids.
- Meet rigorous deadlines, come in on budget.

Representative Agencies
Elite
Ford
Wilhelmina

Account Management

- Negotiate advertising contracts; manage million dollar accounts.
- Produce million dollar plus budgets.
- Oversee billing and talent payments.
- Business agent for clients of representation firm.

Public Relations/Representation

- Represent photographers, musicians, personalities, and screenwriters.
- Adept at subtle, successful management of creative egos.
- Liaison for international clients.
- Maintain extensive worldwide network of business contacts.

Computer Skills

- Word Perfect
- Lotus123
- Harvard Graphics
- Quicken Accounting
- Accpac General Accounting
- Boss

Employment

Senior Photographers Agent **1993 to present**
Superior Representation L.T.D.
New York, NY

- Produce worldwide photo shoots. Scout new clients, negotiate all contracts, and maintain million dollar accounts. Maintain wide network of international business and creative contacts.

Production Manager **1991 to 1993**
Dynamic Productions
New York, Miami, Paris

- Directed production of fifty catalog/advertising photo shoots worldwide, utilizing twenty to forty photo teams. Supervised staff of ten. Coordinated location, scheduling, budgets, and casting.

Sole Proprietor and President **1990 to 1991**
David R. Fuery Talent, Inc.
New York, NY

- Independently engineered and established private company. Represented artistic professionals as business agent and manager.

Director **1986 to 1990**
Fashion Model Management
New York, NY

- Booked top models for print and show. Negotiated advertising contracts, scouted worldwide, and established new client base. Supervised staff of fifteen.

Education

M.A. in Fine Arts in progress — **Pratt Institute**
New York, NY

B.A. in Marketing, 1985 — **American College Paris**
Paris, France

AEROBICS INSTRUCTOR

JENNIFER CASHMERE, CAI

13446 West Ocean Boulevard
Palo Alto, CA 92303
(415) 555-6729

CREDENTIALS

Certified Aerobics Instructor
Former U.S. Miss Fitness, 1988-89
Former Miss California Fitness, 1990

EDUCATION

Masters Degree, USC
Health & Fitness, 1992

Bachelor of Science, USC
Health & Nutrition, 1990

Effective industry-specific graphic design
Simple yet highly effective format
Strong credentials under "Key Professional Achievements"

KEY PROFESSIONAL ACHIEVEMENTS

Produced Cashmere Video Training Tapes for TLT Enterprises
Worked with Cory Everson in Producing TV ESPN Show "Gotta Sweat"
Consultant to Scandinavian Health Spa Aerobic Program (Corporate)
Fitness Competitor in Five World Class Events Annually
Personal Trainer for Selected Celebrities

Work Experience:
Cashmere Fitness Consultants, International, Palo Alto, CA
Health & Fitness Expert, 1993 - Present

Global Gym, Chicago, IL
National Aerobics Program Coordinator, 1990 - 1993

Member:
American Fitness Association (Board of Directors)
Aerobic Association for Better Health (Board of Directors)
National Health & Fitness Association of America
International Aerobics & Fitness Association

Professional References:
Portfolio of References Gladly Furnished Upon Request

ART DIRECTOR

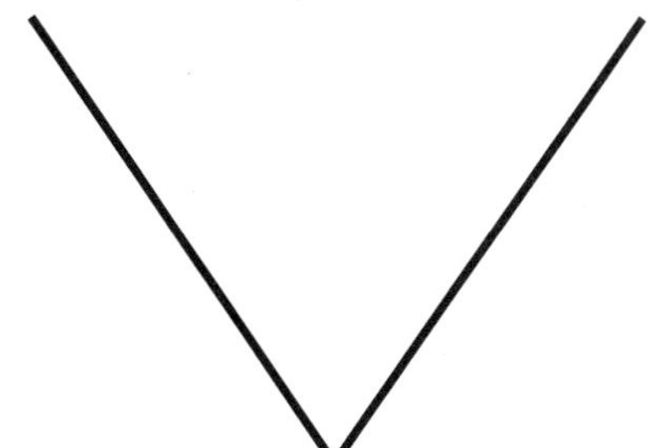

R E S U M E

> *Simple but effective graphics*
> *Solid work experience accompanied by contributions and successes*
> *Easy-to-read, one-page resume that sparks interest in the reader*

Cynthia Dannington

333 McAfee Lane
Trenton, NJ 08000
609-555-8430

PROFILE

> Art Director and Print Production Manager with over 10 years of experience in a wide variety of environments, including a comic strip syndicate, an advertising agency, and the film industry.

> Computer: Macintosh, Quark XPress, Adobe Photoshop, Adobe Illustrator, Paache Airbrush.

EXPERIENCE

KING FEATURES SYNDICATE, New York
Art Director / Print Production Manager (1985 - Present)

Supervise 25 employees in the page layout and printing of syndicated comics, newspaper articles, and puzzles for national newspapers. Oversee weekly page makeup and client contact for personal ads in 15 nationwide publications. Manage electronic prepress section. Schedule and quality-check four-color promotional ads for licensing, sales, and comic art departments. Set prep quality standards. Design and quality-check covers for syndicated newspaper TV guides.

> Successfully converted 85% of work to electronic page layout.
> Department is nationally recognized as leader in in-house printing.
> Broadened scope of department to include more challenging and creative responsibilities.

DANNINGTON STUDIOS, Trenton, New Jersey
Freelance Graphic Artist (1982 - 1985)

Developed concepts and designs for clients in the film, theater, non-profit, and fashion industries. Designed special promotional material, direct-mail brochures, press kits, and corporate identities. Produced exceptional quality work for clients on a tight budget and a tight deadline.

MULTI-MEDIA ADVERTISING, New York
Assistant Art Director (1981 - 1982)

Designed newspaper ads for real estate companies, stores, restaurants, and politicians.

EDUCATION

BFA - Advertising Design, 1981
SYRACUSE UNIVERSITY, New York

ARCHITECT

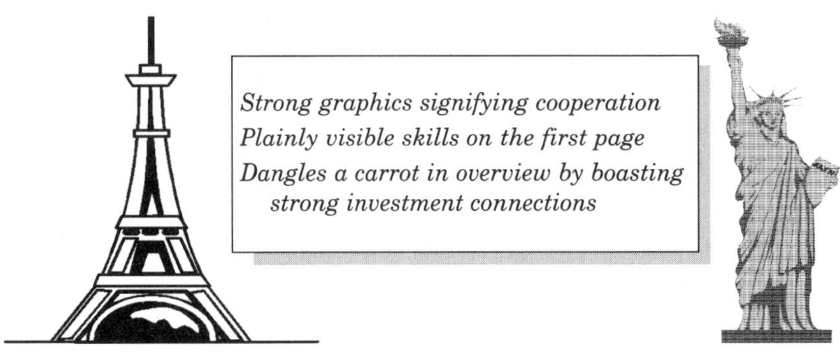

JEAN-LOUIS de MARGUERIE de MONTFORT
2233 Poinciana Island
North Miami Beach, Florida 33160
(305) 555-7537

LICENSED ARCHITECT

Project Development & Real Estate Professional

- Legal U.S. Immigrant -

OVERVIEW: Strong **investment contacts (public & private)** in Europe, specifically in France, desirous of making real estate/business investments in U.S. A solid and *verifiable* **record of achievement** as a French Architect and Project Manager, gaining the trust and confidence of many reputable **corporate leaders and government officials.**

PROFILE OF STRENGTHS: (French Architects are not only involved with the design stage of a project, but the actual construction through final completion—Start-to-finish responsibility).

Residential & Commercial

* **Real Estate Valuation - Feasibility Studies**
* **Estimating, Appraisals, Inspections and Project Budgeting**
* **Negotiating & Contract Administration**
* **Architectural Concept and Design**
* **All Phases of Project Development Through Punch List**

SKILLS AND ABILITIES:

* Sales & Marketing
* Interior Design
* Strategic Planning
* Employee/Subcontractor Management
* Business Management
* International Purchasing
* Finance & Profit Achievement
* Banking and Financing

EMPLOYMENT:

Jean-Louis de Marguerie de Montfort, Architect
French Riviera (Cros Cagnes, Antibes, & Nice) — **Southern France**
LICENSED ARCHITECT — **1972 - Present**

- Specializing in French Architecture and Interior Design -

Architect specializing in residential homes ranging in price from $1.5 million to $5 million homes and estates (3,400 - 15,500 sq. ft.). In addition, have solid design and construction experience in commercial projects including: office buildings, schools, churches, hotels, and restaurants. Expertise in project renovations (minor - major).

EMPLOYMENT (Continued):

* Established a **regional reputation** for excellence and developed a loyal following in Europe. Manage all phases of project development - from design to completion. Highly successful for project profitability and investor ROI.

* Strong **management skills,** including personnel and project scheduling, employee and subcontractor supervision, budgeting and finance, problem solving, client relations, and quality control.

* Seasoned **sales and marketing skills.** Demonstrated ability to gain trust and confidence of prospects. Personable, a sense of humor, and highly ethical.

EMPLOYMENT OTHER: Draftman, Architect's Project Manager, 1959 - 1966
Architect Designer (Spain), 1966 - 1972

EDUCATION: Licensed Architect: Ministre de l'Environement and du Cadre de Vie, May 1980

- Specific References & Supporting Documentation Furnished Upon Request -

ASSOCIATION DIRECTOR

Demonstrates broad experience
Easy to read with bullets under experience
Strong ending on page two—Education, Professional Development, Honors and Activities

Deborah A. Stone

37 Fredicks Boulevard
Old Bridge, New Jersey 55555
(908) 555-2114

Summary

Broad-based responsibilities in the following areas:

- Program Development
- Strategic Planning
- Marketing
- Team Building
- Research
- Statistical Analysis
- Recruitment
- Training

Profile

Results-oriented manager with excellent team and coalition building skills.....promote cohesiveness within the organization......utilize creativity and risk-taking abilities to develop and implement organization-wide programs.....enhance corporate visibility, public relations, and alternate sources of revenue.

Experience

Children with AIDS Foundation, Central Jersey Chapter, Cranbury, NJ

Director of Community Services 1991-Present

- Developed a major health education program. Designed a marketing plan to obtain corporate sponsorship and regional work site implementation.
- Recruited, interviewed, and trained volunteers for program implementation. Increased volunteer base by 200% and program implementation by 150%.
- Increased public awareness through press releases, radio interviews, and creating promotional pieces for various chapter activities. Promoted cross-marketing activities within the regional service area. Designed and facilitated chapter needs assessment.
- Planned, budgeted, and implemented local, statewide, and regional professional education conferences. Developed and implemented chapter program plan.
- Supervised Communications Coordinator and secretary.

Resolve Health Services, Inc., Philadelphia, PA 1987-1991

Program Development Manager

- Authored and submitted proposals to various institutions totaling over $420,000; generated $200,000 in additional revenue.
- Researched and analyzed macroenvironmental trends and utilization patterns within fifteen-county service area. Identified opportunities for program expansion, increased productivity, and diversified funding.
- Implemented community development efforts. Headed up development of a Luzerne County Interagency Network.
- Researched and organized statistical data, developing a database for corporate needs assessments and program evaluations.
- Secured and supervised student intern.
- Conducted the annual agency HIV prevention/AIDS in-service.

Experience (continued)

Pennsylvania Department of Health, Northeastern District, Kingston, PA
Statistical Consultant 1986-1987
Intern 1985

- Statistical Consultant to Wyoming County Interagency Council Health Watch project. Designed a county-wide survey; conducted training in proper interviewing techniques and supervision of interviewers.
- Organized implementation through coordinating Interagency interests and scheduling deadlines; administered survey input and interpreted results.
- Designed, researched, and authored a model Pennsylvania Department of Health Northeast Regional Directory for 10 counties. Regional Directory included information on organizations, staff, service areas, programs, and clinics.
- Researched the impact of Regional Services on health problems and the relationships to other agencies in the community.

Education

Masters of Health Administration, Wilkes University
Graduated 1985, with distinction

Bachelor of Arts in Education, Westchester University
Graduated 1983, Cum Laude

Computers:

WordPerfect 5.1 for DOS and Windows, Word for Windows, Lotus 1-2-3, SPSS

Professional Development

- Annual Institute of Nursing Child Health Conference
- Teen Forum: Model Programs to Promote Adolescent Health and Delay Pregnancy
- Grantsmanship Training Program
- Fourteenth Annual Region III Primary Care Conference

Honors and Activities

- Planning Committee, Central New Jersey Maternal and Child Health Consortium
- Community Speaker, Prevent Child Abuse—New Jersey
- Newsletter Editor, National Society for Fundraising Executives, Greater Pocono Northeast Chapter
- Community speaker regarding HIV infection and AIDS, American Red Cross

ATTORNEY

Backscreen to add effect
Education showcased in the center of page one
Functional format with list of employers on page two

MILTON N. WRIGHT
Attorney at Law

300 Rainbow Lane
Houston, Texas 77777

(713) 555-3367 (Home)
(713) 555-4495 (Fax)

SUMMARY OF QUALIFICATIONS

- **Juris Doctor** with 5+ years of expertise in **Corporate Law; Employment Law; Oil and Gas Law;** and **Litigation.**
- Licensed to practice in the **State of Texas** and Northern and Eastern **U.S. District Federal Court; State of Colorado** (License Pending).
- Proficiency in transactional type and contract matters; legal research and analysis; strategy development; composition of complicated contracts, briefs. Working knowledge of Westlaw and Lexis Legal Researching.
- Experienced in oil and gas title work; liens; lease analysis; interpretation of laws.
- Demonstrated ability to successfully negotiate/litigate cases to productive conclusions.

EDUCATION

ST. MARY'S UNIVERSITY - San Antonio, Texas
Doctor of Jurisprudence Degree (1989)

TEXAS A&M UNIVERSITY - College Station, Texas
Bachelor of Arts Degree in History (1986)

PROFESSIONAL HIGHLIGHTS / ACHIEVEMENTS

- Directed complex employment litigation matter; conducted week-long jury trial; resulted in satisfactory jury verdict; resolved case with settlement.
- Wrote personnel and drug testing policy manuals for three corporations.
- Researched case law and statutes involving federal procedures and forum selection provisions of contracts. Initiated extensive legal research of contractual forum selection clauses in contracts. Wrote briefs. Resulted in obtaining desired relief from Federal District Court.
- Analyzed facts and circumstances; researched law applicable to facts and contract provisions; developed successful strategy and negotiated satisfactory resolution involving issues of production, expenditure, and management for corporation.
- Successfully negotiated settlement for client possessing $3 million in assets and $15 million in debts; resolved case for $1 million without resulting in bankruptcy.
- Negotiated coverage dispute with independent insurance company; instituted lawsuit; through effective discovery and litigation strategy, negotiated settlement to fully compensate client for damages/expenses.
- Represented Defendant in oil and gas dispute; Plaintiff sought $200,000 in damages plus denial of right-to-operate $6 million project. Through shrewd research and investigation, found damaging discovery to Plaintiff; resulted in obtaining right-to-operate for client with no damages due.
- Efficiently and profitably manage law practice and office staff; establish procedures and policies; budget time, money, and resources; handle full caseload of litigation and transactional matters.

MILTON N. WRIGHT, Attorney at Law **Page Two**

PROFESSIONAL EXPERIENCE

LAW OFFICES OF MILTON N. WRIGHT — Houston, Texas
Attorney at Law — 1994 - Present

LAW OFFICES OF TRIMBER & BOREN, P.C. — San Marcus, Texas
Associate Attorney at Law — 1989 - 1993

BROWN, HOPEWELL, AND SMITH — San Antonio, Texas
Law Clerk — 1987 - 1988

COMMUNITY / VOLUNTEER ACTIVITIES

Member, Houston Chamber of Commerce (1990-Present)

Member, National Multiple Sclerosis Society (1991-Present)

March of Dimes Volunteer

PROFESSIONAL AFFILIATIONS

STATE BAR OF TEXAS

Corporate Division
Real Property Trust and Estate Division

—References Furnished Upon Request—

AUTO FINANCING

Teddy G. Hartez

555 Elm Street, Elkview, ID 05071
(555) 555-7974

Career Objective

Automotive dealer financing manager position with the opportunity for growth into regional F&I director responsibilities

Summary of Professional Qualifications

Successful 18-year career as F&I manager in automotive industry, including the largest Ford and Chevrolet dealerships in the state of West Virginia
Extraordinary ability to arrange financing, with career closing history of 85.7%
Loan processing accuracy record of 97.1% for the last three years
Consistently average $650 per retail unit of add-ons sold
City-wide reputation for being goal-driven, reliably successful, and highly ethical
Work consistently well under high stress, always maintaining good PR

Personal Characteristics

Present a highly professional, polished image
Aggressive in financial dealings and extremely self-confident
Efficient, accurate, honest, and hardworking; extremely high work ethic
Excellent interpersonal skills; good with coworkers and customers alike
Strong family values; married with two young children

Employment History

Business Manager • 1989 to Present
BERT WOLFE FORD-PORSCHE-AUDI-TOYOTA — ELKVIEW, IDAHO
Second highest volume dealer in Idaho; largest Ford dealer in the state
Business Manager • 1985 to 1989
Joe Holland Chevrolet-Geo-VW-Isuzu-Hyundai, Inc. — Elkview, Idaho
Business Manager • 1980 to 1985
TAG GALYEAN CHEVROLET — Elkview, Idaho
Largest Chevrolet dealer in the state at the time (dealership sold in 1985)
Business Manager • 1977 to 1980
VINCE PATERNO PONTIAC — Elkview, Idaho

Education

Bachelor of Science Degree in Industrial Relations, with a Minor in Economics
Idaho Institute of Technology, Montgomery, Idaho

A highly targeted resume
Accomplishments blended nicely with Personal Characteristics
Sections separated by lines for easy reading

BANKER

Profile Summary allows flexibility relative to career goals
A neat, nicely presented one-page document
A solid presentation of skills, qualifications, and accomplishments

Brad Barker

15 West Maple Street • Saddle Brook, New Jersey 07663
(201) 555-5353

PROFILE SUMMARY:

Experienced professional with a successful career in banking, business development, and administration • Excel at interfacing with others at all levels to ensure organizational goals are attained • Proactive approach has resulted in capturing numerous accounts and expanding client base • Possess excellent interpersonal, analytical, and organizational skills • Excel within highly competitive environments where leadership skills are the keys to success • An effective manager with the skills necessary to direct, train, and motivate staff to its fullest potential.

BANKING EMPLOYMENT:

UNITED JERSEY BANK New Jersey
Assistant Vice President *1994 - Present*

- High-profile management position accountable for soliciting community business accounts and developing strategic alliances with clientele.
- Develop tactics to increase assets and profitability within a territory consisting of 6 franchises throughout Bergen County, New Jersey.
- Devise and implement innovative marketing principles and promotional sales events for commercial and consumer projects to further support financial growth.
- Counsel high net-worth individuals and corporate clients with regard to investment opportunities, risk analysis, and monetary returns.
- Cross-sell banking services and products to clientele.
- Participate in community events to position the Bank as a leader within the territory.

Highlights:

- ♦ Generated over $100,000 in revenue and fee income within a 4-month period.
- ♦ Developed a strategic marketing campaign targeting accountants, attorneys, and medical professionals which has generated substantial referrals.

REPUBLIC NATIONAL BANK of NEW YORK New York, New York
Assistant Treasurer *1987 - 1994*

- Directed daily operations for a retail bank, including branch sales, business development, customer service, and credit analysis.
- Managed a staff of 15 Customer Service Representatives and Tellers.
- Analyzed financial statements and pertinent information to determine creditworthiness of prospective customers.
- Negotiated and secured terms, pricing, and conditions.
- Counseled corporate clients and high net-worth individuals with regard to their borrowing needs.

EDUCATIONAL BACKGROUND:

Bachelor of Arts in Social Science (1986)
St. Bonaventure University • St. Bonaventure, New York
Dean's List

CERTIFICATIONS:

Financial Statement Analysis
Business Development Skills
Mortgage Specialist

BANKER

Effective inventory resume—management, sales, leadership, and training

One-company experience showing four positions of increasing responsibility

Well presented—neat and clean one-page resume

Rebecca A. Price

649 Lotus Drive ♦ Mason, MI 48000
313-555-8843

Career Summary

Branch Manager with 17 years of progressively responsible positions in the financial industry. Strong managerial, administrative, interpersonal, and problem-solving skills, with proven leadership ability.

operations management Manage operations, personnel, budget, profit planning, and audit & compliance for branch with assets up to $19 million. Proven ability to achieve success given difficult situations. Turned around Mason Branch within three months, bringing branch within audit compliance. Maintained excellent audit ratings. Effectively managed branch throughout merger process. Able to plan, organize, delegate, administer, and direct in order to meet branch goals and corporate mission.

sales Sales Team Leader; strong customer service orientation. Of 79 offices, Mason Branch was #1 in Cross-Sell Ratio for 1990. As individual, placed second in Cross-Sell for that same year. Outstanding achievement in cross-sell ratio for 1992. Increased branch average monthly deposit balance by $1.5 million from 1992-1993.

leadership & training Strong leadership skills with the ability to generate enthusiasm among staff. Supervise, develop, and direct staff of seven. Determined staffing levels and reorganized job responsibilities to effectively utilize resources during merger. Implemented a Retail Sales Performance System to train employees to be part of sales culture.

Professional History

MAJOR NATIONAL BANK - SOUTHEAST MICHIGAN ♦ 1978-present

Branch Manager, Mason Branch (1985-Present)
Collector, Loan Collection Department (1982-1985)
Head Teller, Rockwood Branch (1980-1982)
Teller, Rockwood Branch (1978-1980)

Education

UNIVERSITY OF MICHIGAN
Bachelor of Business Administration, Finance (1992)

Continuing education and seminars in sales, business development, commercial lending, and human resources.

Community Reinvestment

Treasurer, South Rockwood Rotary, 1994-1995; Board Member, Credit Women International; Junior Achievement–Certificate of Appreciation, 1994; Big Brothers/Big Sisters, 1990-Present.

CAROL PAPPAS

6342 Okeechobee Boulevard
Miami, FL 33309

(305) 555-8372

BANK TELLER
Offering Highly Seasoned Customer Service Skills

PROFILE:

A competent, personable, and highly motivated banking professional, having over three years' successful experience as a bank teller. Recognized for ...

- Competency and thoroughness
- Going the "extra mile"
- Strong communication skills
- Work well under pressure
- Superb customer service skills
- Patience and composure
- Analytical aptitude
- Upbeat and positive attitude

COMPUTER SKILLS:

IBM & MAC
Baltimore 8500
Quicken
WordPerfect
TF-5000 Banking System
Teller-All
Windows 95

> *Bank teller with good portfolio of skills, including computers*
> *Clear, easy-to-read, one-page format*
> *Strong education (internship) and employment achievements*

EDUCATION:

Stetson University, St. Petersburg, Florida
Associate Degree: Accounting

Internship:
Barnett Bank, Tampa, Florida
Internship, Teller, Records, Vault Services 1989-90

University of Miami, Extension, Coral Gables, FL
Currently Enrolled—Nights: Bachelor of Science Degree: Accounting
(Expected graduation date: 5/98)

EMPLOYMENT:

Great Western Bank, Kendall Lakes, FL 1993 - Present
Bank Teller / Customer Service

- Customer service handling daily transactions
- Resolving customers' problems; working with other departments to this end
- Promoting new bank services, bank credit cards, and loan programs

Achievements

- Train and supervise new hires
- Named "Rookie of the Year," for most productive new teller, 1993
- Recognized for highest level of accuracy of all 18 tellers, 1995

INTERESTS:

Volleyball, tennis, sailing, horseback riding, hiking, surfing the Internet

- Supporting Documentation and Professional References Furnished Upon Request -

Good portfolio of skills, including computers
Clean, easy-to-read, one-page format with sections separated by lines
Minimization of weak education by experience and inclusion of company training

BOOKKEEPING

BRIDGET D. SHANAHAN

15 Grove Street ❑ Patchogue, New York 11772 ❑ (516) 555-8203

❐ PROFILE

Professional abilities in general bookkeeping. Excellent analytical skills; develop operative systems to reduce expenses and protect revenue. A versatile team player who can work effectively and independently in challenging environments. Proficient on Lotus, Great Plains accounting software, and Officewriter programs.

❐ ACHIEVEMENTS AND QUALIFICATIONS

- ❑ **Designed original program to correct inefficient hotel reservation system;** reduced expenditures by clarification of authorizations and billing.
- ❑ **Partnered with CEO to develop detailed medical coverage cost analysis schedule.**
- ❑ **Authored clearly understandable manuals** on accounting office systems and procedures.
- ❑ **Developed financial tracking system** to maximize dollars spent on temporary help.
- ❑ **Created innovative procedures** that dramatically increased data entry productivity.

❐ PROFESSIONAL DEVELOPMENT

Arrow Electronics, Yaphank, NY
Accounts Payable Manager 1989 to present

Oversee accounts payable department of electronics production facility ($115M sales).

- ❑ Coordinate and implement all aspects of general bookkeeping. Reconcile bank statements and accounts. Utilize chart of accounts to code vouchers and enter accounts payable invoices. Prepare cash disbursements, apply cash receipts, research bills, check batches and day reports for accuracy. Generate computerized end of month reports. Utilize trial balance for various schedules.
- ❑ **Develop and execute numerous special projects.** Determine budgets, establish hotel accounts, travel arrangements and itineraries for conventions etc. Maintain individual files and process payroll of each freelancer and temp used on jobs. Compile monthly special reports, prepare American Express schedule. Act as back-up for vacation coverage in department.

Video Today Magazine, New York, NY
Accounts Payable Manager 1987 to 1989

General accounting with concentrated focus on vendor and customer relations.

- ❑ Addressed and resolved client problems and concerns. Performed customer credit verifications. Entered and prepared cash disbursements, invoices, and cash receipts. Assembled and tested voucher packages and coded account distribution. Monitored aging report, tracked collection of past due accounts, reviewed expense reports.

❐ EDUCATION AND TRAINING

Hofstra University, Uniondale, NY Courses toward B.A. in Liberal Arts.

Company training: Journal entries, adjustments and accompanying schedules. Client billing systems (actualizations, etc.).

Strong, one-page resume—skills-oriented
Gap in employment (1995 to present) overshadowed by achievements
Employment gap must be addressed in strong cover letter.

BROADCAST INDUSTRY

GERALD HINKLEY

(904) 555-3131 ▲ 1111 Applebee Square ▲ Deltona, Florida 32700

CAREER PROFILE

Well-qualified producer, director, and cameraman, with over 10 years' experience in television production and broadcast in the news and entertainment industry. Qualifications include:

- Electronic News Gathering
- Electronic Field Producing
- Network News Production / Research / Direction
- Investigative Reporting
- Remote / In-the-field Reporting
- Aerial Photography (Helicopters)
- News Copywriter
- Shooting
- Lighting
- Film Editing
- Soundman
- Audio / Multi Channel Board
- Movie Technician / Soundman
- Commercials
- In-House Promotional Videos
- Instructional / Training Videos
- Music Videos
- Staff Management / Direction

CAREER ACHIEVEMENTS

- Producer of "Eye on Asia" for a leading PBS station
- Directed lighting and ran camera for Award Winning 30-second PSA spot for Hale House
- As executive producer and cameraman, produced a promotional video of the Sands Hotel to attract investors for new casino being built in San Juan
- Cameraman for "Simon & Garfunkel, Reunion in Central Park for HBO Special"
- Pioneered and broke a story on the underground life in the abandoned subways of New York City
- Produced a promotional video for Lansphere, an exclusive spa in Connecticut
- Soundman, VCR operator, and editor of live broadcast for the "Flamenco Mass" at St. Peter's Church in New York City
- Senior cameraman of syndicated talk show, "Power Breakfast Club"

EMPLOYMENT HISTORY

Owner/Operator A.B.C. PRODUCTIONS, New York — 1990-1995

Producer, director, and editor of commercial and industrial video productions company. Freelance cameraman for numerous broadcasting networks. Extensive independent experience in ENG and EFP. Traveled throughout Haiti, Cuba, and the U.S. covering news stories for Univision Spanish Network.
Other major clients included CNN, All American Video, Telemundo, Artel, UN Television.

Cameraman, Soundman SUNRISE VIDEO, New York — 1989-1990

Field producing, motion picture soundman.

Cameraman, Soundman, Producer, Editor UNIVISION NETWORK NEWS, New York — 1987-1989

Cover and broadcast international news to 175 countries.

Backstage Coordinator SHUBERT ORGANIZATION, New York — 1984-1985

Coordinated theatrical productions.

EQUIPMENT KNOWLEDGE & SKILLS

CAMERAS	Sony Betacam SP, BVW3A/30, BVW-105 & 405 – Ikigami HL-79E Hitachi SK-98, SK-81
VCRs	Sony BVU-110, VO-6800, BVU-800s – JVC4900 – Hitachi-HR 100 portables
EDITING	Sony RM BVE 500 & 440
COMPUTERS	Character Generators – Editing – Lighting/Sound Controllers (Eagle)
LANGUAGES	Spanish – Read, Write, and Speak Fluently

EDUCATION

CENTER FOR THE MEDIA ARTS, NY • **Certificate in Television Production and Editing**
RCA INSTITUTE, NY • **Television Production**
BOROUGH OF MANHATTAN COMMUNITY COLLEGE, NY • **A.S. Degree**

CAREER COUNSELOR

BEVERLY BASKIN, M.A.

6 Alberta Drive, Marlboro, New Jersey 07746
(908) 555-4860 - home

Effective functional format on page one
Impressive presentations and publications at bottom of page one
Strong education section at conclusion

STRENGTHS AND ABILITIES

- Career and Mental Health Counseling
- Organizational Consulting
- Empowerment Counseling
- Training and Development

PROFESSIONAL ACCOMPLISHMENTS

Individual Counseling and Organizational Consulting

- Serve as Executive Director of Baskin Business and Career Services, a private practice specializing in career and mental health counseling, as well as issues facing employees in the workplace.
- Conduct nationwide three-day outplacement seminars and one-on-one executive coaching sessions for Fortune 500 corporations.
- Currently negotiating "Lunchtime Career Seminar" series for 1996 with NOVA Corp., Princeton, New Jersey.
- Served as Keynote Speaker and workshop leader, Professional Association of Resume Writers Convention, 1991 and 1992. Chosen Keynote Speaker for the New Jersey Home Economists in Business, 1994-1995 Conference.
- Enlisted as guest speaker on New Jersey Talk Radio, WCTC, "The Liz Maida Show," and WRFM, "About Money."

Seminars/Training

- Presented "Multimodal Therapy, the Cutting Edge of Psychotherapy Today," with Dr. Alice Whipple, New Jersey Mental Health Conference, Rider University, October 1995.
- Recommended by the New Grange Community Center for Adults with Learning Disabilities, Princeton, New Jersey. Developed a program entitled, "Making the Correct Vocational Choice," 1994 conference. Presented workshop to members of the Monmouth County Board of Social Services, 1994.
- Contracted as a workshop leader for Brookdale Community College Community Services Division. Assist with career workshops, business seminars, and women's conferences.
- Listed with the NJEA's Speaker's Bureau. Conducted a full day seminar entitled "Career Education in the Public Schools" for the Sayreville Public School System.
- Lead half-day seminars for Rutgers University Student Services, Monmouth County Library Headquarters, and Monmouth County Vocational School Districts.

Presentations and Publications

Contributing Author - *Key Careers,* by Robert Noe. Contributing Author - *Targeted Cover Letters* by Mark Ince. Contributing Author - *Executive Job Search Strategies,* by Robert Hines. Contributing Author - *Using WordPerfect in Your Job Search,* by David Nobel.

EXPERIENCE

EXECUTIVE DIRECTOR

1984-Present
Baskin Business and Career Services
Offices in Woodbridge, Princeton, and Marlboro, New Jersey

Additional Counseling Experience:

Beverly Baskin, M.A. - Private Counseling Practice
Dr. Alice Whipple, Licensed Psychologist, Princeton, New Jersey
Jewish Family Services, Edison, New Jersey

WORKSHOP LEADER, ***Community Services Division***

Brookdale Community College, Freehold, New Jersey 1984-Present

ADULT EDUCATION TEACHER

Freehold Township Public Schools, Freehold, New Jersey 1981-1984

BUSINESS EDUCATION TEACHER, ***Facilitator of Co-Op Program***

Jamesburg High School, Jamesburg, New Jersey 1971-1981

EDUCATION

MA in Counseling Services, Rider University, Lawrenceville, New Jersey
Graduate Studies, Career and Vocational Counseling, Rutgers University
Selected by the New Jersey Employment Counselors Association as recipient of a Counseling Student Grant to further my education
Bachelor of Science in Education, City University of New York, Baruch College

American Counseling Association and
New Jersey Counseling Association and Affiliates
National Career Development Association
National Association of Employment Counselors
Member, Career Planning and Adult Development Network
Member, National Association of Job Search Training
Middle Atlantic Career Counseling Association
American Psychological Association, Student Member

JOSEF M. HUBERNESH
138 Commonwealth Avenue
Boston, MA 01960
(617) 555-0878

> *Powerful presentation with targeted title*
> *Strong Overview and Areas of Expertise sections*
> *Forceful ending with excellent credentials*

EXECUTIVE CHEF

Specializing in Italian, French & Continental Fine-Dining Cuisine

Dynamic, Results-Oriented & Team-Spirited

OVERVIEW

Over fifteen years of professional cooking and kitchen management experience. Exemplify leadership qualities and professionalism, backed by a consistent, verifiable record of achievement.

Consistently maintain 5★/5✦ and Micheline 2★ rated restaurant establishments including: the *Hubernesh Imperial* (Boston, MA), the *Hubernesh Imperial* (Vienna, Austria), *Boulderfrach International* (Transkai, South Africa), and *Klosterbrau* (Seefeld, Austria).

AREAS OF EXPERTISE

Master Chef designation
Executive/Sous-Chef experience with million-dollar, upscale establishments
Trained by Paul Bocuse, Gaston Lenotre, Roger Verge, M. Matt and R. Gerer
Training & development specialist; teaching instructor
Successful catering experience (1,200+ people)
Maximizing kitchen productivity and staff performance

PROFESSIONAL EXPERIENCE

The Hubernesh Imperial, Boston, MA — 5★/5✦
GM / EXECUTIVE SOUS-CHEF — 1993 - Present

Executive Sous-Chef for restaurant serving Italian, French, and Continental cuisine, producing $2.4 million in revenues. Hire, train, and direct six cooks/chefs. Plan menu, assure quality control, and minimize waste.

The Hubernesh Imperial, Vienna, Austria — 4★/4✦
GM / EXECUTIVE CHEF — 1987 - 1993

Supervised 28 cooks/chefs, managed back house operations, and performed purchasing function for this $7 million upscale establishment specializing in Italian and French cuisine.

Les Chef de France, Epcot Center, Orlando, FL — 5★/5✦
CHEF - FOOD PRODUCTION FACILITY — 1989 - 1990

Managed 15 people and oversaw production of high-volume establishment, for this $16 million upscale restaurant specializing in French cuisine.

EXPERIENCE (Continued)

Hotel Klosterbrau, Seefeld, Austria — 5★/5✦ & Micheline 2★
EXECUTIVE SOUS-CHEF — 1987 - 1989

Supervised 35 cooks/chefs, for this internationally renowned hotel boasting two award-winning restaurants ($7 million in food volume/year). One of just two restaurants in Austria with a Micheline 2★ rating.

SUN International, Transkai, South Africa — 5★/5✦ & Micheline 2★
SOUS-CHEF — 1986 - 1987

Oversaw 48 people for Chico's Restaurant, one of the hotel's 14 restaurants producing a total of $50 million/year in food revenue.

Hotel Palaise, Vienna, Austria — 5★/5✦ & Micheline 2★
CHEF — 1985 - 1986

A landmark hotel with a 400-year history, considered one of the top upscale hotels in Europe. Served Traditional and Continental cuisine. Annual F&B revenues of $20 million.

EDUCATION & QUALIFICATIONS

W.I.F.I., Innsbrook, Austria
Graduate: CERTIFIED MASTER CHEF

Silver Medalist:	International Cooking Olympics, Germany, 1983
Guest Chef:	Cuisine de Chefs, Paulos Cafe Restaurant Les Chef de France Epcot Center, Orlando, FL
Instructor:	Culinary Arts to Aspiring Sous/Executive Chefs
Guest Appearance:	Sunny 104.3 FM Radio - *Kevin's Kitchen*

- References & Supporting Documentation Furnished Upon Request -

CARTOONIST
SPORTS / HUMOR

JERRY P. KOONZ
1824 5th Avenue
New York, NY 10021
(212) 555-8263

Light and entertaining industry-specific graphic
Emphasis on well-known publications that accentuate his value
Probably accompanied by a portfolio of his work

PROFILE:

More than 12 years of successful experience as a freelance cartoonist specializing in the field of sports and humor. Have appeared regularly in the following publications:

*	Golf Digest	1987 - Present
*	Golfer's World	1990 - Present
*	Sports Illustrated	1990 - 1994
*	Sporting News	1989 - 1993

Recent Work:

- Six-year contract with British Golfing Journal, 1990 - Present
- Seven-year contract with Walt Disney Publications, 1989 - 1996
- Eight-year contract with PGA of America (Promotion's Dept.), 1989 - 1996
- Eight entries with the New Yorker Magazine, 1989 - 1995
- Three entries in NBA All-Star Program, 1989, 1992, 1993

Education:

B.A.: Animation Science; University of Vermont, Burlington, VT
With Honors, 1986

Awards:

ACA National Honorable Mention (1988-1996)
NACA National Recognition (1991-1996)
IACA International Recognition (1987 - 1996)

References and Professional Portfolio Furnished
Upon Request

An author's favorite—a creative and fun resume
Excellent graphic presentation at the bottom
Solid Summary of Qualifications section

LISA JOHNSON

402 Rally Drive • Belleville, Illinois 62221 • (618) 555-8

SUMMARY OF QUALIFICATIONS

Six years experience as the Head Coach of highly competitive basketball, volleyball, and softball teams for a quality NAIA women's intercollegiate athletic program in the American Midwest Conference (formerly the Show-Me Collegiate Conference). A successful track record for graduating student-athletes (97%), managing athletic programs, recruiting, and developing talent at the high school, junior varsity, and varsity levels. Actively involved in faculty, athletic, and student affairs committees. Proven athletic administration skills include:

Budgeting	Travel Planning	Public Relations
Staffing/Scheduling	Academic Standards	Recreational Programs

- Graduated 60 Academic All Conference volleyball and softball players in the last five years. Coached volleyball teams that qualified for post-season play each year and softball teams that have finished no less than fourth in the conference, including a regional championship and a 4th place national finish.
- Member of the American Volleyball Coaches Association, National Softball Coaches Association, and National Association of Intercollegiate Athletics.
- Served as the Director of Public Relations for the St. Louis Steamers Soccer Club from 1985-1987. Accustomed to developing a strong rapport with local media contacts.
- Hold an M.A. Degree in Speech Communication from Southern Illinois University at Edwardsville and a B.A. Degree in Communication from St. Louis University. Earned Academic All Conference honors in basketball as an undergraduate. Taught various Physical Education (activities and theory) and Communication courses over the last six years including Public Speaking, Interpersonal Skills, Small Groups, and Persuasion.

COACHING HIGHLIGHTS/COMMITTEE WORK

Head Volleyball/Softball Coach, McKauliffe College, Livingston, Illinois 1989-Present

- 1995: American Midwest Rating Committee, Volleyball
- 1995: 4th Place, NAIA National Softball Championship, the highest national tournament finish for any athletic team at McKauliffe College
- 1995: NSCA Exposure Camp Director
- 1995: NAIA Executive Committee, Softball
- 1995: NAIA Midwest Region Champions, Softball
- 1995: NAIA Midwest Region Coach of the Year, Softball
- 1994: NSCA Exposure Camp Staff
- 1993: NAIA District #20 Chair, Softball
- 1992: Show-Me Collegiate Conference Champions, Volleyball
- 1992: Show-Me Collegiate Conference Coach of the Year, Volleyball

	1990	1991	1992	1993	1994	1995	Totals
SOFTBALL							
Won/Loss	29-14	19-9	21-10	22-8	28-18	41-16	160-75 (68%)
NAIA All Americans	1	n/a	n/a	n/a	n/a	2	3
All Conference	2	3	3	4	5	5	22
Academic All Conference	1	1	5	7	8	9	31
VOLLEYBALL							
Won/Loss	18-10	24-20	18-11	25-13	28-13	16-21	129-88 (60%)
NAIA All Americans	n/a	n/a	1	1	2	2	6
All Conference	2	2	3	4	3	3	17
Academic All Conference	2	2	5	6	7	7	29

COMPUTER TRAINING

Effective presentation with skills leading the way
Good chronology of employment with specific achievements
Incidental employment handled in the Related Experience section

Jan Abercrombie

98033 North Addison ■ Chicago, Illinois 60000 ■ (212

COMPUTER TRAINING & TECHNICAL SUPPORT PROFESSIONAL

Sales Automation ■ Marketing ■ Network Support

Results-driven training and support specialist with proven record of achievement in computer training and technical support. Produced measurable results in sales force automation through training and support of sales reps in multiple divisions. Outstanding project management, technical, networking, training, and presentation skills. Extensive PC software experience:

- WordPerfect
- Lotus 123
- Microsoft Excel
- Lotus Freelance
- DOS
- Norton Utilities
- cc:Mail
- Windows 95
- Procomm
- Laplink Pro
- Paradox
- Microsoft Access

PROFESSIONAL EXPERIENCE

Technical Administrator 1994-Present
SHELTON HOMES, INC., Chicago, IL

Manage, support, troubleshoot, and maintain sales automation system for 2 major divisions of large homebuilding corporation. Provide onsite training and telephone support for multiple sales offices for general PC projects. Produce computerized/multimedia presentation materials for employee meetings and other functions. Involved in development, testing, and training of new software programs distributed throughout the region to additional users.

- Solely responsible for installation, training, and sales support of WinSell program, a Windows-based sales/prospecting program for the homebuilding industry, resulting in 37% increase in sales rep efficiency.
- Instrumental in diagnosing major system problem and implementing solution in regional office affecting 25+ users. Kept repair costs under budget and completed job in 50% of projected time.

Information Resource Specialist / Network Administrator 1991-1994
ALUMINUM RECYCLING ASSOCIATION OF NORTH AMERICA, Chicago, IL

Managed and maintained online electronic bulletin board system for 2500+ users. Supervised holding library and database, information acquisition program, and publication ordering system. Developed procedures and other in-house documents.

- Learned Novell Network system independently; promoted to system administrator and liaison to outside vendor support after 1 year.
- Trained and supported 40 employees during network upgrade and installation of WordPerfect.

Membership Coordinator / Trainer 1989-1991
AMERICAN ASSOCIATION FOR MENTAL RESEARCH, Washington, D.C.

Managed database of 8000 members for 16 divisions. Identified and solved problems related to annual meeting registration and management of general session meeting.

- Served as back-up to computer manager and liaison to vendor support.
- Provided training and support to member associations during conversion to proprietary software system.

RELATED EXPERIENCE

Operations Assistant 1988-1989
MAJOR DOMO ENTERPRISES, INC., Washington, D.C.

Supervised pre-show activities and pre-exhibitor fact books and information sheets. Supervised convention hall personnel and onsite registration.

General Manager 1986-1988
JAMES RADISSON PROPERTIES, Washington, D.C.

Supervised hotel employees; managed accounts for hotels, condominiums, and private customers. Extensive computer operation and accounting.

Public Relations Intern 1986
CINCINNATI BLUE BIRDS HOCKEY CLUB, Cincinnati, OH

Served as marketing liaison with local media, developed marketing strategies, compiled market analysis information, prepared statistical analysis of team performance for media distribution.

EDUCATION

Bachelor of Science Business Administration 1986
ILLINOIS STATE UNIVERSITY, Normal, IL
Financed 100% of educational expenses.

Additional Training:

- "How to Teach People to Use Computers" (3 days), SoftBank Institute, Washington, D.C. 1995
- "Understanding the Internet," National Seminars Group, Bethesda, MD 1995
- "Computer Training & Support Conference," SoftBank Institute, Orlando, FL 1995
- "Advanced PC Troubleshooting, Essential Seminars," Tysons Corner, VA 1994

References furnished upon request

COMPUTERS—DATA PROCESSIN

Strong portfolio of skills to open the resume
Emphasis on skills and abilities
Strong finish with education and computer proficiency

JUANITA D. SMITH

3045 Information Highway, Villa #B-6, Cyberston, Mo
(750) 555-2345 • E-mail: juansmi@aol.com

PROFILE

- **Expertise in Information Systems Development.** Over 15 years' direct experience in the analysis - design - development - quality assurance - testing - and implementation of large-scale information systems for both private and government clients. Proficient in software, applications, and database development. Successful in aligning IS strategy and architecture with corporate mission. **Professional Trainer. Willing to travel, relocate, or accept contractual assignments.**

- systems analysis, integration, lifecycle	- client-server technology
- Wide Area & Local Area Networks	- multi-vendor environment
- strategic IS planning	- telecommunications integration
- configuration management	- technology security
- business disaster recovery	- cost reduction through technology
- operations and process reengineering	- Continuous Improvement
- Deming Management Method	- ISO-9000
- Statistical Process Control (SPC)	- MRP II utilization
- Total Quality Management (TQM)	- APICS-certified
- Just-in-Time (JIT)	- distributed processing
- technical training (all levels)	- university-level curricula design

SELECTED ACHIEVEMENTS

TWENTY-FIRST CENTURY TECHNOLOGIES, LTD.

PROJECT LEADERSHIP

- **Directed the strategic and tactical growth and development of a Wide Area Network** (WAN) consisting of over 125 nodes and incorporating DOS and UNIX-based systems. Mobilized special task force to determine feasibility and technical requirements for this project.
- **Participated in strategic network planning and special studies** to enhance network utility. Optimized network availability and performance of all network resources.
- **Defined and developed software standards and documentation.**

PROGRAM IMPLEMENTATION

- **Trained line and senior management** on use of microcomputers and installed software (introductory, advanced, and recurring classes). **Served as key technical advisor** to CEO and his direct reports regarding Information Technology issues.
- **Spearheaded and co-managed the search and implementation of a fourth-generation MRP II package.**
- Served in several critical **leadership roles:** (Chair) Emerging Technologies Steering Committee - (Co-Chair) Reengineering Strategies Committee - (Member) Project Team Mobilization.

PROCESS REENGINEERING

- **Modernized the company's Information Systems department** to meet current and future data processing, transmission, and communication requirements.
- **Significantly improved Department's ability to manage the network.** Standardized software and hardware applications which decreased user training and equipment acquisition costs.

ALLIANCE DATA & TELECOMMUNICATIONS SERVICES CORPORATION

COST REDUCTION

- **Saved company $1 million annually by automating the production planning process.** Designed/directed an Ethernet-based LAN (Local Area Network) system to use MRP II technology (all company plants and product lines).
- **Wrote software that forward and backward-scheduled shop floor operations** and introduced a Just-in-Time use of raw materials.
- **Restructured inventory management procedures** using a time-phasing approach which decreased storage costs and resulted in **$345,000 annual savings.**
- **Conducted company-wide systems training** on use of MRP II software - microcomputers - micro-to-mini communications - word processing - spreadsheet and database managers - development software.

SELECTED ACHIEVEMENTS (continued)

UNITED STATES NAVY

PROJECT MANAGEMENT & COORDINATION

- **Provided end-user training and documentation of computer and security systems.** Designed and instructed in use of Wide Area Network. **Received several commendations for improvements to command-wide training management systems.**
- Streamlined mission planning and reporting processes through use of automation. Certified computer systems for the processing of classified information.
- **Authored numerous Naval training manuals and developed procedures** for aircrew qualifications, testing / scoring, performance measurement, and certification. Served as Flight Examiner and Instructor Pilot on naval ship the U.S.S. Connecticut.
- **Technically prepared 175-member crew** for qualifications in General Damage Control and Firefighting. **Designed curriculum and performance measurement tests.**

WORK HISTORY

- TWENTY-FIRST CENTURY TECHNOLOGIES, LTD., Quality, Montana
  (HIGH-TECH DIVISION OF FORTUNE 1000 TECHNOSTAT & AN IS0-9000-CERTIFIED ORGANIZATION)
  Information Systems Manager (10/87-present)
- ALLIANCE DATA & TELECOMMUNICATIONS CORP., Secret City, Montana
  Manager, Innovation & Technologies Department (8/84-8/87)
- UNITED STATES NAVY (prior to 1984)
  - **Lieutenant Commander: Honorably Discharged**
  - Training Director: Naval Conference Center
  - Recipient: Meritorious Service Medal (2)

EDUCATION

- **Master of Science - Systems Management**
  Montana State College of Technology, Secret City, Montana
- **Bachelor of Science - Computer Science**
  Montana State College of Technology, Secret City, Montana
- American Production & Inventory Management Certification:
  Certified in Production & Inventory Management (CPIM)
- Numerous continuing education workshops: detailed list upon request.

COMPUTERS & SYSTEMS PROFICIENCY

OPERATING SYSTEMS

- NOVELL Netware 2, 3 - IBM AIX 3.2, 3.4 (UNIX) - OS/2 version 3 - WINDOWS 2.0, 3.0, 3.1 - PCDOS & MSDOS versions 3.0 through 6.22.

PROGRAMMING LANGUAGES

- PROGRESS - "C" - BASIC - dbase III, IV - PL/1 - COBOL (ANSI & pre-ANSI) -FORTRAN (ANSI & pre-ANSI) - IBM Assembly.

APPLICATIONS

- Word processors: WordPerfect - Microsoft Word / Works - PCWrite.
- Spreadsheets: Excel - QuattroPro - Lotus 123.
- Database Managers: PROGRESS - Access - PCFILE - dBase II, III, IV.

COMMUNICATIONS

- Hyper Access - IPX and TCP/IP protocols - Procomm and Procomm Plus - Internet and other online services.

Simple, one-page resume with emphasis on hardware/software knowledge
Skills and achievements highlighted in lieu of education information
Educational deficiency needs to be addressed in the cover letter.

David A. Doss
136 Marsh Lane
Addison, Texas 7500
(214) 555-2000

Qualifications Summary

Systems Programmer established in technical support and systems support with strong emphasis on troubleshooting and installation and maintenance of third-party software. Over 8 years MVS Systems Programmer experience, including SNA networking with VTAM, NCP, and SSP. Over 10 years VM Systems Programmer experience. First-hand knowledge of computer operations, operations management, and applications programming.

Hardware: IBM 30XX and 37XX, VM/XA SPA, MVS/XA, JES2, VTAM, NCP.
Software: SSP, TSO/E, ISPF/PDF, SMP/E, ACF2, RSCSv2, TCP/IP.

Experience

9/87-Present — Kelly Air Force Base
Consultant — San Antonio, Texas

Provide all installation, maintenance, and upgrade support for VM/XA 2.1.0 and MVS/XA 2.2.0 operating systems on IBM 4381 designated as a Mission Critical Computer Resource (CBIPO, CBPDO, SMP/E). Control all system and resource access as System Manager (includes ACF2 Administrator). Manage all direct access storage backups and recovery. Authored operations manuals and procedures. Proficient in ACF/VTAM (3.2.0), ACF/NCP (4.1.0), and ACF/SSP (3.2.0).

- ❑ Compiler support for Automated Test Equipment including rehost implementation, verification, and documentation. Technical support, user support, and training.
- ❑ Recovered BETA compiler system used to program ATE equipment in support of F-111 aircraft avionics.
- ❑ Developed and implemented fiber optics link in support of Operational Readiness Inspection alternate site requirements.

3/85-9/87 — Santa Rosa Medical Center
Systems Analyst/Programmer — San Antonio, Texas

Maintained and upgraded hospital accounting applications. Authored batch applications to provide input data for Shared Medical Systems RJE host.

Systems Programmer

Installed and maintained MVS/XA operating system and all subsystems.

Headed DOS/VSE to MVS/XA conversion team. Developed unique procedures for sharing databases between DOS-based DLI and IMS on the MVS/XA system during the conversion. Authored an application to recover "lost" CICS transient data transactions resulting in the recovery of over $80,000 in hospital revenues.

Personal Data

Top Secret Cryptographic Clearance, United States Air Force

CONTROLLER

EMMELINE E. WHITCOMB

1244 N.W. 97th Avenue | Res. (305) 555-3312
Miami, Florida 33111 | Fax (305) 555-4312

QUALIFICATIONS

CORPORATE CONTROLLER — Fifteen years' experience with high-volume manufacturer, demonstrating consistent record of impacting profit performance throughout tenure. Instrumental in reducing overhead $2.9 million (16%) and contributing to operational goals and personnel relations. Strengths include general ledger, financial statements, financial analysis, budgeting, cash management, and internal and external reporting. Prior experience in public accounting with leading international firm.

Clean, neat, and effective presentation
Experience complemented by education
Experience effectively highlighted by "Selected Contributions" layout

EDUCATION, PROFESSIONAL REGISTRATION

Certified Public Accountant

M.S., Taxation — Wharton School of Business

B.S., Business Administration — Princeton University

PROFESSIONAL EXPERIENCE

MECHANICAL MANUFACTURERS, Miami, Florida — 1981-Present

CONTROLLER: Manage financial and accounting functions for manufacturer generating annual sales in excess of $195 million. Accountability extends to financial statements, profit flow/cash flow analysis, and management of lines of credit. Hire and supervise accounting staff of ten. As management team member, participate in strategic planning, including expense forecasting, tax planning, and cash management/investment strategies.

Corporate interface with lenders and auditors (international accounting firm, IRS, Property Tax Assessors). Report directly to CEO. Promoted from Director of Accounting/MIS in 1989.

Selected Contributions:

- Provided financial data and accounting services in connection with change in ownership, including licensing requirements, conversion from S corp to C corp, and collaboration with attorney.
- Reduced primary expense category from 50% to 34-36%, saving company approximately $1.2 million through implementation of purchasing controls.
- Directed conversion of 401(k) program from company-directed to employee-directed program, reducing employer liability and labor costs of approx. $135,000 by off-loading management of funds.
- Established overhead budgeting system using Microsoft Excel to improve expense tracking.
- Introduced cafeteria plan and designed bonus system to improve employee morale during downsizing.
- Improved relations with and reduced turnover among mid-management and support staff.

TOUCHE ROSS, Miami, Florida — 1978-1981

SENIOR AUDITOR: Supervised audit team. Representative client list included securities firms, manufacturers, government entities, and financial institutions.

♦ ♦ ♦

CONVENTION PLANNER

Solid and effective one-page resume
Strong portfolio of skills at opening
Right-to-the-point information on employment responsibilities and achievements

MARIA LANE

1504 Ocean Reef, Jupiter, FL 33477 Telephone (407) 555-8978

Experience and education have provided excellent working knowledge in the following key areas:

Sales & Marketing
Market Analysis
Sales Forecasting
Account Development
New Business Development
Seminars & Presentations
Program Development
Budget Planning

Highly regarded for consistently achieving *superior sales results* through leadership, planning and effective implementation. Management style is to lead by action, assess the situation, and create consensus through effective communications.

Senior Groups & Meetings Manager
PALM BEACH COUNTY CONVENTION & VISITOR'S BUREAU West Palm Beach, FL 1994 - Present
Joined the bureau, serving 37 Gold Coast communities (1 million population), to cover the association, incentive, and corporate markets in the Midwest, West Coast and Canada. Named Senior Sales Manager, after three months of goal-exceeding performance. Presently direct the Mid-Atlantic region.

- In late spring, 1995, monthly goals for confirmed bookings were at 325%, and 80% for the calendar year.
- Arrange sales missions to major cities and familiarization trips for association leaders and corporate travel planners.
- Increased sales leads 46% for 1994/95 by executing a high-volume direct mail campaign aimed at targeted prospects.

Director of Convention Sales
FRESNO CITY & COUNTY CONVENTION & VISITOR'S BUREAU Fresno, CA 1984 - 1994
Played a key role developing aggressive short-term strategic marketing plans that recaptured Fresno's top ranking as a convention site during economic doldrums. Joined the Bureau as Membership Director. Named Senior Convention Sales Manager in 1988, and promoted to Director in 1990 for a Bureau serving a half-million population in Central California.

- Led the convention sales department in the reversal of a three-year downturn. Fresno moved from fourth place as a state, regional, and district convention site in 1989, to third in 1990 & 91, and second in 1992.
- Starting in 1989-90, which saw a $36.6 million decrease from the previous year, began producing consistent revenue increases, totaling more than $91 million, over four consecutive years.
- Increased sales leads to 207 in 1992-93 from 60 in 1989-90, with a corresponding 25% growth in actual bookings.
- Advanced average convention attendance by 50%, and increased revenues to $38 million from $10 million.
- Launched a national athletic marketing program, resulting in 10 events and $7 million in future business.
- Successfully orchestrated several sales blitzes, one of which led to $3 million in future business.
- Earned the *Outstanding Achievement Award* in 1991 from the Western Association of Convention & Visitors Bureaus, and *Business Associate of the Year Award* in 1993 from the American Business Women's Association.
- Presented talk, *Getting More Business with Less Money and Fewer Staff Members*, at the 1992 Annual Convention of the Western Association of Convention & Visitors Bureaus.

A.S. Degree Program - Business Administration
Fresno City College, California, 1984

CREDIT MANAGER

One-page resume with lots of information
Solid emphasis on skills and key achievements
Emphasis on achievements to overcome potential educational deficiency

CYNTHIA CITO

15334 Maywood Drive **(201) 555-2275** Maywood, New Jersey 07607

PROFILE SUMMARY:

An ambitious, dedicated, and proactive credit management professional with a strong background that includes: vendor relations; negotiations; client credit management; staff supervision • Confident decision maker • Computer skills include Lotus 1-2-3, Excel, Windows, Microsoft Word, Microsoft Office, and ProWrite • Possess a solid base of knowledge and experience upon which to draw that will assist employers in meeting their credit objectives.

- **Thorough understanding of credit operations and the need for strong management in all financial areas in order to maintain profitability.**
- **Experienced in all phases of credit approval; demonstrated ability to upper management to appropriately and profitability handle large credit limits.**
- **Superb negotiation skills with the ability to interact with clients, establish equitable payment policies, and resolve billing errors to maintain positive relations.**
- **Proven collection abilities - thorough knowledge of acceptable and legal collection practices.**

PROFESSIONAL EXPERIENCE:

B&B/H.W. INTERNATIONAL • Edison, New Jersey **1990 - Present**

CREDIT MANAGER for B&B (1995-Present)

- Determine creditworthiness for a $30 million importer of clothes and vinyl bags.
- Review all incoming and outgoing orders and conduct extensive credit checks with agencies, vendors, and financial institutions.
- Analyze financial statements to calculate credit strategies.
- Research chargebacks and process accordingly.
- Train, develop, and manage accounts receivable staff and allocating personnel.
- Coordinate documentation for Letters of Credit.
- Assist in cash posting and process legal forms.
- Attend monthly credit meetings sponsored by Dun & Bradstreet.

  - ♦ Saved company over $230,000 by strategically holding off shipments to major retailers with poor credit history.
  - ♦ Fostered communications between sales and credit departments to ensure organizational goals were achieved in accordance with credit procedures.
  - ♦ Instrumental in the implementation of monthly credit reports of each account being forwarded to sales force; enabled comprehension of account's creditworthiness and future sales tactics.
  - ♦ Decreased chargebacks through diligent communication with key management personnel of shipping vendors.
  - ♦ Elected by peers to serve as Treasurer for a credit group within the retail market.

ASSISTANT CREDIT MANAGER for H.W. International (1990 - 1995)

- Assisted in maintaining all credit files; accountable for all functions of collections for 3 major vendors, including chargebacks and negotiations.
- Effectively identified and resolved potential posting problems with cash applications.

  - ♦ Streamlined daily procedures and improved efficiency through implementation of computerized credit system.
  - ♦ Saved over $200,000 in shipment expenditures by holding off a shipment to a major retailer with poor credit history.
  - ♦ Assumed departmental responsibility during manager's 2-month leave.
  - ♦ Promoted by upper management for superior performance.

EDUCATIONAL BACKGROUND:

Regularly attend advanced training in credit management through Dun & Bradstreet and New York Institute of Credit Seminars.

Middlesex County College • Edison, New Jersey • Psychology

DENTIST

DOROTHY DePACE, DDS, MSPH

864 East 19th Street • Fort Lee, New Jersey 07024
(201) 555-8638

PERSONAL PROFILE

By nature a powerful, analytical, scientifically disciplined professional seeking an opportunity to utilize demonstrated strengths in the public health sector. Superior technical knowledge, doctor/patient relationship, methodical analysis and research in a biomedical environment.

EDUCATION

DOCTOR OF DENTAL SCIENCE (DDS), December 1980
School of Dentistry, Federal University Espirito Santo
Vitoria Espirito Santo, Brazil

MASTER IN REMOVABLE PROSTHODONTICS, 1985
Thesis: Semi Rigid Prosthodontic Unilateral
Dental Conference in Guarapary, E.S. Brazil

MASTER IN SCIENCE IN PUBLIC HEALTH, 19
University of Alabama at Birmingham, Birmingham, A
Thesis: "Prevention of Caries in Pit and Fissure Using Se
International Dental Public Health

> *A dentist who highlights education and training up front*
>
> *Effective listing of credentials including publications and affiliations*
>
> *Easy-to-read format—pertinent information is accessible*

Resident in General Dentistry, 1981 - 1982
Botafogo Polyclinic, Rio de Janeiro, Brazil

Dental Sculpture, 1981
School of Dentistry Federal University of Rio De Janeiro, Brazil

Dental Nutrition 1100, Six Hour Credit, 1992
Institute for Natural Resources, Miami Florida

CAREER PATH

THE METROPOLITAN ARES OF ESPIRITO SANTO'S CAPITAL, Vitoria, E.S. Brazil **1984 - 1996**
Dentist
Worked as a dentist in a general practice. Spent three years training in prosthodontics. Quickly increased number of patients with a very high retention and loyalty level.

SAO JOSE RURAL HOSPITAL, Colatina, E.S., Brazil **1985 - 1986**
Case Manager
Screened and referred patients to appropriate clinics. Followed up on case studies of the prevalent dental and medical communicable illnesses of patients seen and treated at the hospital. Processed patient information, and maintained active records to assist the appropriate clinic on the research data bank.

SAO JOSE RURAL HOSPITAL, Colatina, E.S., Brazil **1985 - 1986**
Part-time Health Educator
Provided technical assistance and training to patients in the areas of dental and physical health. Conducted lectures on matters such as hygiene, vaccination, nutrition, and the importance of breast feeding.

UNIVERSITY OF ESPIRITO SANTO, Vitoria, E.S., Brazil **1979 - 1980**
Student Instructor
Supervised and assisted dental students with diagnostic, treatment plan, laboratory work, and orientation during their work with patients. Graded each student.

DOROTHY DePACE • (201) 555-8638

(CAREER PATH CONTINUED)...

UNIVERSITY FEDERAL, E.S., Brazil **1979 - 1980**
Part-time Assistant Professional/Instructor
Taught dental procedure techniques. Assisted with diagnostic and evaluation treatment plan during treatments, and laboratory assignments. Graded each student.

CERTIFICATIONS

CERTIFICATE IN INTERNATIONAL EPIDEMIOLOGY OF AIDS, 1993
University of Miami School of Medicine National Institute
of Health Forgaty International, Miami, Florida

ADDITIONAL TRAINING

Worked as Pediatric Dentist, Education, Public Health

Director of Laboratory Safety for Nutrition Laboratories,
Department of Epidemiology and Public Health

INTERNSHIP/CLINIC

Department of Public Health, Internship 325 Hours
Florida State Department of Public Health, Miami Florida

Visiting Research Associate in Dental Public Health
University of Alabama at Birmingham, Birmingham, Alabama

PROFESSIONAL AFFILIATIONS

American Dental Association
Espirito Santo Dental Association
Paulista Dental Association
Federal Dental International
American Academy of Cosmetic Dentistry
Brazilian Dental Association
Rio de Janeiro Dental Association
American Dental Association
West Dade Dental Society
Hispanic Dental Association
American Association of Public Health Dentistry

PUBLICATIONS

Researched and Wrote Biomaterial on Microleage in Gallium, Presented March 11-15, 1992
Meeting AADR in Boston, Massachusetts

Presented a Panel Removivel Prosthodontic with Free Unilateral -
6th Dental Meeting of Espirito Santo, April 18-21, 1986

LANGUAGES

Portuguese, English, Spanish; read and comprehend Italian

DISTRIBUTION

Executive-level resume with emphasis on skills backed by achievements
Employment sections packed with relevant, value-oriented information
Conclusion with powerful education and affiliations sections

DOUGLAS LITCHFORD

119 Old Stable Road
Lynchburg, Virginia 24503
(804) 555-4600

DISTRIBUTION OPERATIONS / WAREHOUSING / TRANSPORTATION EXECUTIVE
Building Profitable, Efficient & Quality-Driven National Logistics Operations

Well-qualified executive with 21+ years' experience in the strategic planning, development, staffing, budgeting, and management of large-scale distribution operations. Expertise includes:

- Multi-Site Operations Management
- Transportation Planning / Operations
- Carrier Selection / Negotiations
- Equipment Acquisition / Asset Management
- Human Resource Affairs / Labor Relations
- EDI / Supplier Partnerships
- Materials Planning / Management
- Capital Project Management
- Facility Design / Specification
- Budgeting / Financial Affairs
- JIT / Quick Response Inventory
- OSHA / DOT Regulatory Affairs

Managed up to 22 distribution sites supplying 130 sites nationwide with an inventory valued at $140+ million and a 140-vehicle fleet. Captured multimillion dollar cost savings through efficiency, productivity, quality, and safety improvements.

PROFESSIONAL EXPERIENCE:

Senior Partner — 1992 to Present
PENSKE TRUCKING, Lynchburg, Virginia

Recruited by executive team of this full-service transportation management firm to provide strategic and tactical leadership for an aggressive business growth and diversification program. Company specializes in the design and delivery of customized logistics operations to reduce costs of product acquisition, transportation, and warehousing for client companies.

Manage client projects from initial consultation, through a comprehensive service improvement, cost reduction and analysis program for design, development, and oversight of logistics operations. Evaluate existing logistics operations and integrate within newly-established programs. Analyze efficiencies of existing warehousing, fleet, and traffic management processes to determine alternative paths of supply management. Provide on-site training to company personnel and personally negotiate carrier price and service contracts.

- Won nine major traffic management contracts which generated over $1 million in revenues.
- Spearheaded three major logistics projects with full responsibility for design of turnkey warehousing, distribution, fleet, and logistics operations.

Vice President of Distribution — 1978 to 1991
THE HOME CENTERS, INC., Lynchburg, Virginia

Senior Operating Executive responsible for the strategic planning, development, and management of a regional distribution program servicing 167 home centers in 10 states throughout the Eastern U.S. Total revenue volume exceeded $650 million. Total SKUs of approximately 20,000 items.

Scope of responsibility included five distribution centers, a 100-tractor private fleet, 400 personnel, a $31 million inventory and the entire domestic / import traffic management program. Managed a $17 million annual operating budget, administered all DOT and OSHA regulatory compliance programs, and introduced a complete safety, health, quality, and productivity improvement plan. Directed distribution, operations, purchasing and vendor management programs.

Conducted ongoing operational analyses to maximize operational efficiencies through redesign of warehousing facilities and realignment of regional distribution network. Analyzed cost factors to determine the need for facility expansion, closure and / or relocation. Negotiated contracts with common carriers to reduce transportation costs and administered union contract agreements for all employees.

THE HOME CENTERS, INC. *(Continued):*

- Created an innovative cross-docking program in cooperation with major suppliers that reduced annual product acquisition costs by more than $15 million.
- Introduced a proactive program for inventory control that reduced shrinkage from $1.4 million to only $250,000 within two years.
- Consulted with professional firm to design and implement leading edge computer technology for the optimal replenishment method for each SKU category.
- Implemented JIT and quick-response inventory and stock replenishment programs that resolved previous problems with merchandise distribution and provided adequate on-hand inventory at all 165 retail locations.

Assistant Vice President of Corporate Distribution 1970 to 1977
BLOOMINGDALES, Lynchburg, Virginia

Promoted from Director of Distribution to Assistant Vice President within one year of hire with responsibility for 22 distribution centers (3 million square feet), 1100 employees, 140-vehicle fleet, $140 million inventory, and $23 million annual operating budget. Directed stock replenishment and merchandise distribution (87,000 hard and soft goods) to 130 stores in nine states. Total revenues exceeded $1 billion.

- Launched a series of aggressive cost reduction initiatives that saved over $9 million in annual expenses. Realized savings through redesign of existing warehousing and transportation programs, negotiation of discounted purchasing and service agreements, realignment of staff requirements, and improved operating policies and procedures.
- Initiated and secured ICC approval for a wholly-owned subsidiary contract carrier. Reduced annual costs to the corporation by $2.5 million through savings in payroll and equipment costs concurrent with a significant decrease in union exposure.
- Restructured the entire distribution network, consolidated operations, and eliminated four distribution centers for a net annual savings of more than $6.5 million.
- Negotiated favorable collective bargaining agreements with three Teamsters local unions and the International Ladies Garment Workers Union.

Traffic Manager / Customer Relations Manager 1966 to 1969
RCA-WHIRLPOOL DISTRIBUTOR, Lynchburg, Virginia

Supervised inbound traffic, public warehousing, customer delivery operations, dealer/customer relations, and warranty/non-warranty repair programs. Facilitated significant improvements in the productivity, efficiency, and quality of operations.

EDUCATION:

Bachelor of Science / Business / Summa Cum Laude, Lynchburg College 1994
Bachelor of Arts / Psychology, Liberty University 1966

Highlights of Continuing Professional Education:

- Traffic Management, Liberty University
- General Transportation Management, Liberty University
- Computer Applications in Distribution, American Management Association
- Warehouse Layout, American Management Association
- Materials Handling Management, International Materials Management Society

PROFESSIONAL AFFILIATIONS:

American Management Association
Council of Logistics Management
International Materials Handling Society
Warehouse Education & Research Council
Private Carrier Council
American Trucking Association
Virginia Motor Truck Association

ENGINEERING

> *Strong portfolio of skills at opening*
> *Emphasis on positions with current employer*
> *Strong finish with education—a triple major*

EDWARD EDMONDS
119 Old Stable Road
Lynchburg, Virginia 24503
Home (804) 555-4600

MANAGEMENT PROFESSIONAL
Engineer / Management / Consultant

Six years' experience in the design, development, and leadership of large-scale corporate actions to improve productivity, quality, and efficiency. Facilitated significant cost savings through expertise in:

- Reengineering
- Continuous Improvement
- Statistical Design/Analysis
- Quality/Productivity Training
- Process Control & Improvement
- Manufacturing Methods
- Team Building/Team Leadership
- Project Management

PROFESSIONAL EXPERIENCE

Advanced Manufacturing & Process Engineer 1991 to Present
CONTINENTAL MANUFACTURING, INC., Lynchburg, Virginia

Recruited into the corporation's Management Development Program and placed on a fast-track career path. Rotated through a series of increasingly responsible assignments in Engineering, Operations, Corporate Quality, Distribution, and Manufacturing at Continental facilities in the U.S., Latin America and Europe.

Manufacturing Division, Lynchburg, Virginia (1993 to Present)

Promoted from Management Development Program to permanent professional position in Corporation's largest operating division (four business units with 5000+ employees and 15 manufacturing facilities throughout the U.S.). Given full responsibility and decision-making authority for design, development, implementation, and leadership of an aggressive waste reduction program for raw materials, WIP, and finished product.

Challenged to advocate program implementation and win the support of manufacturing management and staff throughout this nationwide division. Established cross-functional management teams (e.g., Quality, Manufacturing, R&D, Engineering) at each facility to research and identify specific areas for cost reduction within their organizations. Scope of responsibility includes process redesign, new product introduction, materials handling, and resource management.

- Generated over $10 million in savings within first year with an additional $15+ million projected for 1995.

Manufacturing Division, Caracas, Venezuela (1992 to 1993)

Planned and directed an aggressive program to optimize plant layout and methods for this multimillion dollar converting operation. Established, trained, and managed a continuous improvement team of four professionals to facilitate project implementation and ongoing productivity improvements.

- Decreased material handling by 50% and reduced space requirements by 650 sqm.
- Designed and implemented Kanban system resulting in a 33% increase in productivity and 50% reduction in inventory.
- Decreased CCT by 50% to meet the corporation's performance objectives and reduced production costs by 15%.

Electronic Products Division, Silicon Valley, California (1991)

Introduced improved process control methodologies into an electronic cable assembly operation. Complemented changes to the manufacturing process with on-site training, feedback loops, and designer/trainer involvement.

- Increased yield to 95% to meet IBM's quality supplier status requirements.

Industrial Engineering Consultant 1990
CONSUMER DIRECT, INC., Bogota, Columbia

Completed two-month consulting assignment to troubleshoot and upgrade specific manufacturing areas for this large consumer products manufacturer.

- Designed sampling plan as the foundation for a plant-wide preventive maintenance program.
- Wrote software program to maximize plant capacity with minimal equipment, personnel, and materials.

Assistant Industrial Engineer 1988 to 1990
SMITH SPECIALTY LABS & MANUFACTURING CO., Bronson, Michigan

Recruited for four internships while completing studies at the University of Michigan. Earned an excellent reputation for expertise in statistical theory and application.

- Invented a new measuring tool for shop materials that was subsequently utilized throughout the manufacturing facility.
- Planned and led 17 capability studies of specific product characteristics to determine their compliance with customer specifications. Utilized SPC techniques to measure product tolerances and performance.
- Conducted a large in-plant industrial experiment to identify improved process control methods to upgrade manufacturing and product capabilities.

Assistant Industrial Engineer 1988 to 1989
DETROIT METRO HOSPITAL, Detroit, Michigan

- Conducted a series of productivity monitoring and analysis projects throughout the manufacturing facility to validate worksheet model and variance analysis methodologies.
- Redesigned the corporation's central computer area to improve workflow, productivity, and efficiency of operations. Orchestrated complete reconfiguration of equipment, personnel, and infrastructure.
- Evaluated software prior to acquisition to determine its validity for specific flowcharting and reporting functions.

EDUCATION

Bachelor of Science, Triple Major in Industrial Engineering, Mathematics & Statistics, 1991
UNIVERSITY OF MICHIGAN, Ann Arbor, Michigan

- Completed short-term projects with professors in the Engineering and Mathematics Departments. Conducted research experimentation, collected/analyzed data, and reported results. Wrote code for random number generator algorithms.

PERSONAL PROFILE

Born in U.S. Lived in Portugal, Spain, Brazil, and Denmark. Enjoy windsurfing, skiing, and travel.

ENGINEER

JOSE M. DIAGO

Well focused and targeted resume
Fine blend of skills, responsibilities, and achievements
Good chronological employment history backed by accomplishments

1255 Cobra Drive
Stuart, FL 33999
(407) 555-7690

START-UP ENGINEER

Specializing in Mechanical Equipment, Process Controls, and Instrumentation

---

OVERVIEW

More than 7 years of Power Plant start-up and engineering experience (Fossil, Biomass, & Nuclear). A team leader, highly adaptable to varying environments. An analytical thinker recognized for problem-solving and strong interpersonal skills. Areas of expertise include:

- **A comprehensive and thorough understanding of power plant processes**
- **Working knowledge of test equipment - electronic and mechanical**
- **Redesign and modification of systems and controls**
- **Recognized ability to troubleshoot and resolve highly complex problems**
- **Flexible and adaptive to change; resourceful in getting the job done**
- **Work well independently; interface professionally with all disciplines**

WORK HISTORY

B & R Power Group, Connick, MD **1992 - Present**
START-UP ENGINEER (1995 - Present)
Okeelanta Cogeneration Project, South Bay, FL
Mechanical Start-Up Engineer for main turbine and auxiliaries, feedwater and condensate systems, main and process steam, ash handling, and process control valves. Performed mechanical testing, troubleshooting, and tuning. Directed steam cycle chemical cleaning and steam blows.

PRE-OPERATIONAL TEST ENGINEER (1994 - 1995)
Kennecott Utah Copper Refinery Modernization Project, Magna, UT
Responsible for mechanical and electrical start-up of refinery electrolyte filtering, distribution, sampling systems, condensate systems, and steam plant. Tested, tuned, and troubleshot PLC's, instrumentation, and controls. Provided support to client operations.

- Resolved a serious plant steam supply system problem for refinery. Reworked inadequate controls to keep system reliable and the plant operational at $1 million/day.

START-UP ENGINEER (1993 - 1994)
Chambers Works Cogeneration Project, Carney's Point, NJ
Mechanical and Controls Start-Up Engineer for the auxiliary boiler, ash handling, extraction, and process steam systems. Tested and troubleshot mechanical equipment. Performed BMS testing, and boiler controls programming and tuning. Performed PLC and instrumentation testing, troubleshooting, and programming.

- Directed rebuild of station auxiliary boiler after explosion. Modified boiler controls during recommissioning to improve boiler safety.
- Commissioned pneumatic fly ash system with recycle. Worked with vendor to resolve numerous control problems, which involved significant rewrite to 2,000-rung program.

WORK HISTORY

B & R Power Group, Connick, MD (Continued):

START-UP ENGINEER (1992 - 1993)
Limerick Generating Station, Limerick, PA
Lead Start-Up Engineer for deep bed demineralizer and resin transfer and handling systems installation. Developed system start-up program and performed acceptance tests. Developed training and operational procedures. Responsible for mechanical testing, PLC programming/testing, and control tuning.

- Resolved significant mechanical and controls systems design deficiencies with hydropneumatic resin handling system. Implemented changes to make system reliable with no impact to station operations.

JB Clarke Power Services, Baltimore, MD **1990 - 1991**
SYSTEM ENGINEER (3/91 - 9/91)
Limerick Generating Station, Limerick, PA
Assigned to Philadelphia Electric Company Station Technical Section. Performed heat transfer testing and flow balancing. Developed procedures for major plant maintenance evolutions. Performed tracer calibrations of feed water flow elements.

TEST ENGINEER (7/90 - 1/91)
Limerick Generating Station, Limerick, PA
Assigned to Philadelphia Electric Company Station Technical Section. Performed extensive service water systems flow, heat transfer, and NDE testing. Functionally tested plant modifications. Performed functional testing on 4kV Emergency Diesel Generator and breaker systems.

Aaron & Starr Construction Company, San Francisco, CA **1988 - 1990**
TEST ENGINEER
Limerick Generating Station, Limerick, PA
Assigned to Philadelphia Electric Company Station Technical Section. Provided support to station operations. Troubleshot electrical and mechanical equipment. Wrote operating procedures and logic functional tests. Station Engineer responsible for plant wastewater, room unit coolers, HVAC, and gaseous radwaste.

EDUCATION

Drexel University, Philadelphia, PA
Bachelor of Science Mechanical Engineering, 1989

Gettysburg College, Gettysburg, PA
Associate of Science Computer Science, 1987

COMPUTER SKILLS:
Hardware: Allen Bradley PLC, SLC Series; PC's; VAX; UNIX.
Software: Allen Bradley Series 7200, 1742 PLC Programming; DOS; Windows; MS Excel/Word; Lotus; WordPerfect; PASCAL; Fortran; VAX/VMS; UNIX

INTERESTS: Running, snow skiing, rock and ice climbing, reading

- References & Supporting Documentation Furnished Upon Request -

Comprehensive Summary and Profile sections
A functional format emphasizing qualifications
Strong closing with Education, Qualifications, and Affiliations

Nancy J. Krane

4182 Redmont Drive
Wall Township, New Jersey 07719
Home: (908) 555-5195

SUMMARY

Over 18 years of extensive engineering and managerial experience; 10 years involving the operations and maintenance of power plants. Eight years specializing in mechanical and construction quality control/assurance. Proven strengths in leadership, communication, developing planning and scheduling. Excellent presentation and customer/business focus skills.

Currently working on a special project to reengineer the Enterprise Human Resource Department. Work as part of a team to redesign performance reviews, benefits, and corporate policies which will help to deliver services at competitive pricing in a regulated and deregulated market.

PROFILE

Broad-based responsibilities in the following areas:

- Operations
- Quality Assurance
- Power Plant Setups
- Vendor Negotiations
- Product Allocation
- Team Building/Human Resources
- Maintenance Management
- New Business Development

PROFESSIONAL HIGHLIGHTS

ENGINEERING

- Managed daily operations and maintenance of generating station. Provided competitive focus to daily business decisions, with emphasis on cost of product and asset allocation.
- Installed, operated, and maintained gas turbine and diesel generators in the United States, Egypt, and Republic of Panama.
- Coordinate and participated in construction site development for military maneuvers, and municipal projects.
- Supervised maintenance management program to include scheduling equipment outage, readiness, dispatching and part inventory reporting.

PROJECT MANAGEMENT

- Facilitated Phase One of the Dry Low Nox research and development project on Gas Turbine Engines.
- Supervised the installation and acceptance of combustion controls system on General Electric and Westinghouse units.
- Coordinated planning and scheduling for Salt River Dam and Municipal Upgrade projects.
- Managed logistical requirements for mobile power plant airlifts for Bright Star and Gallant Eagle military missions.

QUALITY MANAGEMENT

- Designed and implemented Quality Services Work Teams. Established employee involvement teams, performance quality measurements, and customer/supplier relationships.
- Lead marketing initiative to automate Customer Satisfaction Index process in order to evaluate online performance and value added improvements.
- Instructed construction materials design courses for roads and airfield runways, emphasis on Quality Control and Assurance.
- Served as Military Mechanical and Construction Quality Assurance representative on civil engineering projects.

EMPLOYMENT HISTORY

PUBLIC UTILITIES: While assigned as Technical Supervisor, served in various engineering capacities.

1994 - Current	Station Planning Engineer
1992 - 1993	Senior Technical Supervisor/Project Manager
1989 - 1991	Technical Supervisor/Quality Services Manager

CORPS OF ENGINEERS: While serving 12 years in the US Air Force Corps of Engineers, held various engineering positions.

1985 - 1989	Senior Power Plant Operator/Maintenance Technician
1981 - 1984	Technical Construction Supervisor/Master Instructor
1977 - 1980	Maintenance Manager/Equipment Repair Specialist

EDUCATION

CIVILIAN:
New York Regents Consolidated Studies (120+ hours), BS, Primary - Social Sciences, Secondary - Business and General Engineering.
University of Maryland, AA, Liberal Arts, General Studies.
Washington High School (Iowa), General Studies.

MILITARY:
US Air Force Engineer School, Prime Power Production Course.
Leadership Management Courses.
Mechanical and Construction Quality Control Courses.
Maintenance Management Course.
Engineer Equipment Maintenance Course.
Master Instructor's Course.

QUALIFICATIONS

LICENSE:
State of New Jersey, Engineer's License, Blue Seal.
National Institute of the Uniform Licensing of Power Engineers, Third Class.

CERTIFICATION:
American Society Quality Control, Certified Quality Technician.

AFFILIATIONS

PROFESSIONAL:
US Air Force Reserve, Sergeant First Class, Information Office Manager.
Association Society Quality Control, Princeton Chapter Member.
American Management Association, National Member.
Non-Commissioned Officers Association, Permanent Board Trustee.

VOLUNTEER:
Project CAN BE Food Drive, Community Relations Representative.
US Air Force Reserve, Career Guidance Counselor.
Local Municipalities, Minorities in Engineering.

Consultant title to indicate "in transition" but still working
Easy access to accomplishment section
Strong ending with Education, Certifications, and Licensure

ERIC PETERSON, CHMM

10 Gary Lane • Rochelle Park, New Jersey 07

(201) 555-0521

ENVIRONMENTAL HEALTH AND SAFETY PROFESSIONAL

A highly experienced professional possessing a comprehensive background in regulatory enforcement. Thoroughly versed in DOT, EPA, NJDEP and OSHA rules and regulations. Experienced in hazardous waste removal and management. Versed in various computer applications and E-mail transmittals. Bilingual in English/French.

ACCOMPLISHMENTS / HIGHLIGHTS:

- ♦ **As a private consultant, expertly identify issues of noncompliance to the environmental health and safety laws/regulations for clients: significantly reduce expenditures and streamline operations.**
- ♦ **Successfully reduced workplace injuries at a major exporter resulting in substantial savings in related costs (workers compensation, down time, OT for additional employees).**
- ♦ **Trained a hazardous waste transportation company in proper handling of haz mat.**
- ♦ **At Freehold Cartage, reduced expenditures by consolidating permits when appropriate.**
- ♦ **Lowered insurance premiums and improved rating by lowering experience modification factor.**
- ♦ **As Sanitarian for 2 townships, appeared in court as an enforcement agent.**

PROFESSIONAL EXPERIENCE:

INDEPENDENT CONSULTANT — 1993 - Present

- Provide consulting services to organizations nationwide with emphasis in health, safety, transportation, and environmental law/regulations.
- Review site plans; perform site visits and audits to ensure compliance with existing or upcoming laws and regulations.
- Outline recommendations in detailed reports that identify areas of noncompliance.
- Interface daily with senior level management.
- Conduct comprehensive training in job-specific activities pertaining to health, safety, and transportation activities.

ENVIRAL, INC. — New Brunswick, New Jersey
Director, Regulatory Services — *1986 - 1993*

- Directed all environmental and occupational compliance for a solid and hazardous waste transportation company, including state and federal transportation regulations.
- Generated permit applications and annual reports for environmental authorities.
- Monitored and coordinated the proper storage and disposal of on-site waste.
- Trained and developed personnel in 7 divisions (encompassing over 160 employees) in all safety and transportation regulations.
- Interfaced closely with insurance companies to ensure low accident ratios through implementation of safety programs and procedures.
- Served as an instrumental member of the Accident Review Committee and Safety Awards Incentive Program.

(continued ...)

ERIC PETERSON, CHMM
(201) 555-0521
- Page Two -

***PROFESSIONAL EXPERIENCE* continued ...**

PARAMUS TOWNSHIP — Paramus, New Jersey
HACKENSACK TOWNSHIP — Hackensack, New Jersey
Sanitary Inspector — *1984 - 1986*

- Reviewed site plan proposals for Health Department concerns, including subsurface disposal systems and drinking water systems.
- Performed engineering review of wastewater and freshwater systems.
- Enforced state/local regulations for recreational facilities and retail food establishments.
- Inspected sites and ensured compliance with local noise ordinances.
- Issued Notices of Violations.

EDUCATION, CERTIFICATIONS, and LICENSURE:

Bachelor of Science in Biology/Environmental Science (1982)
State College, New Jersey

Regularly attend advanced training in:
Hazardous Waste Management • OSHA Regulations • Wastewater Disposal Systems
Underground Storage Tanks • Soil and Site Evaluation

Certified Hazardous Materials Manager, Master Level
Registered Environmental Health Specialist
NJ Sanitary Inspector - First Grade
CDL Class B Hazardous Materials and Tank Vehicle Endorsements

DOT Certified Instructor
DOT/EPA Regulatory Compliance Manager
DOT Cargo Tank Inspector
Transportation of Dangerous Goods Certification, Canadian Regulations
Registered Sanitarian, National Environmental Health Association

PROFESSIONAL MEMBERSHIPS:

Academy of Certified Hazardous Materials Managers
National Environmental Health Association
NJ Environmental Health Association

PERSONAL:

Dual Citizenship: USA/Canada

A neat, one-page resume with emphasis on skills and achievements
A modest but effective title following the Heading
Employment responsibilities joined by key accomplishments

CUSTOMER SERVICE

ANGELA DERBY
1827-B America's Cup Blvd.
Newport, RI 02840
(401) 555-3001

CUSTOMER SERVICE PROFESSIONAL

PROFILE:

- More than 7 years' successful experience in Customer Service & Support with recognized strengths in account maintenance, problem-solving & trouble-shooting, sales staff support, and planning/implementing proactive procedures and systems to alleviate problems in the first place.
- Possess solid computer skills. Excellent working knowledge using both IBM and Mac systems; Lotus 1-2-3, Excel, WordPerfect, MS Word, CT DataTrac.
- Ability to train, motivate, and supervise Customer Service employees. A team player, acknowledged as *"Total Quality Customer Service Professional."*
- Develop plan, conduct audits and variance analyses, process payroll and payroll tax reports and filings, and maintain/update accurate inventories.

Synopsis of Achievements

Increased customer retention by 19%, from 72% to 91%
Reactivated 9 key accounts ($253K/year), utilizing persuasion/mediation skills
Proactive planning led to notable increase in morale in all departments
Created customer satisfaction survey, drastically reducing potential problems

---

EMPLOYMENT:

1990 - Present

Cellular One, Newport, RI
Customer Service Representative
Work with 28 sales professionals covering 2 states (Rhode Island and Connecticut), responsible for over 3,800 individual and corporate accounts.

- Support sales reps in opening new accounts and upgrading existing service
- Quickly and effectively solve customer challenges
- Maintain quality control/satisfaction records, constantly seeking new ways to improve customer service

1985 - 1990

Daniel Southerland, Public Speaker, Newport, RI
Client Support
Worked with nationally acclaimed trainer and public speaker in booking programs. Work entailed heavy cold-canvassing, working with speakers bureaus, and following up on referrals.

- Instrumental in igniting revenues from $58K in 1985 to $686K in 1990
- Received *Red Ribbon Award* from National Speakers Bureau for fine work
- Helped position Southerland to land VP position with Pilzer Seminar Group

EDUCATION:

Southern New England Junior College, Providence, RI
Associate of Arts: Communications & Public Relations, 1985

REFERENCES:

Furnished upon request.

Candidate has a job and is seeking a specific VP position.
Education and work experience complement each other.
Strength is highlighted in three main sections following Education.

Walter A. Harns

123 Timberland Drive • Klamath Falls, Oregon
(503) 555-2121

OBJECTIVE Vice President for Programs with the Wildlife Habitat Enhancement Council.

PROFILE

- Over 15 years experience in ecosystem biodiversity and habitat management.
- Excellent communication, organizational, and time-management skills.
- Belief in straightforward and honest approach for soliciting cooperation.
- Motivated to *do the job well.*
- Fluent in Spanish and French.

EDUCATION

Bachelor of Science - Magna Cum Laude, Wildlife Management and Biology
Humboldt State University, Arcata, CA

RELEVANT EXPERIENCE AND ACCOMPLISHMENTS

ECOSYSTEM AND HABITAT MANAGEMENT

- Designed and introduced plant, fish, and wildlife species surveys, assessment, habitat protection, restoration, and monitoring programs to 3 districts.
- First biologist hired by Law Enforcement Division, US Fish & Wildlife Service, to enforce International Endangered Species Treaty Act.
- Developed and perfected Spotted Owl Survey techniques and identified habitat parameters in National Forest.

ENVIRONMENTAL PLANNING AND DESIGN

- As interdisciplinary team member, participated in development of Master Management Plans of Mt. Baker-Snoqualmie National Forest, Crystal Mountain Ski Resort, and 880-square-mile White River watershed.
- Evaluated and designed projects and plans.

MANAGEMENT

- Supervised 12 people directly and 82 indirectly.
- Promoted team building and collaboration to accomplish all multi-disciplined tasks.

EMPLOYMENT HISTORY

Headquarters, US Department of Agriculture, Forest Service, Washington, DC

1991-present **Resource Director**
Managed all natural resources and disciplines including cultural, recreation, plants, hydrology, soils, fish, wildlife, ecosystems, special uses, and volunteer programs.

1984-1991 **District Biologist**
Developed, implemented, and managed all plant, fish, and wildlife species and habitat programs for 3 National Forest districts.

1975-1984 **Timber Sale Administrator**
Ensured contract compliance of private timber companies' logging and timber sale activity, including erosion control, stream and wetland protection, threatened and endangered species habitat protection, road design and construction, and forest reclamation.

AFFILIATIONS/MEMBERSHIPS

President, Fallbrook Land Conservancy
Member, Habitat Restoration Working Group, The Wildlife Society

> *Executive-level resume with emphasis on skills backed by achievements*
> *Consultant title indicates "in transition" but presently working.*
> *Easy access to specific skills and abilities.*

JOHN JOHNSON
119 Old Stable Road
Lynchburg, Virginia 24503
(804) 555-4600

CORPORATE FINANCE / ACCOUNTING / ADMINISTRATION / MIS

Sixteen-year professional career directing domestic and international corporate finance for challenging and complex operations. Expert negotiation and transaction management qualifications. Skilled decision maker, problem solver and team leader. Fluent in French and Scandinavian languages. Conversational German.

- Merger & Acquisition Management
- Corporate Divestiture & Realignment
- Strategic Planning & Development
- SEC Regulatory Affairs & Documentation
- Securities & Investment Banking
- Public Relations & Investor Relations
- Financial Consolidation & Reporting
- Asset & Liability Management
- General Accounting Operations
- Operations & Financial Analysis
- Pension & Benefits Administration
- Domestic & International Tax

PROFESSIONAL EXPERIENCE:

Present — Since resigning my position with Williams Company, I have completed several contract/consulting engagements:

- Investor Group — Completed due diligence review for acquisition of start-up medical supply manufacturer.
- Software Company — Advised CEO and operating management in the preparation and presentation of capital investment solicitations to the venture capital community.
- Construction & Development Company — Prepared annual financial statement, operating and capital budgets, and forecasts.

WILLIAMS COMPANY, INC., Lynchburg, Virginia — 1981 to 1994

Fast-track promotion throughout 13-year career with this $5.5 billion, 50,000-employee, diversified manufacturer. Promoted through a series of increasingly responsible senior accounting and supervisory positions to final promotions as:

Assistant Controller, Smithfield, Inc., spin-off of Williams Company (1993 to 1994)
Director of Financial Consolidations & Reporting, Williams Company, Inc. (1987 to 1993)

As Director, held full responsibility for directing all accounting operations and monitoring financial performance of each operating division. Defined MIS information requirements to meet operating needs and established corporate-wide accounting policies, procedures, and reporting packages. Led a professional staff of 16 (11 of whom were CPAs with Big 6 experience) with dotted line responsibility for 70+ Division and Group Controllers.

Directed accounting operations for international and domestic taxes, long-term contracts, foreign currencies and derivatives, pensions and retiree medical benefits. Prepared shareholder, SEC, and internal Board of Directors and Management reports, and semiannual consolidated plans. Monitored financial performance of divisions including receivables and inventory management, capital expenditures, R&D expenditures, and general administrative costs. Managed systems implementation and integration of MIS for all operating divisions.

WILLIAMS COMPANY, INC. *(Continued):*

In 1992, selected to lead the management team responsible for orchestrating the spin-off of Williams commercial growth businesses to form Smithfield, Inc. Continued to manage ongoing responsibilities throughout 18-month project. Worked with SEC personnel, investment banking advisors, corporate securities counsel, legal transactions firm, and CFO. Directed strategic financial analysis, asset/liability allocation, and preparation of Form 10 SEC registration statement for new company shares.

Following transition to Smithfield, given full management responsibility for three corporate departments — Business Operations Analysis & Planning, Financial Consolidations & Reporting, and General Accounting. Coordinated with Tax Director on international tax planning and related legal structuring. Directed a staff of 10 headquarters personnel and a worldwide team of Division Controllers.

Career Highlights & Achievements:

- Directed the strategic analysis of Williams which resulted in spin-off of Smithfield.
- Established the entire accounting and financial infrastructure for new corporation. Developed policies and procedures for budgeting, financial analysis, financial reporting, tax accounting, and pension accounting. Coordinated with Treasury Department for international cash management.
- Directed complex financial analysis and integration of all accounting and financial operations for 19 acquisitions worldwide ($500,000 to $258 million). Integrated two acquisitions concurrent with company spin-off.
- Orchestrated accounting and financial affairs for the disposition of over 70 operating divisions of Williams during the company's realignment of its core portfolio. Consulted with Williams U.K. operations to resolve operational and financial issues related to the disposition of international business units.
- Developed economic analysis of impact on stock price of share buyback versus acquisition investment with the company's price/earnings ratio as measure.
- Served as the sole company representative on behalf of Smithfield in discussions and negotiations with the SEC on challenged issues regarding company formation and financial information.
- Successfully represented Williams in an arbitration of a disputed sales contract. Presented and interpreted financial and contractual documentation for the court, and recovered $20.6 million of disputed $21 million for the corporation.

WATSON & WATSON, PLC, Forest, Virginia 1979 to 1981

Staff Accountant promoted to **In-Charge Accountant** promoted to **Senior Accountant** within 18 months. Heavy SEC experience (including 10-K and S-1 filings). Industry experience included oil and gas, manufacturing, and food distribution.

EDUCATION:

Bachelor of Science, Business Administration / Accounting Option, Summa Cum Laude Graduate, 1978
NEW MEXICO STATE UNIVERSITY *(passed CPA examination in 1978)*

ALLEN T. HUNT, JR., CPA, CFP
200 Long Key Road
Palm Beach Gardens, Florida 33410

Clean, easy-to-read resume with focused title
Deemphasized employment dates since candidate has been out of work for a while
Emphasis on skills and abilities—accentuating tax accounting

(Strictly Confidential)

(407) 555-2888

FINANCIAL MANAGEMENT EXECUTIVE

- Corporate Tax Accounting Specialist -

SPECIFIC AREAS OF STRENGTH:

Tax Accounting	Budget & Reporting
Cash Management	Automation and MIS
Streamlining Operations	Audit Management

PROFESSIONAL EXPERIENCE:

Southeastern Export, LTD. — **North Palm Beach, Florida**
CONTROLLER
S.E., Ltd., is a global business organization founded by TV personality David Faulk made up of 12 separate corporations including: S.E. Design, S.E. Equipment, Inc., S.E. Sports Management, S.E. Marketing Services, S.E. Productions, S.E. Publishing, S.E. Financial Services, and S.E. Consultative Group. Annual sales are in excess of $40 million, with over 130 employees. (1991-95)

Responsibilities:
Budgeting, tax planning and compliance, cost control/containment, financial reporting, forecasting and monthly financial analysis, accounts payable, payroll, benefits administration, and audit management.

* Directed all tax work for all 12 corporations and performed all accounting, financial, and tax planning for David Faulk and his family members. Prepared over 400 Federal/State individual and corporate tax returns annually.
* Saved S.E. Products Inc. over $250,000 in tax accounting fees. Saved the firm over $400,000 by studying and adjusting the S.E. Design state allocation method.
* Assisted in the development and implementation of a new network computer system. Consolidated the Accounting Department, improved performance and monthly financial reporting structure. Enhanced cash flow position.
* Analyzed financial status of London office and recommended its closure. Revenues increased and operational efficiencies improved concurrently with these cost cuts.
* Involved with three major out-of-state audits (Sales and Use Tax and Gross Receipts Audits). Successfully limited exposure for the firm.

Mark, Fore & Strike, Inc. — **Delray Beach, Florida**
CONTROLLER
This company consists of 14 exclusive retail clothing stores complemented by a high-volume mail order catalog with annual sales of $23 million. (1985-91)

PROFESSIONAL EXPERIENCE:

Mark, Fore & Strike, Inc., (Continued)

Responsibilities:

Budgeting, cash management including a $1.5 million line of credit, monthly financial statements, accounting and expense controls, year-end audit preparation and coordination, preparation of tax returns, interpretation of balances or trends with recommendations for corrective action, and supervision of accounting personnel.

* Successfully negotiated with major banking institution an increase in the line of credit from $750,000 to $1.5 million. Directed all company audits.
* Saved the firm over $190,000 by successfully negotiating insurance rates. Also saved the company $100,000 in credit card processing fees. Implemented a 401(K) plan. Streamlined monthly reporting period from 60 to 40 days.

Worldmark Corporation / Micro Fusion — **North Palm Beach, Florida**
CONTROLLER / TAX MANAGER
Worldmark is a Forbes 400 privately held company. (1981-85)

Responsibilities:
All areas of operations and accounting including: budgeting, cash management, monthly financial statements, account controls, year-end accounting/audit preparation and personnel supervision.

* Directed tax planning for the firm and prepared consolidated tax provisions for three separate holding companies. Also tax planning and preparation of corporate and individual income tax returns for the company President.

EXPERIENCE OTHER: (Prior to 1985)

Laventhol & Horwath, CPA's — West Palm Beach Florida
SENIOR ACCOUNTANT

Peat, Marwick, Mitchell & Company, CPA's — Providence, Rhode Island
SENIOR ACCOUNTANT

EDUCATION:

Bryant College of Business Administration — Smithfield, Rhode Island
BACHELOR OF SCIENCE: ACCOUNTING (Dean's List)

CERTIFICATIONS & MEMBERSHIPS:

Certified Public Accountant
Certified Financial Planner
Member: American Institute of CPA's
Member: Florida Society of CPA's

- References & Supporting Documentation Furnished Upon Request -

FIRESIGHTER

The Career Profile works here because this career is narrow in scope and hasn't changed over time.

Listing of relevant education and training on page two—important for this career

SEAN MCCONNELL

1234 Myrtle Lane, Temecula, California 92591 ☎ (909) 5

CAREER PROFILE

An experienced **Firefighter** whose professional responsibilities expanded his primary specialty into areas of operational management, staff training, administration and finance, motivational leadership, and decision making. Competent and knowledgeable in all phases of fire fighting with specific expertise in managerial activities. Qualified by:

- A proven record of success with progressively increasing responsibilities based upon experience, knowledge, and superior work performance.
- An innate ability to easily interface between both management and staff as well as with individuals of diverse backgrounds and cultures.
- Excellent communication, motivational, and time-management skills and abilities.
- Organizational and analytical skills, decisiveness in crisis situations, and adeptness in managing multiple tasks simultaneously.
- Hands-on experience in developing and training cohesive, dedicated, and loyal staffs.

PROFESSIONAL EXPERIENCE

NORTH COUNTY FIRE PROTECTION DISTRICT, Fallbrook, California - October 1992 to present

Fire Captain (Acting) responsible for supervising and coordinating day-to-day activities of assigned firefighters engaged in protecting lives and property. Functional authority includes: supervision of personnel; operations and maintenance of fire equipment, apparatus, and station facilities; response to alarms received and initial assumption of fire control activities; planning, supervising, and conducting training, fire prevention, and maintenance programs; station administration relative to personnel, emergency responses, inspections, station facilities, etc., by coordinating and supervising fire company policies, regulations, and procedures; enforcing and implementing department policies, regulations, and procedures; conducting pre-fire planning surveys and developing fire ground methodologies; and conducting preliminary fire company investigations to establish cause and point of origin.

NORTH COUNTY FIRE PROTECTION DISTRICT, Fallbrook, California - October 1986 to October 1992

Engineer responsible for controlling and extinguishing fires, protecting life and property, and maintaining assigned equipment under emergency and routine conditions. Additional responsibilities included performing assigned duties in preventive maintenance and repair of assigned equipment, apparatus, buildings, equipment, and facilities. Collateral duties involved providing instruction to Fire Fighting Team personnel.

NORTH COUNTY FIRE PROTECTION DISTRICT, Fallbrook, California - April 1983 to October 1986

Firefighter/Reserve Firefighter responsible for controlling and extinguishing fires, protecting life, environment, and property, responding to medical emergencies, and maintaining fire fighting equipment.

ACCOMPLISHMENTS

- Secretary and Crew Representative, Fallbrook Firefighters Association.
- Recipient, 5 and 10 year Dedicated Service Awards, North County Fire Protection District.
- Recipient, Crew Representative Service Award, Fallbrook Firefighters Association.
- Developed, implemented, and monitored Apartment and Street Map Books.
- Voluntarily installed new engine equipment and Communications Center upgrade machinery.
- Assisted in construction of Station #4 Apparatus Building and remodel of Headquarters Station.
- Conducted periodic inspections of emergency apparatus identifying numerous, potentially costly problems and initiating corrective actions to eliminate repair time and reduce expenditures.
- Enhanced the overall safety of firefighters and the general public.

RELEVANT COMPETENCIES

- Budget Preparation
- Hazardous Materials
- Station Management
- Strategic Planning
- Communications
- Motivation & Leadership
- Staff Training
- Staff Development
- Codes Compliance

(Continued on next page)

EDUCATION AND PROFESSIONAL TRAINING

Crafton Hills Community College, Yucaipa, California - 10 Credits
- Undergraduate Studies - Major Emphasis: **Fire Science**

Miramar Community College, San Diego, California - 30+ Credits
- Undergraduate Studies - Major Emphasis: **Fire Science**

Palomar Community College, San Marcos, California - 20+ Credits
- Undergraduate Studies - Major Emphasis: **Fire Science**

Santa Ana College, Santa Ana, California - 20+ Credits
- Undergraduate Studies - Major Emphasis: **Fire Science**

Santa Ana College Fire Academy, Santa Ana, California
- **Honor Graduate: Certificated Fire Science Course**

California State Department of Education
- Fundamentals of Radiological Monitoring, 1991
- Oil Fire School, 1983
- Surviving Hazardous Materials Incidents, 1989

California State Board of Fire Services
- Fire Apparatus Driver Operator I, IA, IB, 1988
- Firefighter I & II, 1985 and 1986

California Specialized Training Institute (CSTI) Courses
- Building Collapse, 1991
- Firefighter Safety, 1991
- Fire Hydraulics, 1983
- Fire Instructor IA, 1992
- Fire Instructor IB, 1992
- Fire Investigation IA, 1991
- Fire Management I, 1994
- Flammable Liquids Fire Control, 1988
- First Responder Operational, 1989
- Pipeline Safety, 1987

California State Fire Officer Certification Program
- Fire Prevention IA & IB, 1988 and 1989
- Fire Command IA & IB, 1986 and 1986

MEMBERSHIPS, AFFILIATIONS, ASSOCIATIONS

California Firefighters Association (CFA), Sacramento, California
Fallbrook Firefighters Association (FFA), Fallbrook, California

CREDENTIALS, CERTIFICATIONS, LICENSES

- American Heart Association - CPR Certificate
- California State Certified Fire Officer
- California State Class B Commercial License
- San Diego County, Emergency Medical Services, License: EMT-D
- State Certified Driver Operator

Appropriate personal and professional references are available.

ARTHUR C. GRANT

2344 Shoreline Drive
Boca Raton, Florida 33433

(407) 555-5337

FOOD & BEVERAGE / HOSPITALITY EXECUTIVE

- DIRECTOR OF CATERING & CLUB MANAGEMENT -

OVERVIEW:

A highly experienced, profit-oriented professional with an impressive record of accomplishments in high-volume, upscale dining environments. A management professional recognized for integrity and competence. Areas of expertise include:

Growth & Revenue Enhancement	Profit Attainment
Personnel Management	Member/Guest Relations
Provide High Quality Service	High-Volume Catering
Deliver Solid ROI to Stockholders	Increasing Club Membership

PROFESSIONAL HIGHLIGHTS:

- **Fine Dining Management Experience:** Employed by distinguished establishments including: Premiere Club of the Palm Beaches, Governors Club at Phillips Point, and Coleman's Catering Corporation. A strong list of accomplishments and fine references.

- **Caterer For President's Dinners:** For President Reagan and Vice President Bush, Washington, D.C. Convention Center, 1985. Served 5,600 honored guests.

- **Caterer:** New York Harbor Independence Day Celebration, dedicating the restoration of the *Statue of Liberty.* Served 11,500 guests aboard yachts.

- **Governor's Ball, New Jersey:** Directed all catering operations (seven consecutive years) for the largest black-tie political dinner held under a tent (5,000 guests).

PROFESSIONAL EXPERIENCE:

1991 - Present

Premiere Club of the Palm Beaches, Silver Tower Plaza, North Palm Beach, Florida
GENERAL MANAGER / DIRECTOR OF CATERING - Direct all F&B and catering operations for this exclusive private dining club. Recognized for maintaining high quality food and service during major growth period.

Successfully managed growth as club grew from 345 to 845 members. Stabilized all key positions and significantly reduced turnover.

educed membership sales payroll two-thirds, while exceeding growth pro-
ctions. Simultaneously improved employee productivity and morale.

rectly reported to Club Owner and C.E.O.

ivered a 26% return on investment to shareholders and owners.

The career direction and background clearly addressed in heading. Use of "chef" bullets is a classy touch that distinguishes the candidate. The Overview and Professional Highlights list qualifications and accomplishments, not simply relying on former job responsibilities.

EXPERIENCE (Continued):

1989 - 1991

Governors Club At Phillips Point, West Palm Beach, Florida
DIRECTOR OF CATERING - Directed all catering operations for this upscale private dining club with over 1,200 members. The club was affiliated with *Country Clubs of America (CCA),* a worldwide network of renowned establishments.

Ignited catering revenues from $600,000 to $990,000 the first year and $1.2 million the second season. Catering revenues contributed 50% of total sales—a 25% increase achieved in less than 24 months.

Awarded *Catering Director of the Year,* receiving recognition from CCA, for strong pioneering efforts in promoting catering within the private club industry. Trained Catering Directors throughout the region.

1977 - 1988

Ballard's Catering Corp., Morristown, New Jersey
PRESIDENT - Over 11 years, owned/operated three successful catering firms targeting specific markets, including affluent clientele and government officials.

Built business from ground zero to a highly profitable $6.5 million organization, employing over 600 people.

Directed formal black-tie affairs for Presidents Nixon, Ford, Carter, and Reagan (5,600 guests/function). Catered major events including the Governor's Ball (NJ) and Independence Day Celebration (NY Harbor).

Began Associated Catering, 1979 (mid-price catering). Began Catering by Albert K, 1980 (Jewish clientele). Restored a historical railroad station to a 175-seat restaurant. All ventures were profitable and sold.

1964 - 1977

Coleman's Inc., Newark, New Jersey
VICE PRESIDENT / GENERAL MANAGER - Joined in an entry-level capacity and ascended to positions of increasing responsibility over 13 years. Positions held: Sous-chef; Steward; Food & Beverage Manager; Director of Purchasing; Director of Operations; Vice President/General Manager.

EDUCATION:

Adelphi University, Long Island, New York
BACHELOR OF SCIENCE DEGREE
Major: Hotel/Restaurant Management; Minor: Personnel Management

INTERESTS:

Skiing, HO trains (hobby), and gardening. Member: International Geneva Association, Confrerie De La Chaine Des Rotisseurs, and Ordre De La Mondial

REFERENCES:

Furnished upon request.

Education first because she is a recent college graduate. (Note the inclusion of conferences attended and her certification.)

The tree graphic is a classy touch for a position in forestry.

She uses the Highlights section as a summary and then moves into her work experience.

JENNIFER D. SOUTH

8400 Industrial Parkway
Dublin, OH 43016

Home: (614) 555-2484
24-Hour Message: (614) 555-7615

EDUCATION/TRAINING

Bachelor of Science, Natural Resources, Ohio State University, 1995
Major: Urban Forestry
Honors: Cum laude with distinction in **Forest Resource Management**
National Golden Key Honor Society, **Gamma Sigma Delta**

Certified Arborist, International Society of Arboriculture, 1995
Ornamental Plant and Shade Tree Pest Control, Ohio Public Operator's License, 1995
Conferences: Ohio Nurseryman's Conferences, 1994-95, 1996-97;
Urban Forestry Conference, 1994-95, 1996-97
Accounting Certificate, Columbus Business University, 1982
Bachelor of Arts, Psychology, Ohio University, Athens, 1978

PROFESSIONAL HIGHLIGHTS

- Skilled project coordinator and team supervisor; effective in prioritizing, delegating, and motivating; effective problem solver with ability to maximize resources
- Experienced working with municipal agencies and local governments
- Educated in the infrastructure between urban forestry and city
- Assigned by Horticulturist to maintain large perennial beds in eight city parks
- Experienced crew leader, ensuring all street sites were marked by OUPS (Ohio Utilities Protection Service) before planting of street trees; oversaw planting and maintenance of street trees and public gardens
- Implemented Landmark Tree Program:
  - Sought and gained approval from City Council to initiate a Landmark Tree Program in Marysville, Ohio
  - Researched and documented large tree criteria of surrounding communities and states
  - Established guidelines to certify Landmark Trees

WORK EXPERIENCE

CITY OF MARYSVILLE — Marysville, OH
Park Tree Inventory Specialist — 1997-Present
- Locate, identify, and perform health assessment of all park trees; record and later input into in-house tree inventory computer program

Assistant City Forester — 1994-1997
- Supervised and maintained city street trees. Entailed planting, mulching, pruning, watering, staking, fertilizing, and the ability to operate machinery and small power equipment as well as the use of hand tools. (Tree population - 5,000)
- Participated in the following activities:
  - Pruning approximately 1,950 trees (increase of 76% over previous year)
  - Fertilizing approximately 460 trees (increase of 150% over previous year)
  - Managing citywide tree planting by various landscape contractors and the City of Marysville Parks crews: Established street tree locations; followed up on tree inspections; initiated verbal and written correspondence with developers and landscape contractors; and notified homeowners of tree plantings
  - Organizing City of Marysville, Tree City USA Program

OHIO STATE UNIVERSITY — Columbus, OH
Full-time Student — 1992-1995
- Gained valuable horticulture field knowledge experience
- Volunteered for campus tree planting program

CITY OF MARYSVILLE — Marysville, OH
Account Clerk, Finance and Mayor's Court — 1989-1992

BENNETT & BENNETT, INC. — Columbus, OH
Bookkeeper — 1983-1989

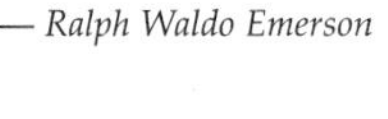

The creation of a thousand forests is in one acorn.
— *Ralph Waldo Emerson*

FUND RAISER

RACHAEL PETERS
1776 Spirit Way
Seattle, WA 91000
(606) 555-2468

Example of resumap format, centralizing the career objective and surrounding it with supportive information
Repetitive skill used to emphasize an important element of this industry
Achievements that represent results

Skills:

* *Raising money*
  * Budgeting & cost control
    * *Raising money*
      * Employee management & supervision
      * *Raising money*
    * Strategic program planning
  * *Raising money*
* Maximizing donations for direct giving

Achievements:

* Raised over $4.2 million in past 5 years for the United Way & Save The Children.
* 5-year consistent record of attaining projected fund raising targets.
* Reduced volunteer turnover of 38% to less than 8% annually. Increased donations 123%.
* Play pivotal role in assuring highest % of donations going to program - 81% (STC).

PROFESSIONAL FUND RAISING - PROGRAM DEVELOPMENT

NATIONAL / INTERNATIONAL CHARITIES & FOUNDATIONS

Employment:

United Way, Seattle, WA
Regional Coordinator 1981 - Present
Fund Raiser

Save The Children, Seattle, WA
Fund Raiser 1988 - Present

Education:

Wharton School of Business - U. of Penn.
MBA with Honors, 1979
B.A. in Organizational Behavior, 1975

Affiliations:
Member: United Way, Save The Children, Special Olympics, March of Dimes

Management Style:

* Team Player - Goal Oriented
* Seasoned Trainer & Motivator
* Highly Ethical

Personal & Professional References
& Supporting Documentation:
Furnished Upon Request

HABILITATION TECHNICIAN

Untraditional but easy-to-read layout of each section—Resumap format The central point of the resume is the job definition.

KENNY SHAFFER
21 Main Street, Apt. 10
Danville, Illinois 62215
(618) 555-7776

Qualifications

- Five years experience working with students (pre-K to adults) with behavioral disorders and developmental disabilities
- Additional background as a Nurse's Aide in a skilled and intermediate nursing home setting

Experience

- Chart progress based on established IEP's
- Assist with motor and daily living skills
- Provide support to students either individually or in small groups

HABILITATION TECHNICIAN

FOR DEVELOPMENTALLY DISABLED

Employment

Individual Teacher's Aide (1995-Present)
Warren G. Murray Center, Centralia, Illinois

Substitute Teacher's Aide (1990-Present)
Centralia High School, Centralia, Illinois

Nurse's Aide (1988)
Emerald Garden Health Care Center, Lebanon, Illinois

Education

Paralegal Studies, Sanford Brown Vocational College, St. Louis, Missouri
Business Administration, Kaskaskia Junior College, Centralia, Illinois
Paralegal Studies, Belleville Area College, Belleville, Illinois

REFERENCES AVAILABLE UPON REQUEST

HEALTHCARE ADMINISTRATION

Easy-to-read overall layout

Under the most recent job, highlighting of experience in each discipline to easily communicate experience and accomplishments

JOHN BRADFORD BRITTON, MHSL

1124 West Anandale ■ Long Island, NY 10055
(212) 555-8876

PROFESSION, QUALIFICATIONS

SENIOR HEALTHCARE ADMINISTRATOR with significant experience in managed care environments. Initiated and inspired management and clinical teams to achieve measurable successes in administration, marketing, MIS, physician relations, and patient care. Strengths include:

- Business Management, Operations, Organizational Restructuring
- Strategic Planning, Positioning in Anticipation of Industry Trends
- Marketing, Advertising, Sales Strategy Development
- Community, Physician, Employee & Industry Relations

MANAGEMENT EXPERIENCE

ADMINISTRATOR — **Imaging Associates,** New York, New York 8/88-Present
Direct accountability for full scope of operations for New York's premier freestanding radiology center.

Administration, Finance
- Increased net profit in excess of 350% within 2-year period.
- Controlled $10+ million operating budget and $1 million capital equipment acquisition budget.
- Negotiated radiology equipment service agreements, realizing savings of $900,000 over 5-year period.
- Engineered organizational restructuring, developed new service lines, and facilitated transition from top-line to bottom-line organization, addressing recent nationwide decline of imaging center services.
- Handled complex and highly sensitive physician-related matters with malpractice liability insurance company, patients, and legal counsel.

Marketing, Public Relations
- Led effort in collaboration with marketing/communications consultant toward design and execution of Center's first Strategic Marketing Plan.
- Involved in industry at national level as Past President of Board of Directors for American Imaging Association; fought successfully against onerous federal and state legislative efforts.
- Developed successful sales strategies to address influx of competition and control major market share.

Information Systems
- Implemented Center's first computerized patient scheduling and registration network.
- Involved in decision processes to ensure information resource architecture is consistent with strategic goals.
- Participated on national task force to survey advancing technology (Picture Archival & Comm. Systems).

Human Resources
- Managed hiring and patient-focused training for management, clinical, and support staff.
- Introduced flexible benefits plan and 401(k) retirement plan for staff of 65.

PRIOR CAREER SUMMARY
- Manager, Syracuse County Health Department, Syracuse, New York 10/87-7/88
- Associate Director, Allied Ambulance Service, Syracuse, New York 8/84-10/87
- EMS Instructor, County General Hospital, Rochester, New York 2/81-8/84

EDUCATION, CERTIFICATION

Masters in Health Systems Leadership, University of Chicago 1987
Bachelor of Science, Organizational Behavior, University of San Francisco 1983
Professional in Human Resources, Human Resource Certification Institute 1991

■ ■ ■

HOSPITALITY/EDUCATION DEFICIENCY

Highly targeted resume
Effective 2-column resume format
5 key skill areas bolded in left column
Education de-emphasized and no degree listed

GREG FANTIN

19986 U.S. Highway Ten
Roswell, GA 30075

MANAGEMENT EXECUTIVE
COUNTRY CLUB, RESORT, & PRESTIGIOUS COMMUNITY DEVELOPMENTS

EXECUTIVE PROFILE

Twenty years experience directing high-caliber properties nationally and internationally.

▼ **Operational Management**:
* Manage Large-Scale Properties
* Direct Multiple Profit Centers
* Establish Quality Standards
* Maximize Operational Assets

▼ **Recreation Facility Management**:
* Golf & Country Club Properties
  Course Management
  Golf Academy
  Membership Development
  Tournament & Event Coordination
* Yacht Club & Marina Operations
* Tennis & Swimming Facilities
* Clubhouse Operations

▼ **Financial / Budget Management**:
* Budget Analysis & Strategies
* Financial Objectives
* Asset Evaluation & Enhancement
* Payroll and Cost Controls
* Inventory Requirements
* Systems and Data Processing

▼ **Personnel Management**:
* Develop "Team Spirited" Organizations
* Perform Employment Needs Analysis
* Review Policies and Procedures
* Multinational Staff Recruitment
* Manage Over 350 Employees

▼ **Specialized Management Experience**:
* Turnaround Situations
* Workouts / Reorganizations
* Start-up Operations
* Equity Conversions

PROFESSIONAL EXPERIENCE

Executive Manager
Dubai Creek International Golf & Yacht Club
Dubai, United Arab Emirates (1992-Present)

Competitively selected from over 800 candidates worldwide to manage the pre-opening (final design review and changes) and opening of international resort. Full management responsibilities for an 18-hole championship golf course, 9-hole Par 3 floodlit course, golf academy, and golf club. Recruited multinational staff and senior executives. Coordinated European PGA Tournament on opening day. Directed yacht club operations (115-slip marina) achieving 60% occupancy in first 9 months.

Pre-sold 50% of Club memberships prior to grand opening. Created zero-based budgets, projecting a first year profit of $1.2 million.

Vice President: Hospitality
Bald Head Island
Bald Head, North Carolina (1991-92)

Recruited to the Executive Board, in charge of formulating new development plans and budgets for 1,800-acre Planned Unit Development (PUD). Managed final design and opening of Bald Head Island Golf & Tennis Club. Directed golf & recreational operations, mainland & island marinas, ferry operations, island cafe, and chandlery.

Increased income by constructing a new club and expanding Food & Beverage facilities. Acquired third ferry (secluded island—no access by car) to accommodate growth projections. Remodeled pool and tennis facilities. Reorganized property management division for 105 units. Established quality standards for entire resort operations, enhancing overall resort experience.

Professional Experience (Continued):

President
B.K. Nelson Associates
Tequesta, Florida (1988-91)

Point man for various assignments focusing on organizational development, design review, operations analysis, budgeting, and financial evaluation of community development and resort properties. Restructured and repositioned country club and other service industry concerns in meeting growth objectives.

Executive Manager
Mountain View Associates
White Field, New Hampshire (1987-88)

Recruited by majority owner to staff and direct a 235-room hotel facility on 80 acres with golfing, dining, and "carriage trade" related services. Worked on preliminary plans in developing an adjoining 259-acre parcel with single and multi-unit residences including an additional 18-hole golf course.

President: Club & Recreational Division
Heathrow
Orlando, Florida (1986)

Responsible for division—a multiunit PUD residential/commercial property. Hired to enhance design and establish a "world-class" operational philosophy. Redesigned facilities, recruited senior management staff for the Club, 18-hole golf course, 10 tennis courts, and aquatic facility. Staged Heathrow International Tennis Grand Prix.

Vice President: Operations
John's Island, Inc.
Vero Beach, Florida (1983-86)

Directed operations for this 3,500-acre PUD (3 golf courses, 20 tennis courts, a 105-unit hotel, golf & beach clubs, & 4 dining areas) directing over 350 employees. Established progressive management systems and personnel. Reversed Food & Beverage division to a profitable status.

John's Island, Inc. (Continued):

Reduced payroll ($1 million to $675K) in 7 months while revenues increased 190%. Assisted in multi-million dollar equity conversion from developer to membership-owned status. Achieved asset appreciation of $22 million in 36 months.

General Manager
Hobe Sound Company
Hobe Sound, Florida (1979-83)

Executive manager for the Hobe Sound Company and two subsidiaries: Jupiter Island Club (one of the most exclusive resort communities in the U.S.) and Hobe Sound Water Company. Formulated a well-managed organization establishing business goals, incorporating strong financial, operating, and maintenance programs for the island consisting of:

- 18-hole golf course
- 10 tennis courts
- Health spa
- 4 dining rooms
- 3 club houses
- 60-slip marina
- Movie theater
- Island services

Proactive marketing yielded a 26% increase in hotel occupancy. Reduced pension expenses by $32K. Realized a 100% increase in water plant production. Turned F&B around ($99K loss to $139K profit). Reversed a $300K negative cash flow to a $1.1 million surplus.

Manager
Topnotch at Stowe
Stowe, Vermont (1975-79)

Created and directed dynamic growth ($162K to $4.2 million) for this emerging world-class New England resort. Built solid management team in developing facilities and services to accommodate rapid development. Established quality standards (Mobil Four Star Award) and "award-winning" dining facilities (recognized through membership in the *Leading Hotels of the World*).

EDUCATION:

University of Hawaii, Honolulu, Hawaii, 1970
Business Administration
(Foreign Trade, Management, Economics)

HUMAN RESOURCES

The heading communicates the discipline clearly and effectively profiles the candidate.

The job descriptions focus on accomplishments, not responsibilities.

JASON P. GRAHAM

342 93rd Avenue S.E.
Mercer Island, WA 98041
(206) 555-1697

HUMAN RESOURCES

RECRUITMENT ... TRAINING ... ORGANIZATIONAL DEVELOPMENT ... COUNSELING

Twelve years of domestic and international experience in executive recruitment, staff training and development, budget administration, and employee assistance programs. Strong record of accomplishments working with senior managers to recruit highly qualified work teams and personnel. Particularly successful directing outreach, personnel, and marketing programs for human resources. Graduate degree in Psychology and training as a senior-level psychologist in the occupational field.

CAREER HISTORY & ACCOMPLISHMENTS

EXECUTIVE RECRUITER/ PRODUCTIVITY MANAGEMENT CONSULTANT — DRAKE INTERNATIONAL, *1990-Present*, *Sydney, Australia and Seattle, WA*

With more than 800 employees, Drake International provides executive recruitment, staffing, sales, training, management consulting, and employee assessment services in nine countries. Responsible for executive recruitment and marketing in the greater Seattle area.

- Named one of top five executive recruiters for the company out of 70 total recruiters worldwide. Billed over $190,000 during a 12-month period.
- Administered extensive psychological testing and screening to prospective employees to ensure a good match between applicants and the employer.
- Selected by senior management to market and provide technical training on a brand new psychological assessment product called "Triage." Led marketing effort to introduce the product to major companies in the Pacific Northwest market.

REHABILITATION CONSULTANT/ PSYCHOLOGIST — ANDERSON REHABILITATION GROUP, *1989-1990*, *Melbourne, Australia*

Anderson provides work rehabilitation, stress management, and other human resources and psychological services to individuals who have suffered some work injury. Responsible for psychological testing, counseling and therapy, medical and legal report writing, business planning, and liaison with corporate employers.

- Successfully negotiated a significant number of "return to work" contracts with corporate employers.
- Named acting manager for six months. During that period directed day-to-day business functions with no problems or interruptions in business activity.
- Established a network of clients and developed strong business relations for repeat referral business.

Previous experience (1986-1988) as **Client Services Supervisor** with Community Services Victoria, a state government department. Conducted training programs and provided information on legislation and policy development. Started career as **Youth Projects Coordinator** (1983-1985).

EDUCATION

M.A. (equivalent) and B.A. in Psychology, Monash University, Australia.
Completed University of Washington's Executive Management Program, 1995.

Sharon Margaret

14 Briarcliffe • Collinsville, IL 62234 • (618) 555-9968

The Heading is very creative, with the enlarged first initial and reverse print address.

The Professional Profile is easy to read and understand.

The Key Accomplishments format is perfect for this or a sales discipline.

Professional Profile

For the last two years, Sharon Margaret has proven herself to be a highly productive agent for Best Insurance Company. Her peers and policyholders appreciate her keen sense of quality service and knowledge of underwriting rules, procedures, and policy contract. She has expanded her personal lines more than 60% and currently manages more than 1,100 household, 1,200 auto, 600 fire, 300 life, and 200 health insurance policies.

Sharon is a valuable team member who always contributes professionalism, continuous improvement, and a winning attitude. Together with her operation partners, she was part of the 1995 instructor team that visited the campus of Eastern University last summer. Her "Multi-Lining" presentation was part of a program that earned outstanding reviews as "the best campus seminar ever" by many attendees.

Sharon holds a B.A. degree in Communications from Southern Illinois University at Edwardsville. In addition, she is completing Best Insurance Company's Advanced Life Curriculum Program as well as Part 2, Business Life Insurance, of the Life Underwriting Training Council to receive her L.U.T.C.F. designation.

Key Accomplishments

- Millionaire Club 1994; 93 paid apps, $25,447 paid premium
- On Time, Life Honor Program, 1995
- Multi-Illini Club (4x4), twenty-seven month streak
- RVP Club (8x4), twenty-six month streak
- Star Level IV 1994
- On Time Star Level IV, 1995
- LUTC I Graduate
- Monthly Average = 65 total apps (30 auto, 15 fire, 10 life, 10 health)
- FIC = 960 to date
- Course School 2, Field Period Leader, 3rd Place
- Course School 3, Field Period Leader, 1st Place

Professional Organizations

- Life Underwriters Political Action Committee
- East Side Life Underwriters
- National Association of Life Underwriters
- Metro-East Professional Women's Association
- Illinois Legislative Action Network

Community Service

- Volunteer, Big Brothers/Big Sisters
- Contributor, Illinois State Police Department
- Contributor, Collinsville Police Department

References Available Upon Request

INTERIOR DESIGNER

D I A N E A. J A C O B
172 River Street ◆ Douglaston, NY 11363 ◆ (516) 555-4201

PROFILE

Interior Designer responsible for layout of 44,000-square-foot furniture showroom and for complete design needs of showroom customers.

Expert in trend analysis, merchandising, and management. Highly creative, capable, and motivated; readily inspire confidence of clients. Direct comprehensive projects in home, office, or retail environments.

REPRESENTATIVE ACCOMPLISHMENTS

- **Design and coordinate furniture showroom of major department store.** Produce semiannual floor plans; consistently rework floor to react to current trends and new merchandise.
- **Achieved second place award** in eleven-store display competition; participated in interior design showcases.
- **Organized and facilitated design seminars** for store events and for community organizations.
- **Nassau Coliseum Home Show designer.** Developed and set up 20′×40′ vignette.

PROFESSIONAL SKILLS

Conceive and draft floor plans and designs for homes, offices, and commercial space.

Determine all components of interiors: color schemes, furnishings, lighting, accessories, window treatments etc. Emphasize client needs assessment; relate well to all types of people.

Develop and implement retail client design service programs.

Determine client needs; draft plans and create design proposals. Recommend merchandise necessary for fulfillment of goals. Provide home visits, in-store consultations, coordinate finalization of projects.

Supervise furniture store operations.

Plan and arrange complete furniture store room settings. Generate sales through effective visual display techniques. Responsible for customer service, sales supervision, opening/closing building, security, cash vault.

RELEVANT EMPLOYMENT

Macy's Furniture Store. Farmingdale, NY	**Designer/Manager**	1993 to present
Levitz Furniture. Garden City, NY	**Interior Designer**	1991 to 1993
Ethan Allen. Hicksville, NY	**Interior Designer/Sales**	1990 to 1991
Classic Galleries. Huntington, NY	**Interior Designer/Sales**	1989 to 1990
Georgetown Manor. Westbury, NY	**Interior Designer/Sales**	1986 to 1989

EDUCATION

Metropolitan Institute of Interior Design, Plainview, NY. Interior Design Certi

Fashion Institute of Technology, New York, NY. AAS, 1975

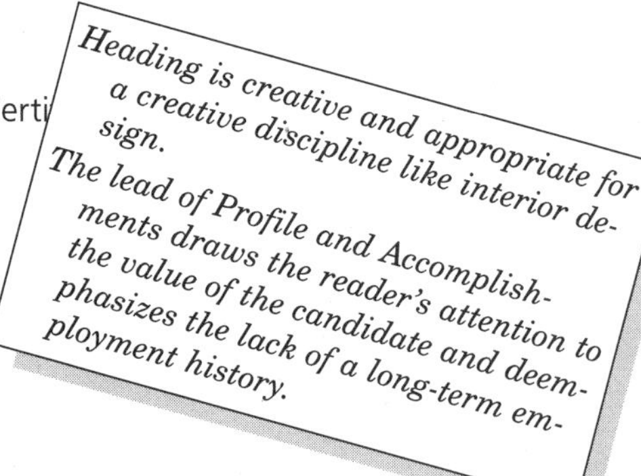

INTERNATIONAL BUSINESS

The Summary effectively ties togethe candidate including tangible ski
Education is listed in front of Worl is a more impressive credential tions in the five years since gr
The paragraph format of Job D friendly.

DARCY L. ABRAMSON

Foreign Trade & International Business Operations

19314 247th ...
Issaquah, WA 980..
(206) 555-4364

SUMMARY

Demonstrated achiever with exceptional knowledge of international markets, business practices, and trade regulations. Strong marketing and finance background combined with fluency in several languages, including "Advanced Level" U.S. State Department certification in Russian Language Reading Comprehension. Skilled at learning new concepts quickly, working well under pressure, and communicating ideas clearly and effectively. Extensive computer training, including knowledge of multiple networking environments and business software packages. Enthusiastic and experienced in overseas travel.

EDUCATION

Masters Degree in Russian & East European Studies (1990)
George Washington University (The Elliott School of International Affairs), Washington, D.C.

B.A. Degree in Foreign Languages (1988)
University of Miami, Coral Gables, FL
Concentration in Russian, Spanish, French, & Italian; graduated cum laude with 3.8 G.P.A.

Completion of Intensive Language Training Program (1989)
Leningrad Polytechnic Institute, Leningrad, U.S.S.R.

CAREER HISTORY & ACCOMPLISHMENTS

Assistant to the Director of Business Development, HEALTHINFUSION INC. *1994*

Worked directly with Director of Business Development and Director of Strategic planning of this large, publicly-traded provider of home health care services. Researched and wrote marketing, financial, and feasibility reports concerning new business acquisitions and acquisition prospects. Played key role in preparing a successful $5 million federal grant proposal to provide the company's Home Infusion Therapy to rural U.S. areas. Prepared corporate financial reports and service contracts for the CFO.

Russian and East European Coordinator, TRANS-CHEMICAL CORPORATION *1993*

Held key responsibility in this small import/export company for helping facilitate trade deals with the Former Soviet Union and Eastern Europe. Served as interpreter and translator for Vice President in major business negotiations. Reviewed company compliance with all applicable customs laws and procedures. Initiated multiple overseas joint ventures and served as liaison for foreign customers on business in the U.S.

Administrative Assistant to the Vice President, FORD MOTOR COMPANY *1991-1992*

Handled administrative functions for the Vice President of Ford's Executive Car Lease Program, a sales division catering primarily to the diplomatic community and the federal government. Assisted in preparing contracts and sales proposals for customers. Established reports to track products throughout the United States and develop further customer contacts for Ford Motor Company.

MEMBERSHIPS & AFFILIATIONS

Founding member of the Former Soviet Union Florida Chamber of Commerce
Member, American Association for Advancement of Slavic Studies
Member, World Affairs Council

James A. Trigali

36 Mary Avenue • Portland, Oregon 97201 ... 55-0936

The shaded box of testimonials is a unique approach that will work if they are complimentary and from key contacts.

"Jim's leadership, organizational skills, and initiative have been exemplary, evidencing his consistent commitment to excellence and strong customer service results ... It has been a pleasure and privilege to work with him." *(Supervisor, 8/93 to 5/95)*

"Jim provides an unassuming but very supportive and strong style of leadership that not only team members but members of the whole unit respect and value. He is a true team player." *(Manager, 5/94 to 9/94)*

"Jim Trigali is definitely an employee that any manager would welcome—he is supportive of management ideas but has the confidence and strength to raise critical concerns that only make the organization a better one." *(Manager, 5/94 to 9/94)*

HIGHLIGHTS

- Comprehensive knowledge of defined contribution 401(K) pension concepts and regulations
- Effective leadership and team-building skills
- Extremely well organized
- Proven customer service skills
- Excellent PC skills, including Windows, WordPerfect, and defined contribution 401(K) daily processing, stock, and mutual fund system logic

EXPERIENCE

CIGNA RETIREMENT & INVESTMENT SERVICES, Portland, OR
Plan Analyst I-IV (1990 to 1996)
Processed all contributions, loan repayments, benefit disbursements, fund transfers, and nonfinancial changes for daily/periodic 401(K) pension record-keeping transactions, including cash, mutual fund, stock, and guaranteed investment contract money movements. Resolved client questions and problems. Interfaced productively with team, department, field, and sales personnel. Completed, verified, and mailed all required client reports, plan year packages, and auditors' requests. Processed ADPs/ACPs and correction of year-end participant tax information.

Achievements:

- Promoted four times in four years
- Consistently met or exceeded all established standards for timing and accuracy
- Selected as one of first two people to participate in changeover to a daily 401(K) processing environment from a monthly processing environment, and quickly adapted to new system
- Chosen to train new hires and other plan analysts transitioning to the daily processing environment
- Served as technical liaison with systems personnel in identifying, communicating, and resolving processing problems with the new system
- Served effectively as team leader and account manager for new *pilot team* concept while maintaining own book of business

AWARDS

PRESIDENT'S CLUB AWARD (1994)
Awarded for contribution to the development of the defined contribution 401(K) daily processing record-keeping system.

EDUCATION

PACIFIC NORTHERN COLLEGE, Portland, OR
Bachelor of Science, Business Administration (1990)

KARATE INSTRUCTOR

Excellent graphic illustration
Proper lead of Credentials and Certifications for an instructor's position

CHU SONG LEE
112 Capital Drive, #4A
Washington, DC 20015
(202) 555-4672

INSTRUCTOR: TAE KWON DO

CREDENTIALS & CERTIFICATIONS:

* Certified Instructor by Korean Tae Kwon Do Academy, 5th Degree Black
* Certified Instructor by American Tae Kwon Do Association, 5th Degree Black
* Certified Sparring Instructor by American Tae Kwon Do Association, 5th Degree Black
* Completed 6-Month Intensive Training under Grand Master Chung, Seoul, S. Korea
* B.A. Degree in Education: Emory University, Atlanta, GA; Cum Laude

TAE KWON DO TEACHING EXPERIENCE:

* South City Gymnasium and Boys Center, Washington, DC — 1994 - Present
* Jue Lee Kwang's Tae Kwon Do, Washington, DC — 1992 - 1994
* Master Tom Duvall, Atlanta, GA — 1988 - 1992
* Lee's Tae Kwon Do Academy, Seoul, S. Korea (Student/Instructor) — 1970 - 1987

Additional Credentials:

CPR Certified - American Red Cross
Certified Weapons Trainer - NRA
Black Belt Attainment in:
* Shorin Ryu Karate
* Kung Fu

OTHER EXPERIENCE:

* The Sign Masters, Washington, DC - Sign Installations — 1992 - Present

LEGAL SECRETARY

Sharon L. Coolidge
510/555-1212

12345 Mission Blvd., Apt 678
Hayward, CA 95303

♦ ♦ ♦ ♦ ♦ ♦ ♦ ♦ ♦

For an administrative-oriented position, the lead of Skills Summary is very important.

STRENGTH: **Law Firm Accounting Clerk**

SKILLS SUMMARY

- **Highly proficient in Elite Law Office Billing System.**
- **SQL; Lotus 1-2-3; Excel; Microsoft Words, Windows, DOS.**
- **10-key by touch.**
- **Effective problem solver; prioritize and manage heavy work flow without direct supervision.**
- **"Can do" attitude; work very cooperatively with legal and nonlegal staff.**
- **Excellent working relationship with billing attorneys.**
- **Additional skills include customer service, general office support.**

PROFESSIONAL EXPERIENCE

Accounting Clerk 3/90 to Present
Law Offices of Mason & Matlock, Sun City, CA

- Facilitate conversion of client accounts from manual to computerized billing using Elite Billing System.
- Generate SQL reports; assist in month-end processing.
- Manually post and reconcile checks; back-up and assistance for A/P.
- Process and distribute daily checks, review check requests.
- Interaction with and response to 13 partners, 3 associates, and clients regarding A/R matters.
- Assign attorney numbers; maintain rate changes; maintain safe contents.
- Maintain monthly employee postage charges; petty cash back-up.
- Train new accounting staff on accounting procedures.

Accomplishment

- Increased the effectiveness of the Elite Billing System by determining a more efficient way to do re-bills resulting in significant savings in time, money, and billing errors.

Assistant Store Manager 4/88 to 2/90
Wilson's House of Suede and Leather, Sunnyvale, CA

- Opened and closed store; supervised sales staff.
- Bookkeeping; payroll; bank deposits.
- Supervised shipping/receiving and inventory control.

Accomplishments

- Increased store sales from 35% to 60%.
- Positive evaluations from secret shoppers increased from 30% to 90%.

CERTIFICATES OF COMPLETION

Sun City Legal Secretary's Association (SULSA), May 1991
Computer Applications, Regional Occupations Program, Newark, CA

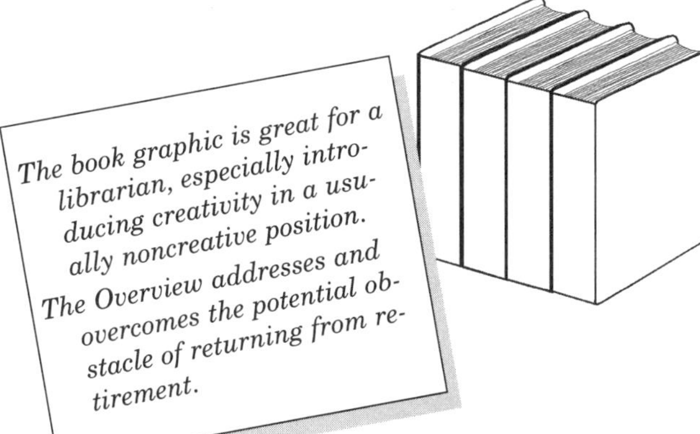

LIBRARIAN

BETTY C. BROWN
810 Clear Water Avenue
Palm Beach, Florida 33401
(407) 555-1199

LIBRARY POSITION

- Public or Private Facility -

OVERVIEW: A retired Elementary School Principal who would like to conclude her career contributing to the growth and organizational enhancement of a library. Desirous of promoting educational excellence through reading and contemporary library services.

SPECIFIC QUALIFICATIONS:

Chairperson:	City of West Palm Beach Library Board, 1991 - 1994. Active Member, 1983 - 1994
Active Member:	West Palm Beach Library Long-Range Planning Ad Hoc Committee, 1994 - Present
Delegate:	To the Florida Governor's Conference on Library and Information Services, December, 1990
Delegate:	To the White House Conference on Library and Information Services, July, 1991
Librarian:	Five years experience as Pharmacy Librarian, Florida A&M University, School of Pharmacy, 1957-62
Change Agent:	Recognized for effecting operational/educational changes as mandated by school committee

PROFESSIONAL EXPERIENCE:

Palm Beach County School System, Florida — 1963 - 1995

Principal	**1986 - 1995**
Assistant Principal	**1983 - 1986**
Reading Consultant	**1974 - 1983**
Reading/English Teacher	**1963 - 1974**

READING CREDENTIALS:

* One of 55 educators selected from Southeastern U.S. to participate in Reading Program sponsored by Southern Association of Secondary Schools & Colleges
* One of 35 educators selected to participate in a Summer Reading Workshop for High School English Teachers (Southern Education Foundation)
* One of 30 educators selected from the U.S. to participate in a Summer N.D.E.A. Institute in Secondary Reading (Conducted by Dr. Ruth Strang)

Laubach Method: Trained to teach illiterate adults.
Maximizing Library Utilization: Recognized for increasing library service utilization, establishing library facilities as a centralized technological hub.

EDUCATION:

M.A. Education, Harvard University
B.A. Education, Boston College

> *The two-column format is creative and still conveys all the important information.*

CHARLES B. WHITCOMB

440 E. Princeton Palo Alto, CA 95555
(510) 555-7006

LOSS PREVENTION MANAGER

Safety ✦ Loss Control ✦ Workers' Compensation
Hazmat ✦ Environmental ✦ Fire Suppression

QUALIFICATIONS SUMMARY

LOSS PREVENTION MANAGER with impressive 14-year career highlighted by contributions in the areas of:

- **Risk Management:** Developed safety, loss control, workers' compensation, hazmat, environmental, and fire suppression programs for commercial and industrial accounts that resulted in a 60-80% reduction in losses.
- **Operations Management:** Turned around departmental operations with poor performance history to rank first in the nation. Developed and implemented TQM programs that reduced losses by approximately 33%.
- **Marketing:** Instrumental in developing new business valued in excess of $57 million.

EDUCATION, CREDENTIALS

Bachelor of Science, Microbiology
University of California, Los Angeles

Registered Environmental Assessor
California Environmental Protection Agency

Certified Health & Safety Technologist
American Board of Industrial Hygiene

PRESENT EMPLOYMENT

EXECUTIVE OFFICER

Sierra Medical, Richmond, CA — 6/95-Present

Manage medical clinic with $26 million budget including supervision of 54 professional and technical staff.

PROFESSIONAL EXPERIENCE

V.P., SAFETY MANAGEMENT
American Insurance, Los Angeles, CA — 1986-1995
($900MM workers' compensation and liability carrier)

Managed loss control department providing customized service for approximately 60 accounts totaling $125 million in premiums. Surveyed accounts for workers' compensation, general liability, products, completed operations, and auto/fleet coverage. Prepared and administered $350,000 departmental budget.

- Reversed department's poor internal audit ratings from #13 (lowest division in the nation) to #1; awarded "Department of the Year" in 1993, 1994, and 1995.
- Active member of business development team; increased revenue from $18 to $125 million in a 4-year period and met premium renewal goal of 100% renewals for four consecutive years.
- Recommended risk management programs for high-tech, construction, agriculture, distribution, and manufacturing accounts that yielded a 60-80% reduction in losses within the policies' first year.

LOSS CONTROL REPRESENTATIVE
World Insurance, Los Angeles, CA — 1982-1986
($200 billion property and casualty carrier)

Surveyed and recommended loss control programs for national accounts throughout the US and Asia. Investigated and analyzed loss trends.

PROFESSIONAL AFFILIATIONS

American Industrial Hygiene Association
American Society of Safety Engineers
National Fire Protection Association

MAINTENANCE

The Summary really says all that is relevant.

The paragraph format of Job Description is good for this discipline, which is more dependent on skills and experience than on accomplishments.

CARL ROBB

12 Hyacinth Drive
Freehold, New Jersey 07728
(908) 555-7270

OBJECTIVE

Career as a maintenance employee in a corporate environment.

SUMMARY

Hands-on experience in the following areas:

- Masonry
- Plumbing and Electrical
- Scheduling
- Reading Blueprints
- Carpentry
- Troubleshooting
- Estimating Materials
- Client Contact

CONSTRUCTION

Adept at discerning cause and effect relationships between trades. Work with carpenters, plumbers, and electricians to achieve a problem-free and orderly job. Develop, implement, and troubleshoot cost-effective alternatives to leveling floors in completed condominiums. Cut costs by half. Enjoy working as part of a team; known as an excellent craftsman who can be counted on to "get the job done."

ESTIMATING

Estimate jobs by physical inspections, notes, and analyzing blueprints. Determine grades and elevations. Develop cost-effective alternatives. Estimate and troubleshoot jobs concerning brick and blockwork. Follow established procedures for replacing concrete work in large condominium complexes throughout the state.

BUSINESS MANAGEMENT

As a Mason Contractor, develop leads and contacts through advertising, telemarketing, and personal interviews. Meet with customers and hire personnel. Organize jobs and coordinate inspections. Prepare weekly payroll. Perform masonry tasks, meet deadlines, and troubleshoot problems through working with other trades, architects, and contractors.

EMPLOYMENT

1984-Present
■ Cornerstone Masonry, Manalapan, NJ
Mason Contractor

1986-Present
■ Astor Remodeling, Matawan, NJ
General Trades

1987-Present
■ Artisan Construction, Keyport, NJ
General Trades

EDUCATION

Graduate, Raritan High School, Raritan, NJ

COMPUTERS

Data Entry, Windows

MANAGEMENT

Leading with the profile of the candidate and accomplishments works well to get the reader's attention.

The layout is well spaced and organized—easy to read.

MAXWELL S. PERKINS

119 Old Stable Road
Lynchburg, Virginia U.S.A.
Phone (804) 555-4600 Fax (804) 555-4700

SENIOR OPERATING & MANAGEMENT EXECUTIVE

Building & Leading Start-Up, Turnaround, & Fast-Track Growth Corporations

Talented, creative, and profit-driven executive recognized nationally for pioneering efforts in product development and industry leadership. Expertise in sales/marketing, global business expansion, manufacturing, corporate finance and business process development. Harvard University Graduate. Distinguished honors and credentials include:

- "Person of the Year," *Printing Magazine*'s highest award in the Promotional Products Industry (1985). Honored as the founder of a billion-dollar consumer products market.
- U.S. Delegate to the 1987 People-To-People Economic Conference in Beijing, China. Long-term career in developing cooperative business ventures with Pacific Rim partners.
- Well-respected public speaking career at national and international trade associations, universities, and professional industry conferences.
- Impressionist painter with works in private and corporate collections in 15 countries worldwide. Earned prestigious designation as a Signature Member of the National Oil & Acrylics Painters Society (N.O.A.P.S.).
- State Masters Racquetball Champion. Ranked #6 in the U.S.

CAREER HISTORY:

Executive Marketing & Management Consultant 1991 to Present

Senior Associates, Inc., Lynchburg, Virginia

Consult with U.S. and Asian companies to provide top-flight expertise in strategic business planning, product development, global marketing, sales promotion, and marketing communications.

- Identified joint venture partners and researched international trade/tariff regulations for diversified Asian manufacturer seeking expansion into the Latin American market.
- Guided insurance company in the preparation of 5-year business plan and capital funding request.
- Orchestrated successful introduction of well-established U.S. mail order company into the promotional products market. Developed budget, defined infrastructure requirements, and designed product promotions (e.g., catalogs, literature, customer communications).
- Currently consulting with premier U.S. supplier of holographic products to provide situational analysis and market development strategies and for successful product positioning.

Chief Executive Officer 1972 to 1991
Graphics International, Lynchburg, Virginia

Senior Operating Executive of this printed apparel and textile manufacturing company supplying the promotional products, premium, department store, and mass merchant markets nationwide. Initially directed operations from Lynchburg-based headquarters. Subsequently directed company's start-up of subsidiaries in Columbus, Georgia and Kowloon, Hong Kong. Chaired the Board of Directors.

Held full P&L responsibility for the entire corporation, all design and production operations, key sales and business development programs, human resource affairs (staff of 350), technology acqu , capital improvement, materials sourcing and the complete finance/accounting function. Directed a four-person senior management team, on-site plant and production management staff, and Managing Director of Hong Kong trading company.

- Built company from $600,000 in annual revenues to $17.8 million and ranking as the fifth largest screen printer in the U.S. Produced over 22,000 orders annually.
- Pioneered development of industry-leading products, technologies, and production methods currently the foundation for a multi-billion dollar industry. Achievements included development of the first 10-color textile printing presses in the U.S., introduction of original packaging standards for major activewear mills and, most significantly, the first multi-color textile apparel printing processes.
- Launched the successful introduction into the global market through development of both import and export operations (combined annual revenues of $1.5+ million).
- Identified tremendous market opportunity for the efficient design and production of small custom orders virtually ignored by major competitors. Developed innovative printing techniques, captured millions of dollars in sales, and won dominant market positioning nationwide.
- Built a nationwide network of 2200 distributors that generated over 50% of total company revenues. Personally directed and negotiated sales programs direct to major accounts including Sears ($2 million annually), Walmart, Target, J.C. Penney, and Wards.
- Introduced sophisticated technologies into the manufacturing, administrative, and financial departments that consistently enhanced quality, productivity, and profit performance.

President 1968 to 1972
Perkins Promotions, Inc. (Subsidiary of Mitchell & Associates), Lynchburg, Virginia

Senior Operating Executive of sales promotion firm servicing its parent advertising agency and major national accounts. Worked in cooperation with teams of advertising executives and creative staffs to plan, design, and produce (via contracted manufacturing) theme-based promotional and internal incentive products in concert with national ad campaigns.

- Completed projects for major U.S. corporations including Anheuser-Busch, McDonald's, Cadillac, Ralston Purina, and Southwestern Bell.

(NOTE: Established Perkins Promotions, Inc. in 1966 and sold to Mitchell & Associates in 1968. Subsequently purchased it back in 1972 as the foundation upon which Graphics International was founded.)

EDUCATION:

HARVARD UNIVERSITY GRADUATE SCHOOL OF BUSINESS ADMINISTRATION
Graduate, OPM Program

UNIVERSITY SCHOOL OF FINE ARTS

Three EURAM International Marketing Conferences (Amsterdam, London, Paris)
Five AMA President Association Programs
Certified Advertising Specialist (C.A.S.) Designation

The shaded box of qualifications is both creative and professional. Highlighting the responsibilities of each position for each employer clearly shows the accomplishments and career progression.

GARY SHAFER

6669 May Court • Hackensack, New Jersey 07601 • **(201) 555-1022**

SUMMARY of QUALIFICATIONS

- **Successful executive level sales management experience with Profit & Loss responsibility.**
- **Proven ability to manage corporate marketing functions including product management, advertising/sales promotion, sales training, and telemarketing.**
- **Experienced with various channels of distribution including direct sales, distributors, dealers, and telephone carriers.**
- **Product expertise includes facsimile equipment, cellular telephones, pagers, and office systems.**
- **Excellent analytical, organizational, and interpersonal skills.**
- **Practical knowledge and understanding of Japanese management techniques.**

PROFESSIONAL EXPERIENCE

PANASONIC COMMUNICATIONS and SYSTEMS COMPANY - Secaucus, NJ **1987 - Present**

An international, multi-billion dollar leader in office automation, office systems, consumer electronics, office equipment, and communications equipment.

VICE PRESIDENT (1989-Present)

- Profit & Loss responsibility for a $150 million division in cellular telephone and paging equipment sales.
- Generated cellular telephone sales of $97 million in 1996.
- Achieved 105% of pager sales budget in 1996.
- Maintained divisional profitability in a volatile and competitive marketplace.
- Preserved market share despite declining economy and changing distribution patterns.
- Departmental productivity totals nearly $3 million per staff member vs. company standards of $1 million per employee.

GENERAL MANAGER - DIRECT SALES (1987-1989)

- Directed the functions of a $76 million direct sales organization in facsimile equipment sales, including staff management of 110 sales representatives.
- Achieved 120% of sales budget and 289% of profit budget for 1989.
- Increased sales rep productivity 18% within 2 years.
- Reduced sales rep turnover despite changing distribution patterns in the industry.
- Implemented a successful Major Account Program to insure the long-term profitability of the direct sales organization.

RICOH CORPORATION - West Caldwell, New Jersey **1977 - 1987**

A multi-billion dollar manufacturer of office equipment and camera products.

DIRECTOR of MARKETING - SYSTEMS PRODUCTS (1983-1987)
DIRECTOR of PRODUCT MARKETING (1979-1983)
DIRECTOR of MARKET PLANNING (1978-1979)
MARKETING SUPPORT MANAGER (1977-1978)

- Directed the planning and marketing of systems/office automation products. Promoted to direct the Company into new business/product areas.
- Responsible for the development and implementation of all phases of marketing in the data communications/office equipment field.
- Developed business, marketing, and launch plans for facsimile products. Successfully introduced several major products that accounted for over 90% of the Group's sales.

PROFESSIONAL EXPERIENCE continued

RICOH CORPORATION **experience continued ...**

- Accountable for the Group program/product management functions.
- Directed OEM sales of peripheral products.
- Developed and managed national account sales programs and successfully negotiated largest sales order in Company's history.
- Initiated and managed the Corporate Telemarketing Program which generated over $4 million in additional revenue.
- Constructed and activated the Sales Training Program which increased sales productivity 18% over two years.
- Directed the advertising, public relations and trade show functions resulting in increased measured brand awareness (20%) and generated over 10,000 sales leads in one year.

BURROUGHS CORPORATION **-** Danbury, Connecticut **1972 - 1977**
A manufacturer of facsimile products with revenues of $100 million.

SALES DEVELOPMENT MANAGER (1975-1977)
STAFF MARKETING PLANNER (1973-1975)
SENIOR MARKETING ANALYST (1973)
MARKET PLANNING ANALYST (1971-1972)

- Developed strategic and profitable programs in sales support, sales development, market planning, and market research.
- Supervised and motivated staff to peak levels of performance.

EDUCATION

MBA (Marketing), New York University Graduate School of Business - New York, NY (1969)

Bachelor of Science (Marketing), Fordham University - Bronx, NY (1967)
Ranked in top 5% of class

The bullets in the introduction section are easy to read.

The Selected Achievements are well defined and relate to the candidate's value.

Richard M. Lawrence, Jr.

8 Waterford Street
River City, VT 07777
(717) 555-7347

Professional Profile

Management professional attuned to the ever-changing needs of business. Extremely service-oriented with a unique combination of intuitive and analytical abilities. Astute in identifying areas in need of improvement, with the vision to develop and implement successful action plans. Consistently demonstrate exceptional knowledge and sound decision-making abilities in the following areas:

- Financial Management
- Organizational Reengineering
- Computer Technology and Programming
- Automated Systems and Procedures
- Customer Relations
- Human Resource Management/Development
- Promotional Activities
- Problem Analysis and Resolution
- Quality Improvement
- Strategic Planning

Management Experience

Harper Valley Auction Co., Inc., Green Hills, Vermont
A nationally recognized antique auction company specializing in firearms, fine glass, toys and dolls, advertising items, Americana, Victoriana, and estates, with annual sales in excess of $6 million. Average of 12–16 specialty auctions conducted each year with absentee bidders from around the world. Budgets for each auction range from $250,000 to $2.5 million.

Positions Held: General Manager (1993 to Present) Managerial Accountant (1988-93)

Selected Achievements:

- Conducted ongoing analyses to evaluate the efficiency, quality, and productivity of all departments. Realigned and automated many tasks resulting in fewer errors, higher production levels, and noticeably improved handling of tasks. Adjusted staffing levels to meet operational requirements. Overall results: Customer service dramatically enhanced, significant company growth and profitability—gross sales nearly doubled and net profit increased by 600% in four years, while general expenses were reduced by nearly 50%.
- Developed and implemented automated accounting system to more efficiently manage the processing and documentation of all financial data. Bookkeeping department was reduced from a staff of 5 (accountant and four support staff) to 1 full-time bookkeeper with assistance from G.M.
- Applied broad knowledge of computer systems—DOS, Windows, UNIX, spreadsheet and accounting applications, hardware and software technical support—to upgrading entire in-house computer system. Extensive programming performed in developing and implementing automated systems to increase accuracy and efficiency.
- Dedicated extensive time and energy to improving communications with personnel, accepting full responsibility for scheduling, performance reviews, employee motivation, and boosting morale.
- Researched and implemented an extensive benefits package that included a 401(k) plan, added a tax exempt short- and long-term disability plan, decreased employee deductibles for health insurance, and increased life insurance benefits by 1000% per employee while successfully reducing cost.
- Transformed shipping department from a "liability" ($5-10K loss per year) to a "profit center" ($5-10K annual profit) by implementing improved practices and tracking systems and converting to a self-insured program for inventory on site and in transit.

Additional Experience

Accountant (3 years) for the following accounting firms: Twitchell & Taylor, CPA, Centerville, Vermont; Foster R. Bouchard, CPA, Cambridge, Vermont; and Judson and Associates, Tax Accountants, Montpelier, Vermont. Prepared individual and corporate tax returns; provided financial and computer consulting; compiled financial statements; prepared payroll deposits; and trained personnel on various computer programs.

Independent Financial and Computer Consultant (6 years) for variety of small businesses. Provided financial management guidance, assistance with personal and corporate tax return preparation, computer and software technical support.

Education

MBA Candidate Local Business College, Green Hills, Vermont (Anticipated Completion 5/96)

Bachelor of Science, Accounting Major University, Boston, Massachusetts, 1986
Achieved GPA of 3.74 while working 40+ hours per week to finance education.

Ongoing Personal and Professional Development: Dale Carnegie course, Managerial and Organizational seminars, Motivational and Self-Improvement tapes and programs.

Affiliations

Institute of Managerial Accountants—Member since 1988

Our Community Rotary Club—Member since 1989; Current President-Elect; Treasurer 1991-93

United States Postal Service Advisory Board—1992-Present

GENERAL MANAGEMENT

> *The Strengths and Abilities section highlights professional experience.*
> *Each bullet under Work History is a tangible accomplishment, or a responsibility where an accomplishment would not work.*

DONALD C. RUSH
7 WASHINGTON ROAD
EAST BRUNSWICK, NEW JERSEY 08816
(908) 555-4097

SUMMARY

Experienced manager with excellent team abilities; strong leadership and presentation skills. Ability to recruit, motivate, and develop long-term employees. Accomplished in repositioning product markets and developing alternative distribution channels.

STRENGTHS AND ABILITIES

- Operations Management
- Merchandising
- New Program Development
- Sales and Marketing
- Strategic Planning
- Field Supervision

WORK HISTORY with RELEVANT EXPERIENCE

MIDAS INTERNATIONAL, Chicago, Illinois 1992-Present

MARKET MANAGER, Central New Jersey

- Maximize the markets' profit contribution to Midas International by increasing sales and controlling expenses. Manage $5.5 million in sales; contribute approximately $600,000 to Midas International in operating income. In charge of unit managers, assistant managers, technicians, and an administrative assistant.
- Administer a $5.5 million sales budget and a $1.4 million payroll budget. Manage a $387,000 advertising budget and a $600,000 controllable expense budget; handle a $650,000 fixed expense budget. Consistently achieve corporate financial goals.
- Responsible for sales and profit, asset management, consumer relations management, safety management, human resource management, and systems management.
- Interface with various internal vice presidents, external vendors including consumer research groups, advertising agencies, and media buying services.
- Assisted in the development and implementation of a shop manager/technician compensation plan designed to reward consumer satisfaction, adhere to specific sales processes, and increase sales.
- Selected as part of the team to develop and implement a new marketing positioning strategy. Involved in the development and implementation of a phone survey designed to measure customer satisfaction. Results of the survey led to an increase in customer service programs.

CARVEL CORPORATION, Farmington, Connecticut 1990-1992

DISTRICT MANAGER

- Oversaw a territory consisting of 76 locations generating in excess of $18.5 million in annual sales.
- Reversed a 10-year negative sales trend. This was achieved by evaluating the strategies, strengths, and weaknesses of direct and indirect competition; determining the market's characteristics and studying opportunities for increased profitability. Created a back to basics business plan, which guided the territory and led to a 5.3% increase over the previous year.
- Expanded Carvel operations into supermarkets, stadiums, and arenas; developed alternative distribution channels. Organized financial and accounting information; measured results against plans.

THE SOUTHLAND CORPORATION, Iselin, New Jersey 1987-1990

FIELD CONSULTANT (1987-1990)
MANAGEMENT TRAINEE (1987)

- Oversaw the turnaround of company owned and operated stores. This was accomplished by putting into place a program that upgraded the facility, improved the stores' merchandising efforts, and trained the staff in customer service techniques.
- Held responsibility for 10 locations. This included the stores' profitability as well as the locations' physical plant and equipment.
- Administrated a $200,000 promotional budget that resulted in a 13% increase in sales.
- Named "1988 Rookie of the Year" and "1989 Field Consultant of the Year."
- Managed a Field Group that consistently outpaced the market in both sales and sales increases over the previous period.
- Maintained records and prepared reports to meet corporate financial reporting requirements. The reports were used by store managers in planning and controlling the business.
- Established contracts with contractor to provide both routine maintenance and emergency repair services.
- Trained and developed seven management trainees.
- Created inventory control systems that provided greater accuracy and reduced losses by approximately 18%.

GARDEN STATE SUPERMARKET, Metuchen, New Jersey 1979-1983

FAMILY OWNED/OPERATED BUSINESS

- Turned around a bankrupt company. Within three months the operation was repositioned and generating a return on the investment for the owners of this privately held business.
- Developed creative marketing and advertising promotions that included sponsoring community events, direct mail, and discount programs.
- Negotiated vendor contracts that reduced expenses by 22.5%.
- Opened a second location in only one year.
- Developed and oversaw an $855,000 budget.

EDUCATION

Bachelor of Science ... Marketing ... Rutgers, The State University, Newark, New Jersey ... 1987

PERSONAL

Enjoy golf, skiing, camping, and working on home improvement projects.

CONFIDENTIALITY REQUESTED **WILLING TO TRAVEL**

> *The Overview tells the reader about the candidate in specific terms and parallels operations in the military and private sectors.*
>
> *The paragraph format of Job Descriptions works well to relate military experience to experience in the private sector.*

MILITARY

KENNETH D. CRYSTAL

6663 Laverne Court
Jupiter, Florida 33458
(407) 555-9921

MANAGEMENT / OPERATIONS / AUTOMATION / LOGISTICS

OVERVIEW: Over 13 years of successful management and leadership experience with a reputation for meeting the most challenging organizational goals and objectives. A pragmatic and focused individual recognized for *"making seemingly impossible situations work."* A proven and *VERIFIABLE* record for:

- Producing higher performance standards and **enhancing productivity during a period of shrinking budgets.**
- Automating departments. As head of the Resources Department for a 14,000 personnel installation, automated major control system, **increasing the effective resource utilization rate from 46% to 97.6% in less than 12 months.** This resulted in a cost savings of over $101 million.
- Controlling growth management - **able to motivate and maximize productivity and employee morale *without* financial incentives.** Took a division with the lowest performance level (out of 54 divisions) and improved to #1 ranking in less than 12 months.
- **Developing and implementing highly successful strategic plans (short and long term).** Established inventory/purchasing control systems that gained accountability for millions of dollars in equipment, thus reducing inventory purchases by $1.1 million.

PROFESSIONAL EXPERIENCE:

United States Army, 1979 - 1996

CAPTAIN - Completed 13-year career with the U.S. Army. Gained upper-level manager status. Participated in the complete revitalization and overhaul of the U.S. Military in general - and the U.S. Army specifically - from the low status perceived in the 1970's to the most powerful and effective military in history.

An active participant in the swift/forceful turnaround of the armed forces that led to the U.S. victory in Operation Desert Storm. Part of the management team that proved that the military could be managed like a well-tuned corporate machine (same size as Exxon Corp.). A successful record for managing complex organizations, supervising thousands of people through hundreds of line-management personnel, responsible for millions of dollars in assets. Specific duties and achievements include:

MANAGEMENT: Led the Army's largest armor company consisting of 14 tanks, 10 APCs, an Engineer Squad and Maintenance Platoon. Managed testings of 14 high-tech, multimillion dollar products that, in less than 12 months, went from conception to production. These systems were highly instrumental in the success of the Desert Storm operation. Upgraded training curriculum and methods, cross-trained personnel in job duties resulting in lower supervision requirements and a significant cost savings in overtime.

Experience (Continued)

OPERATIONS & LOGISTICS: Was the primary logistical advisor to the Commander for 250 men, responsible for $25 million of equipment. Managed a $719,000 budget. Responsible for controlling the procurement of durable and expendable items under the budget. A recognized expert in planning and executing complex operations with 100% accuracy and success including the scheduling and movement of thousands of personnel and the timely transfer of millions of dollars worth of equipment to support and maintain operations.

AUTOMATION & COST CONTROL: Managed and automated the Resource Department on a 14,000-person installation responsible for budgets, materials, and resources. Improved the effective resource utilization rate from 46% to 97.6% in less than 12 months, saving over $101 million in cost with no change in personnel. A highly skilled technical individual, computer literate, able to maximize Management Information Systems to increase profitability.

TRAINING & DEVELOPMENT: Spent the last two years as an Assistant Professor of Military Science (Delta State University, Cleveland, Mississippi). Redesigned comprehensive management training program, (regarded by superiors as the "most aggressive training program within the Brigade"), resulting in subordinates' excelling in all evaluated areas. Developed programs comprising 67 qualifications skills, 19 professional education subjects, and OJT training - leadership curriculum.

EDUCATION: Ohio University, Athens, Ohio
BACHELOR OF SCIENCE DEGREE, 1982
Business Management

* **Combined Armed Services Staff School, Leavenworth, Kansas**
  Effective Management, Public Speaking and Briefings, 1991
* **Company Leaders Course, Monterey, California**
  Management, Leadership & Administrative Procedures, 1989
* **Officers' Advanced Management Level Course, Ft. Knox, Kentucky**
  Advanced Leadership, Management & Problem Solving Analysis, 1986
* **Motor Officers' School, Ft. Knox, Kentucky**
  Equipment Maintenance, Management & Record Keeping, 1982

INTERESTS: Enjoy deep sea fishing, reading (History, Science, & Technology), gardening, cultural activities, and travel.

- References & Supporting Documentation Furnished Upon Request -

LILLIAN SHAW

The easy-to-read format works well here because of one employer. The table works well to illustrate accomplishments.

Résumé

500 Elmwood Drive
Los Angeles, CA 94000

Telephone:
(415) 555-4627

PROFILE

Managing CEO, Credit Union

Fifteen years of progressively responsible positions in credit union management. Strong financial planning, budgeting, and leadership skills. Proven record of increasing profits through investment management and budgeting.

EXPERIENCE

MUNICIPAL EMPLOYEES CREDIT UNION • Los Angeles, CA 1980 - Present

Managing CEO, 1987-Present
Manager, 1982-1987
Office Assistant to Managing CEO, 1980-1982

Manage operations, staff, and $2.9 million in assets. Accountable to Board of Directors. Determine goals and objectives of credit union; develop business plans and design programs to meet objectives. Manage investment portfolio. Budget and P&L responsibility. Approve and process loans. Maintain excellent member relations.

Selected Accomplishments:

- Turned around credit union, which was $100,000 in debt, through effective investment management, budgeting, and loan approval. Since the membership is limited to municipal employees, these improvements were made without a substantial increase in the field of membership.

	1982	1994
Asset Size	$850,000	$2.9 million
Loan Portfolio	$650,000	$1.1 million
Share Portfolio	$700,000	$2.3 million
Cash Portfolio	$ 41,000	$1.6 million

- Spearheaded and successfully managed conversion from a manual system to the Galaxy II online computer system. Result: Greater efficiency and the ability to operate with 50% less staff.

EDUCATION

Bachelor of Business Administration - Finance (1987)
UNIVERSITY OF SOUTHERN CALIFORNIA, Los Angeles, CA

MEDICAL ASSISTANT

MARIANNE HIGGINS DOYLE

8400 Industrial Parkway
Parkside, Indiana 47201
(317) 555-7814

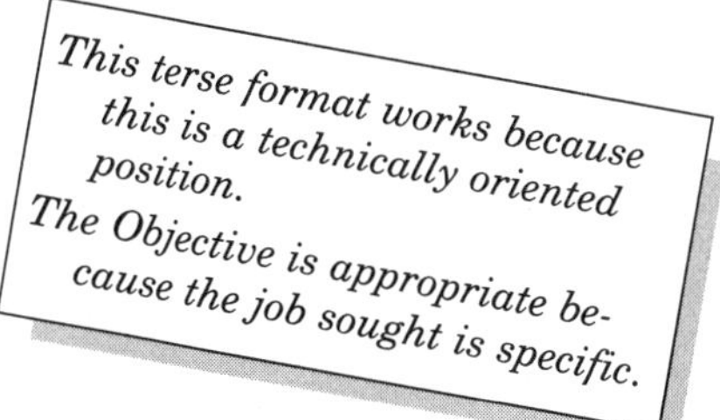

OBJECTIVE

Medical Assistant/Technologist position for a private practice.

PROFESSIONAL EXPERIENCE

Patient Service Technician/Unit Clerk 1989 - Present
COMMUNITY HOSPITAL, Coronary Care Unit, Columbus, Indiana

- Order lab work and x-rays
- Prioritize patient daily care according to acuity and scheduled patient procedures
- Assist patients with A.M. care, take vital signs, prep for procedures, draw blood, and obtain specimens
- Maintain and set up patient rooms
- Perform preventive maintenance on emergency equipment
- Assist with patient and family education
- Assist R.N. with sterile and nonsterile dressing changes
- Perform EKGs
- Trained in Phlebotomy
- Utilize PC to enter and retrieve patient data
- Answer multiline phone, operate fax and copy machine

Office Assistant (6-month part-time position) 1995
HERBERT FOX, M. D., Columbus, Indiana

- Answered phone, scheduled patients
- Greeted patients
- Updated patient charts

EDUCATION

In-house training programs, Community Hospital
EKG, 1993
Phlebotomy, 1993
Tech Class, 1992
Unit Clerk Class, 1990
Nursing Assistant Class, 1989
CPR Certified, since 1989

Columbus State Community College
Computer training: Word Perfect I, Certificate 1995

The Ohio State University
Major: Pre-Veterinarian, 1989-1990

Testimonials from senior officers lend credibility to the candidate.

The Personal Profile focuses on transferable skills and not military-specific skills.

MILITARY

KURT JOHNNEGAN

1342 Alta Vista, San Marcos, California 92200 ☎ (714)

"Straightforward, honest, and firmly committed to the training and welfare of his platoon. Unafraid to ask the hard questions of himself or anyone else." Colonel A. J. Marine, USMC July 14, 1993

"A job-aggressive, enthusiastic, and responsive leader. Among the top 10% (of leaders) ... I have observed in over 13 years." Major Ima Leader, USMC, May 12, 1993

PERSONAL PROFILE

An experienced professional who has survived stiff competition to arrive at positions of responsibility and trust. Competent and knowledgeable in a wide variety of managerial activities with specific expertise in the field of telecommunications systems. Proven record of success with progressively increasing responsibilities. Superb interface between management and labor as well as with individuals of diverse backgrounds and cultures. Excellent communication, motivational, and time-management skills. Organized, methodical, and analytical; particularly adept in simultaneously managing multiple projects. Experienced in training and developing cohesive staffs and in developing and administering budgets. Computer literate in the IBM PC environment with skills in a wide variety of software applications. Project a positive, personable, and professional image at all times.

PROFESSIONAL EXPERIENCE

United States Marine Corps - December 1989 to present

First Lieutenant - Communications Officer whose professional responsibilities have expanded his primary military specialty of telecommunications systems into areas of administration, management, and staff training involving leadership and decision making.

Functional authority included direct supervision of 5 front line supervisors and indirect control of 50+ Marines engaged in all aspects of installation, operation, displacement, and maintenance of telecommunications systems.

Collateral duties included responsibilities as Classified Materials System (CMS) Manager, Computer Information Systems (CIS) Coordinator, and Electronic Warfare (EW) Officer.

Achievements:

- Granted Final Top Secret Security Clearance from U. S. Government based upon Special Background Investigation completed Fall 1991.
- Created and implemented "continual inspection" procedures that resulted in an annual 35% savings of budgeted money allocated for telecommunications equipment batteries.
- Orchestrated maintenance programs presented by subordinate supervisors that corrected inadequacies in preventive maintenance and reduced "wear and tear" of equipment.
- Provided communications specialty training to military personnel that consistently exceeded assigned standards of training.
- Authored communications "How to" manual that standardized organizational operating procedures.

EDUCATION

West Central College, Abiline, Texas - Magna Cum Laude Honors - GPA: 3.85+
B.A. - Major: Political Science and Minor: English

PROFESSIONAL TRAINING AND DEVELOPMENT

- Communications Officer School
- Classified Materials Systems School
- Basic Officer School
- Officers Candidate School

Appropriate personal and professional references are available upon request.

NURSE ANESTHETIST

> *The testimonials are reader-friendly and good references.*
> *All descriptions are terse and quantitative, appropriate for a technical profession.*
> *The style of the candidate's name adds class and distinction.*

Melanie Johnston, CRNA

1555 Main Street • Charleston, WV 25302 • (304) 555-8443

"... exhibits high degree of intelligence and readily grasps new concepts ... has an affable charm ... interacts well with patients, colleagues ... even in the most stressful of situations."

James McCroskey, MD
General Anesthesia Services
Charleston, WV

"... reliable and responsible team player ... willingly shares the workload ... level-headed and competent in an emergency ... proficient and knowledgeable in anesthetic skills and techniques."

Barb Schmitt, CRNA
CAMC-Memorial Division
Charleston, WV

"... an excellent anesthetist who remains calm under pressure ... highest integrity ... exhibits excellent leadership ... has been a tremendous asset to our organization."

Lee Ann Smith, CRNA, BA
Instructor, CAMC School of Nurse Anesthesia
Charleston, WV

"... a very responsible employee ... always volunteering for additional assignments ... prompt and punctual ... has a positive attitude ... a valuable asset to our staff."

Tamy L. Smith, Charge CRNA
CAMC-Memorial Division
Charleston, WV

Professional Profile

- **Certified Registered Nurse Anesthetist**
- Bachelor's degree and four years CRNA experience
- Clinical instructor with over 1,000 hours experience
- Outstanding clinical expertise and proficiency
- Attend weekly continuing education meetings
- Excellent problem solver who works well under pressure
- Reputation as a team player with superb people skills
- Upbeat, personable, and highly energetic

Licensure & Professional Affiliations

- Certified Registered Nurse Anesthetist, Certificate #22250
- Registered Professional Nurse, License #0556500
- Member, American Association of Nurse Anesthetists
- Member, West Virginia Association of Nurse Anesthetists
- Professionally involved with local Women's Health Center

Professional Experience

CHARLESTON AREA MEDICAL CENTER MEMORIAL DIVISION
Charleston, West Virginia 1984-Present

- ☐ **CRNA - Cardiovascular Center -** 1993-Present
  Surgeries include arterial bypasses, hearts, amputations, gall bladders, mastectomies, biopsies, major orthopedics
- ☐ **RN - Medical Surgical -** 1984-1993
  RN and charge nurse duties on a 40-bed med/surg unit, included adolescent ward and peritoneal dialysis

Education

- **Certificate of Anesthesia,** Charleston Area Medical Center School of Anesthesia, Charleston, WV, 1989
  - ☐ Received Josephine A. Reier Memorial Scholarship Award
- **Associate Degree in Nursing,** University of Charleston School of Health Sciences, Charleston, WV, 1983
  - ☐ Received Nursing Student Achievement Award
- **Bachelor of Fine Arts Degree, *magna cum laude,*** Arizona State University, Tempe, Arizona, 1977

NURSE

SHEA ELIZABETH HAINES
11479 Eagle Mountain
San Antonio, Texas 78200
(210) 555-4371

Leads with relevant credentials. Highlights specific areas of experience by bolding.

PROFESSIONAL SUMMARY:

Registered Nurse

- Highly skilled career professional with over 14 years practical experience in **hospital, home health,** and **primary care** environments.
- Established in **STD** and **AIDS patient support** including assessment, counseling, education regarding medications and treatment, lab work, documentation with care plan for diagnosis, and administration of treatment procedures.
- Computer skilled, managing heavy daily patient volume including telephone triage, appointment scheduling, and patient referral. Proficient in all documentation/record maintenance/paperwork to ensure accuracy and patient confidentiality.
- All areas of major and minor surgical procedures performed in hospital environment.

CREDENTIALS:

Board Examination, 1981
License, State of Texas, 1985

EXPERIENCE:

1993-1994	Office/Surgical Nurse, Lisa Rouse, MD, Kerrville, Texas
1989-1991	Supervisor - Home Health Aides, VNA Private Care, Fort Worth, Texas
1986-1989	OR/PACU Nurse, Harris Methodist Hospital, Fort Worth, Texas
1985-1986	ICU Supervisor, Twin Oaks, Fort Worth, Texas
1983-1985	Office/Surgical Nurse, Thomas Virgin, MD, Montgomery, Alabama
1982-1983	Clinical/Classroom Instructor - LVN/EMT/NA, Health Care Institute

EDUCATION:

Associate, Nursing, 1981
Troy State School Of Nursing, Montgomery, Alabama, *St. Margaret Scholarship Student*

AFFILIATIONS:

Texas Nurses' Association, 1985-Current
American Nursing Association, 1981-Current
Alabama Nurses' Association, 1981-1985

COMMUNITY SERVICE:

1989-1991 **AIDS Counselor,** Community Outreach Center, Ft. Worth, Texas

Launched volunteer system and food bank with two other professionals. Provided counseling, information regarding available housing, SSI, food stamps, and other services. Coordinated transportation for medical appointments, personal errands, and outings. Promoted daily activities to sustain positive attitude and quality of life for full-blown AIDS clients.

REFERENCES ON REQUEST

The overall layout makes good use of wide margins so that it is easy to read.
Effective description of past jobs by listing a "project" and then its scope
Classic use of font styles and boldface

PHOTOGRAPHY

Robin Tucker

4635 Montgomery Road, Cincinnati, Ohio 45211 (513) 555-7777

PROFILE

- Strong foundation in photography, commercial art, and computer applications complemented by knowledge of business operations and the need for customer-focused service.
- Track record of initiative and achievement – seeking out freelance projects, expanding job description boundaries, volunteering and being selected for positions of responsibility within chosen field.

EDUCATION

Xavier University • College of Design, Architecture, Art and Planning • Cincinnati, Ohio
Bachelor of Fine Arts, 1995

EXPERIENCE

Commercial Photographer • Freelance

Successful completion of commercial photography assignments requiring planning, follow-through, and results that meet client objectives.

- ***Project:*** Marketing brochure for independent producer of specialized archery equipment (Fall 1995). ***Scope:*** Worked with client to select and position products; shot and developed photos; made brochure layout recommendations and gave technical input regarding reproduction of photographs.
- ***Project:*** Real estate catalog for Architectural and Design Services, Xavier University (Fall 1994). ***Scope:*** Met with client to determine project goals; selected shots and photographed University-owned properties from numerous perspectives; working with strict budget limitations, researched developing options and selected vendors based on quality and price; organized and presented finished photographs.

Night Manager • Starlight Restaurant, Cincinnati, Ohio (1994-Present)

- Train and supervise employees.
- Promote positive customer relationships by focusing strong attention on meeting customer needs and ensuring their enjoyment.
- Coordinate and book entertainment; develop and place related advertising.
- Introduce new product lines following analysis of current operations and growth opportunities.

Lab Monitor • Xavier University, Photography Department (1993-1994)

- Supervised and provided expert assistance to beginning photography students.
- Operated and maintained darkroom equipment.

Exhibit Assistant • Images Center for Photography, Cincinnati, Ohio (1994)

- Participated in the installation of exhibits for photographic-art gallery.
- Monitored gallery shows and provided information to visitors.

COMPUTER SKILLS

Macintosh Systems
Applications: Adobe Illustrator, Adobe Photoshop, Sculpt 3D, Authorware

ADDITIONAL SKILLS

4x5, 2 1/4, 35mm cameras
Black/white and color film processing and printing

EXHIBITS

Student Works • College of Design, Architecture, Art and Planning (1994, 1995)
Undergraduate Ceramic Exhibit • 840 Gallery (May 1994)
Undergraduate Painting Exhibit • 840 Gallery (May 1993)

Portfolio and references available on request.

JACQUELINE BREWSTER, A.T.C.

444 Derby Circle
Louisville, KY 86342 *(880) 555-7202*

CERTIFIED ATHLETIC TRAINER

Offering Solid Credentials in Athletic & Injury Rehabilitation

CREDENTIALS:

* Certified Athletic Trainer, experienced working in rehabilitative environments with *547 hours of clinical practice and 2,125 hours of internship as Trainer.*
* Averaged in the *90th percentile* on the Allied Health Professions Admissions Test. Completed additional courses in *Vertebrate Anatomy, Physics, Chemistry and Biology.*
* Highly competent in evaluations, injury management, rehabilitation, and administration. Successfully work with top college varsity athletes on timely and effective rehabilitation programs.
* Certified *Water Rehabilitation Trainer.* Have clocked over 179 hours of water rehabilitation training to fellow trainers (NATA Program).

Solid opening with a portfolio of credentials
Simple, yet highly effective one-page resume
Emphasis on athletics, with the door left open for other rehab work

EDUCATION:

Marshall University, Huntington, KY (Currently Enrolled)
Master of Science: Health & Physical Education

University of Kentucky, Louisville Campus, Louisville KY 1992
Bachelor of Science: Exercise & Sport Sciences, GPA: 3.62

RELATED WORK EXPERIENCE:

Marshall University, Huntington, KY 1993-Present
Graduate Assistant Athletic Trainer (All Sports)

Louisville Rehab Center, Louisville, KY 1991-93
Athletic Trainer / Exercise Instructor

Caldwell High School, Caldwell, KY 1989-91
Assistant Athletic Trainer, (Internship), Football

VOLUNTEER WORK:

Westerman Rehabilitation Center, Louisville, KY 1989-Present
Post-Op Hip Replacement Therapy

Hendersen Nursing Facility, Caldwell, KY 1990-95
Senior Citizen Injury Rehabilitation

AFFILIATIONS:

* National Athletic Trainers' Association
* Athletic Trainers' Association of Florida
* American College of Sports Medicine

- References Furnished Upon Request -

PHYSICIAN

DONNA M. NEWTON, M.D.

"Diplomate American Board of Anesthesiology"

Home Address
18 Anna Court
Vera, IL 60148
(312) 555-7609

Business Address
1801 Spiro Street, #101
Slaven, IL 60145
(312) 555-1099

LICENSES & CERTIFICATION:

State of Illinois (#303214), State of Wisconsin (#207772), State of Florida (#36485068)
Board Certified: American Board of Anesthesiology, 4/79 (#9999)

QUALIFICATIONS:

General Anesthesia	**Open Heart**	**Pre-Op Consult**
Local	**Pain Clinic**	**Post-Op Consult**
Hypothermia	**Hypotensive**	**Inhalation Therapy**
Regional Anesthesia	**Intravenous**	**Nerve Blocks**
(Spinal, Epidural, Caudal)	**Emergency Treatment**	

PROFESSIONAL EXPERIENCE:

Anesthesia Associates of Lombard County, P.A., Lombard, IL — 1990 - Present
Practice of Anesthesia / Partner: Ursula Pels Heart Institute

North Broward Medical Center, Chicago, IL — 1979 - 1990
Practice of Anesthesia

Medical College of Wisconsin, Milwaukee, Wisconsin — 1976 - 1977
Assistant Professor

EDUCATION:

University of Medicine, Zagreb, Yugoslavia
Degree: Medical Doctor: (1966-71)

K.B.C., Zagreb, Yugoslavia
Internship: (1972-73)

Medical College Of Wisconsin, Milwaukee, WI
Residency
V.A. Hospital / Milwaukee General Hospital

Hospital for Children
Toronto, Canada
Pediatric Anesthesia: 1975

Institute Za Tumore, Zagreb, Yugoslavia
Research on Electro Anesthesia
V.A. Hospital

University of Arkansas
Little Rock, Arkansas
Obstetric Anesthesia

Continuing Education:

Open Heart Workshops (AMA Certified, annually, 1987 - Present)
TE Workshops, (Vail, CO, 1989, 1992, 1996)
Meet AMA Yearly Mandates for Continuing Education

CV Format
Appropriate for a physician's resume, leading with licenses and certifications
Simple listing of qualifications, experience, and education—no unnecessary details

MEMBERSHIPS:

- American Medical Association
- Illinois Medical Association
- American Society of Anesthesiologists
- Illinois Society of Anesthesiologists

LIABILITY INSURANCE:

Over 17 years of professional practice. Never had a judgement or settlement in any professional liability case. Present coverage: C.N.A., Professional Liability Company

- Professional References & Supporting Documentation Furnished Upon Request -

PHYSICIAN ASSISTANT

Good use of title and specialization
Like the physician's resume, focus on listing qualifications and experience

LANCE POWELL, P.A.-C.

15392 78th Drive North
Fort Lauderdale, FL 33401-7319
(407) 555-7722 (Home)
(407) 555-8698 (Cellular)

PHYSICIAN ASSISTANT
Specializing in... Orthopedic Surgery

OVERVIEW: A high-energy, peak-performing *Physician Assistant* with 17 years of above-average success in the medical field. Manage full caseload, providing high-quality professional care. A reputation for strong rapport-building skills and for contributing to the growth of a successful medical practice. Areas of expertise include:

- Pre/post operative management
- Performing initial evaluations
- First Assistant
- Setting fractures
- Total hip & knee procedures
- General orthopedics
- Hand surgery
- Arthroscopic surgery
- ER calls
- Teaching & training

EDUCATION:

SURGICAL INTERNSHIP / RESIDENCY
General Surgery House Staff 1978 -1980
Orthopedic Surgery House Staff 1980 - 1982

Montefiore Hospital and Medical Center, Bronx, NY
Associated Hospitals:
- Hospital of Albert Einstein College of Medicine
- Bronx Municipal Hospital
- North Central Bronx Hospital

ASSOCIATE IN APPLIED SCIENCE 1976 - 1978
Cincinnati Technical College: Physician Assistant Program, Cincinnati, OH

PRE-MEDICINE 1969 - 1971
University of Missouri, Columbia, MO

LIBERAL ARTS / ENGINEERING 1962 - 1963
Syracuse University, Syracuse, NY

PROFESSIONAL EXPERIENCE:

Ben C. Cotter, Jr., M.D., Palm Beach Gardens, FL 1987 - Present
PHYSICIAN ASSISTANT - Orthopedic Surgery; Private Practice

George P. Gonzalez Ergas, M.D., New York, NY 1982 - 1987
PHYSICIAN ASSISTANT - Orthopedic Surgery; Private Practice

TEACHING:

On-going *shadowing experience* 1991 - Present
For budding PA and high school students contemplating careers in medicine and health-related fields.

University of Florida, Gainesville, FL
Preceptor-Externship; Physician Assistant Program 1994

Barry University, Miami Shores, FL
Guest Lecturer - Occupational Therapy 1991

	Touro College P.A. Program, Brooklyn, NY **Guest Lecturer - Orthopedic Surgery**	1981 - 1982
	Stony Brook P.A. Program, Stony Brook, NY **Clinical Instructor - Orthopedic Surgery**	1981 - 1982
LICENSES & CERTIFICATIONS:	**CERTIFIED:** National Commission on Certification of Physician Assistants (#790322)	1979 - Present
	FLORIDA LICENSE: #1542	
	PROFICIENCY EXAMINATION IN SURGERY Administered by the National Commission on Certification for Physician Assistants	1980
	RE-CERTIFICATION NCCPA including extended core examination Component in Surgery	1985
	RE-CERTIFICATION NCCPA extended core examination Component in Surgery and Primary Care	1991
	NEW YORK REGISTRATION: #001031	
AFFILIATIONS:	**FELLOW STUDENT** American Academy of Physician Assistants	1976 - Present
	CHARTER MEMBER Palm Beach County Hand Society	1989 - Present
	REPRESENTATIVE, HOUSE OF DELEGATES	1979
	Member: N.Y. State Society of Physician Assistants	1978 - 1990
	American Academy of P.A.'s Conference Planning Committee	1980 - 1981
MILITARY:	United States Marine Corps, Honorable Discharge Recipient: Meritorious Service Award for Individual Achievement	1965 - 1969
INTERESTS:	Private Pilot, Certified Diver, Fishing, Music (Trumpet), Photography, Sailing, Golf	

- References & Supporting Documentation Furnished Upon Request -

PILOT

The table is reader-friendly and clearly lists very relevant information of flight hours.

Like the medical resume, the focus is on certifications and licenses.

Thomas Keller

1397 LaCienega, Inglewood, California 90219 ☎ (619) 555-1212

QUALIFICATIONS

COMMERCIAL HELICOPTER PILOT qualified by a combination of substantial flight time experience, augmented by formal undergraduate level studies and enhanced by specialized professional training. Competent and knowledgeable in the field of aviation with specific expertise in the Hughes 300C Helicopter. Proven and verifiable flight and safety record. Adroit, agile, and physically fit. Capable, reliable pilot requiring minimal instruction or supervision. Superb interface with individuals of diverse cultures and backgrounds. Present a positive, professional image.

LICENSES AND CERTIFICATIONS

General Helicopters, Rostall, California

- Commercial Rotorcraft Rating, 1989
- Turbine Rating in Hughes 500, 1989

U. S. Parachute Association, Washington, D. C.

- Jumpmaster, 2,756 skydives
- Certified Jump Instructor - Class AAAA

FLIGHT HOURS: Total Time: 4,796

- Pilot in Command 3,990
- Night 144
- Cross Country 653
- 19,254 Take-offs and Landings

- Hughes 300C 4,389
- Hughes 500 35
- 206 324
- L-3 48

PROFESSIONAL EXPERIENCE

ACME HELICOPTER SERVICE, Preston, California - 1983 to present

Commercial Helicopter Pilot - Primarily engaged in flight and pilot obligations conducting sightseeing tours in Reno, Nevada. Ancillary responsibilities include: prevention and management of front control procedures in Southern California avocado and citrus groves; performing aerial photography; and participation in television and film work such as the Los Angeles Marathon, Baja Road Rally Races, etc.

Accomplishments:

- Experienced 3 total engine failures in Hughes 300C while carrying passengers and resulting in no injury to the passengers or damage to the aircraft.
- Recognized as Distinguished Stunt Pilot within the Hollywood, California Motion Picture Industry.

EDUCATION

National University School of Aviation, San Diego, California

Graduate Studies - Concentration: Aviation Management

Florida Institute of Technology, Melbourne, Florida

Bachelor of Science - Major: Aviation Management and Flight Technology

PLANT OPERATIONS

The Key Accomplishments section lists an activity and its result. The Professional Profile section communicates background effectively.

JAY WASSERMAN

304 Moon Lane
Freedom, Illinois 62243
(618) 555-7772

PROFESSIONAL PROFILE

Extensive background managing all plant operations for a $7M commercial printing company, with successful track record for maximizing resources, sales, production, quality, and overall profitability. Hands-on knowledge of 4-color and aqueous coating processes. Areas of expertise include:

Warehousing	Manufacturing	Inventory Management
Vendor Relations	Sales Targeting	Industry Standards
Quality Control	Estimating	Customer Service

CURRENT POSITION

Adsell Printing, St. Louis, MO 1985-Present

Printing Plant Manager: Oversee operations in five departments: Prep, Pressroom, Bindery, Shipping & Receiving, and Warehousing. Supervise 85 employees. Coordinate paper buyouts, prep and press inventory, layout for printing jobs, and all printing and binding production.

KEY ACCOMPLISHMENTS

- Redesigned prep department to allow business to handle modernized mailing requirements. ***Result:*** Doubled press capacity while cutting binding costs in half.

- Restructured relationship with major paper supplier, allowing stock to be purchased on an "as needed" basis from a designated off-site supply. ***Result:*** Company required 30% less inventory space in-house and earned a 20% discount on all merchandise in return for exclusive business.

- Started a new estimating program on large print orders. ***Result:*** Saved $500-$1000 per week previously lost in negotiating paper prices that were inconsistent with original estimates.

- Implemented and managed an in-house consignment plan that replaced the costly and time-consuming process of purchasing key printing and proofing supplies as needed. ***Result:*** Company maintained and replenished a $15,000-20,000 inventory, significantly decreasing press downtime.

- Learned a previously unused computer function to track supply inventory levels. ***Result:*** Negotiated better pricing through extensive knowledge of actual usage and sales trends.

- Negotiated an exclusive two-year deal with a major manufacturer. ***Result:*** Company was given more than $45,000 worth of processing and proofing equipment to replace its manual systems. In addition, vendor supplied engineers to oversee a relocation and create an efficient business layout.

EDUCATION

Towson State University, Baltimore, MD
Bachelor of Science, 1985

PLUMBER

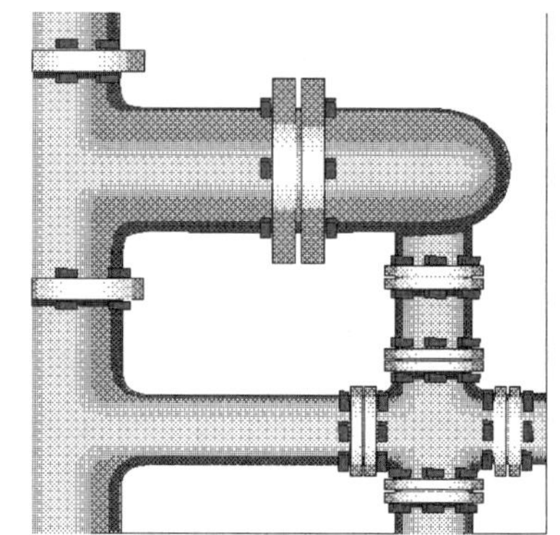

WALTER DYER

848 Blue Ridge Circle
Clarkston, MI 48829
(810) 555-3824

LICENSED MASTER PLUMBER

#CFCO-18290

15 Years Residential & Commercial Experience

Qualifications:

- Leaks
- Fixtures
- Backflow Repair
- Sprinklers & Irrigation
- Lift Stations
- Backflow Certified
- Repairs
- Sewer & Drains
- Cleaning Service
- Septic Tanks
- High Velocity Water Jetting
- Hot Water Heaters

Highlights of Experience:

Introduced TV Sewer Line Inspection as an additional service, generating 6% more income to company's bottom line.

Have successfully directed over 27 plumbers working on 7-10 jobs simultaneously. Hire, train, and assure quality performance of all workers for all projects.

Completely renovated (plumbing) *The Brewster House,* a 160-year old historical structure in Dearborn, MI. This $105,000 job was completed 3 weeks ahead of schedule and came in 18% under budget, without compromising quality.

Over past 15 years, have done major construction/renovation on 82 restaurants, 14 health clubs, 32 manufacturing facilities, 31 warehouse units, 24 high-rise office buildings, 23 hospitals, and over 360 private residences.

Managed high-volume, high-pressure repair operation in Detroit for French company (SOS Depannage). Directed 18 plumbers in 3-county area responding entirely to emergency plumbing and water heater repairs.

Effective graphic
Proper lead of license
Qualifications properly listed early—more relevant than accomplishments

Employment:

Master Plumber for:

Master Rooter, Pontiac, MI	1993 - Present
Dawson Plumbing, Pontiac, MI	1990 - 1993
SOS Depannage, Detroit, MI	1989 - 1990
Pontiac Heating & Plumbing, Pontiac, MI	1981 - 1989

Education:

Wilbur Technical Institute, Norwood, MI, 1979-81
Master Plumber Training and Certification

Interests:

Coach Little League, flag football, and soccer; Executive Board Member: Clarkston Youth Athletic Association; enjoy golf, fishing, and jazz.

SETH MILLER

150 West 156th Street, #778
New York, NY 10019

(212) 555-9256 (Home)
(212) 555-6290 (Fax)
E-mail: bluebird@ix.netcom.com

PRODUCTION & PROJECT COORDINATOR

Interactive / Digital / Multimedia Environments

- Utilizing Solid Computer & Communications Skills -

Career change—strong emphasis on skills, not experience
Nice use of graphics for bullets
Effective Education section for a candidate without a formal degree

OVERVIEW:

A high-energy, peak-performing *Production/Project Coordinator,* with more than 2 years of successful exposure to producing documentary news, television programming, research, and copywriting. Ability to take technical, complex projects from inception to completion. Areas of knowledge include:

- ✗ Multiple Project Coordination
- ✗ Interactive Software Development
- ✗ Knowledge of Diverse Industries
- ✗ Problem-Solving
- ✗ Meeting Demanding Deadlines
- ✗ Budgeting & Finance
- ✗ Team Leadership
- ✗ Strategic Planning/Implementation

COMPUTER SKILLS

- Macintosh proficiency: Own SE30, Quadra 840AV, PowerBook 5300c
- Scripting and basic coding with: Director, HyperCard, HTML 3.0, AppleScript
- Photoshop, Illustrator, Premiere, AfterEffects, Painter, and SndEdit Pro
- Netscape Browser, Telnet, NewsWatcher
- Microsoft Word and Claris Mac Write

INSTRUCTOR:

Albert Merrill School, New York, NY
Instructor: Taught basic electronics through digital technology

PROFESSIONAL EXPERIENCE:

Honeywell, New York, NY — 1988 - 1996
CORPORATE TRAINER

Kaye Construction Corporation, New York, NY — 1983 - 1988
SUPERVISOR

EDUCATION & TRAINING:

New York University, New York, NY
Building & Construction Management - emphasis on Project Management
City College of New York, New York, NY
Electrical Engineering (City College of CUNY)
The New School, Computer Instruction Center, New York, NY
MacroMedia Director Coursework

OTHER - DRAMA:

Laban Institute of Movement Studies, New York, NY
The Medicine Show Theater, New York, NY
Nina Martin/Francis Becker, New York, NY

- References, Reels & Supporting Documentation Furnished Upon Request -

PSYCHIATRIST

PERDEEP M. JAGALUR, M.D.

21 Shoreview Drive, Apt. 3
White Plains, NY 10605
(914) 555-1996

OBJECTIVE

A position as Staff Psychiatrist which will benefit from my ten-year medical track record and utilize my broadbased experience in both psychiatry and general medicine to the fullest.

PROFILE

- Dedicated medical professional with strong detail orientation and exceptional follow-through abilities.
- Demonstrated ability to effectively prioritize a broad range of responsibilities in order to consistently meet deadlines.
- Possess strong diagnostic and problem resolution skills.
- Strong interpersonal skills, proven ability to work effectively with individuals on all levels; team player.
- Demonstrated ability to work well under pressure.
- Strong background in general medicine and surgery.
- Significant expertise in neurology, possess background in substance and alcohol abuse.
- More than three years' experience in Emergency Room settings dealing with all psychiatric disorders.
- Experienced in *partial hospitalization* settings.

The Objective works because the candidate is targeting a specific career.
A Personal section is included.
The focus is on skills and experience rather than on employment experience.

TRAINING

ELMHURST HOSPITAL CENTER, Elmhurst, NY
Psychiatric Resident July 1993 - Present

- Serve as primary therapist; run both group and individual counseling sessions.
- Provide ongoing treatment to more than twenty patients in the outpatient clinic, for long-term care.
- Provide psychiatric consults to Emergency Room physicians.
- Receiving training in ***Electroconvulsive Therapy.***

KINGS COUNTY HOSPITAL, Brooklyn, NY
Psychiatric Resident July 1992 - June 1993

- Provided treatment to more than ten inpatients per day.

EDUCATION

JJM MEDICAL COLLEGE, Davanagere, India
Psychiatric Resident February 1986 - December 1987

- Received diploma in ***Psychological Medicine.***
- ***Commended*** for volunteer effort on behalf of educating general practitioners, in remote areas, in ***psychiatric case management*** and ***managing medications used in treating psychiatric disorders.***

BELLARY MEDICAL COLLEGE, Bellary, India
Medical Doctor (M.B.B.S.) June 1985

THE NATIONAL COLLEGE, Basavanagudi, Bangalore, India
Pre-Medical Studies June 1977 - June 1979

EXPERIENCE
1987 - 1996

FAMILY PRACTICE, Bangalore City, India
General Practitioner

PERSONAL

Married   Citizenship: India   Visa Status: J1

REFERENCES

Available upon request.

MICHAEL S. DUDASH

23657 Londonderry Drive
Novi, MI
(810) 555-3628

REAL ESTATE AGENT

HIGHLIGHTS OF QUALIFICATION

- 14+ years successful experience selling residential and commercial real estate
- Recognized for attaining top listings and developing qualified prospects
- Active member and former Vice President of the Curry County Realtors Association
- State licensed broker and real estate agent since 1982
- Received primary listing for sale of 42,000 sq. ft. warehouse that sold for $3.9 million
- Member of the *TPC* ("Top Pro Club" -$10 million/year+ in real estate sales, 1988-96)

EDUCATION & LICENSES

Central Michigan University, Mt. Pleasant, MI
Bachelor of Arts Degree: Anthropology, 1979

Thomlin School of Real Estate, Thomlin, MI
Real Estate Program Completed, 1981
Graduated top 5% of Class

Certified Residential Professional (CRP), 1982
Certified Commercial Professional (CCP), 1985

Simple format used in residential real estate
In this profession, the Highlights say it all. The actual employment history is less important than the sales achievements and Education section.

PROFESSIONAL EXPERIENCE

Sandra Jeffries Realty, Inc., West Seger, MI — 1990 - Present
BROKER ASSOCIATE

Silver Bullet Commercial Realty, Main Street, MI — 1988 - 1990
BROKER ASSOCIATE

Century 21 Realty, West Seger, MI — 1982 - 1988
BROKER ASSOCIATE

• References & Additional Information Furnished Upon Request •

REAL ESTATE—CONSTRUCTION

JAMES M. HYATT

Seven Timberwood Trace, Woodstone, Colorado 45678
(678) 555-4567 • 402-5678 beeper

PROFILE

- **Senior Construction Project Management and Design experience in industrial, heavy, commercial, manufacturing and residential projects (new construction, retrofit, renovations, etc). Also proficient in sales and product marketing of construction-related services.**

Very detailed resume that is very comprehensive in its coverage of skills
A unique way of listing the company and responsibilities, and almost using the Work History as an appendix

- preconstruction services
- construction administration
- architectural operations
- contract administration
- contractor & subcontract liaison
- project feasibility analysis
- materials purchasing & management
- total quality management
- multimillion dollar budget oversight
- claims avoidance & resolution
- turnkey project management
- project specifications write-up
- architect & engineer interface
- contract interpretation
- subcontract selection
- bid proposal & cost estimating
- vendor / supplier negotiations
- CPM scheduling
- cost control
- safety coordination & training

- **Proven ability to deliver major projects on time and under budget. Skilled in using computer-driven estimating systems and computer-aided design. Author of "state of condition" reports (for structural analysis).**

SPECIFIC ACHIEVEMENTS

BUILDERS INTERNATIONAL CORPORATION

PROJECT MANAGEMENT
- **Oversaw all design and construction of manufacturing facilities:** modifications, renovations, and new construction for domestic and international projects.
- **Hired consulting engineers / architects** and met with key management personnel to determine project specifications.
- **Developed a bid process that acquired competitive bids** on all subcontracted work and materials.

PROJECT CONSULTING
- **Extensively traveled overseas on facilities acquisition projects** to consult on construction project requirements: modifications, renovations, new construction.
- **Collaborated and traveled with company owner to advise on materials and processes** required to design and complete private residential estate.
- **Spearheaded introduction of a computer-aided design system** which enabled department to formulate cost and requirements for over 30 building projects and future design projects.

WILSON, TAYLOR & ASSOCIATES

SALES INITIATIVE
- **Successfully grew start-up company from ground zero to over $13 million in sales in six years** by reinvesting all profits into company and strictly monitoring costs.
- Led Sales and Estimating effort during first three years and **experienced sales increases of 58% in second year and 75% in third year of operations.**

COST AVOIDANCE
- **Designed effective expense containment procedures and operational policies** to ensure continued profitability. Administered $10 million budget.
- **Automated accounting and project estimating function** and trained Project Estimator on this system.

SAFETY PROGRAMMING
- **Reduced occupational accidents by 35% in six months** by creating a companywide safety program that involved hiring a retired OSHA Inspector as a consultant.
- **Personally organized an OSHA / HAZCOM Manual** to ensure all project personnel were in compliance with local, state, and federal regulations.

WORK HISTORY

- BUILDERS INTERNATIONAL CORPORATION, Woodstone, Colorado
  Construction Manager - Corporate: Property Development Division (1990-present)
- WILSON, TAYLOR & ASSOCIATES, Nailing, Colorado
  General Contractor (1982-1990, company profitably sold)

EDUCATION

- **Master of Business Administration,** 1993
  Hammerville State University, Nailing, Colorado
- **Bachelor of Architecture,** 1982
  Hammerville State University, Nailing, Colorado
- Continuing Education:
  - **Completed Architectural Registration Exam - Division "C"**
  - Certificate of Construction Techniques
  - Certificate of Effective Construction Management
  - Certificate of Advanced Sales & Estimating
  - Butler Builder Products Course

MEMBERSHIPS

- **President (Woodstone Local Chapter):** Associated Builders & Contractors, 1995
  Past Membership Chair (National): Associated General Contractors, 1993

SELECTED PROJECTS SUMMARY

- **Client:** Colorado College of the Arts
  Architect: Reagan-Ford & Associates
  Project Scope: The Tipper Building - concrete work, demolition, site prep, paving
- **Client:** Washington Memorial Hospital
  Architect: InterArch Alliance, Inc.
  Project Scope: 5,000-square-foot frame building
- **Client:** Jefferson High School
  Architect: Lincoln & Wilson, LLC
  Project Scope: 75,000-square-foot masonry school
- **Client:** Mountain View Corporation
  Architect: Clinton Eisenhower, RA
  Project Scope: 100,000-square-foot plastic extrusion plant
- **Client:** Blue Vista Office Park Associates / Bankonit Service Center
  Architect: Theodore, Ulysses & Carter, Inc.
  Project Scope: 24,000-square-foot banking / computer center
- **Client:** Wyoming National Guard Armory
  Architect: State of Wyoming
  Project Scope: 14,000-square-foot addition
- **Client:** Grant Automotive Industries
  Architect: InterArch Alliance, Inc.
  Project Scope: 95,000-square-foot preengineered metal building

---

RICHARD HARVARD

Permanent Address
153 Blue Bird Drive
North Fort Myers, FL 33
(813) 555-8822
(407) 555-0011 (Fax)

Graphic is a great touch, especially for this industry.
Project Experience is critical career description.
The use of fonts is excellent, as is the layout of employment dates.

Local Address
266 Fallen Oak
Miami, FL 933781
(407) 555-6633 (Home)

CONSTRUCTION MANAGER / SUPERINTENDENT

OVERVIEW:

Over 25 years' experience in Construction, 16 years as Construction Manager/Superintendent. A successful record of working on small/large sized projects ($5 million to $153 million). A **qualified and competent professional** recognized for completing projects *on time and under budget.* Extensive **national/international experience.** A troubleshooter able to turn around troubled projects to meet challenging goals and objectives.

PROJECT EXPERIENCE:

- Water Treatment Facilities
- Subway Systems
- Large Concrete Placement
- Embassy Renovations/New Construction
- Piping
- Culverts
- Excavation
- Power Plants

Have worked on Defense Contracts governed by the U.S. Army Corps of Engineers, Alexandria, Egypt, (1989-90) and Almaty, Kazakhstan, (1994 - Present).

PROFILE:

* Well organized; able to effectively manage **multiple projects** simultaneously.
* A solid record of **working well with people** at all levels including: government officials, laborers & expats and clients' representatives.
* A proven and *verifiable* record for **profit attainment.** Recognized for containing costs, meeting stringent schedules, and earning profits.

EXPERIENCE:

4/92 - Present

Bill Harbert International, Birmingham, AL ***(Project Site - Almaty, Kazakhstan)***
QUALITY CONTROL MANAGER - Hired and selected to take over as Quality Control Manager in charge of the construction and renovation of the new U.S. Embassy in Kazakhstan ($62 million project). Reestablished good working rapport between the contractor and the U.S. Army Corps of Engineers. During this 8-month assignment, inspected all phases of construction, directed all preparatory meetings and assured that all products used met original specifications. Project was successfully completed in December of 1994.

3/82 - 4/92

L.A. Water Treatment Corp., City of Industries, CA ***(Project Site - Egypt)***
SITE MANAGER - Hired to complete a troubled project (Potable Water Treatment Facility - Provincial Cities Development Project, $22 million project). Finished the project in 5 months and supervised **Plant Start-up. Disinfected & Sterilized 25 kilometers of pipe.**

10/84 - 10/86

Howard, Harbert, Jones, J.V., Greensboro, NC ***(Project Site - Egypt)***
AREA SUPERVISOR / CIVIL FOREMAN - Upgraded sewer & pump stations. In addition, worked on the construction of a $125 million fresh water treatment facility. Poured over 8,000 meters of concrete and completed the project on time and under budget. Used an innovative approach to solve a pouring problem by designing and fabricating a *"Tapered Wall-Tie"* to pour concrete against dead-head concrete.

EDUCATION:

Educational Institute of Pittsburgh, Pittsburgh, Pennsylvania
A.A. Degree: Architectural & Mechanical Design (1965-66)

MILITARY:

United States Marine Corps
Honorable Discharge - Rank of Sergeant; Marine Corps. Silent Drill Team. Top Secret Clearance for *White House Details* and Presidential Guard at Camp David.

- References Furnished Upon Request -

RECRUITER

Barbara Lawrence
147 Middlewood Road
East Brunswick, New Jersey 08816
(908) 555-4113

Profile

Fifteen years of professional experience in personnel and recruiting for both retainer firms and contingency agencies.....background includes applications in operations, business development, and human resources.....possess strong organizational and interpersonal skills.

Summary

Broadbased responsibilities in the following areas:

- Recruitment
- Research Analysis
- Screening and Interviewing
- Candidate Development
- Job Development
- Consultative Sales
- Employer Liaison Functions
- Search Plan Development

Experience

- Developed candidates for executive level positions in the health care industry.
- Worked on Director Level searches for Marketing and Sales, Business Development, Strategic Planning, Environmental Affairs, and Formulations.
- Wrote search plans for clients, detailing information.
- Extensive experience in recruiting of professionals for engineering and manufacturing environments.
- Create advertising campaigns and develop sources of qualified applicants through an extensive network of referrals and corporate recruiting techniques. Market candidates to fill a variety of positions.
- Perform the following functions: prescreening and collection of candidates, interviewing and reference checks, and employee orientation.
- Work closely with Presidents of companies, Hiring Managers, and Human Resources to assess technical personnel needs.
- Directly supervised a staff of five recruiters. Performed extensive training and development of professionals specializing in technical areas.
- Strong background in business development efforts including client needs assessments, acquiring new accounts, and cultivating existing relationships.
- Conduct client presentations and negotiate contract terms. Provide ongoing support to promote future business development.
- Responsible for managing projects from start to completion. Staffed entire departments for newly formed corporations.

Reader-friendly fonts for the section headings
Adequately detailed and descriptive Profile and Summary sections

Employment

1995-Present **Smith Farrell International,** Princeton, NJ
Associate

1991-1995 **Lawrence Associates, Inc.,** Iselin, NJ
Recruiter/Manager

1981-1991 **John Raymond Associates,** Sayreville, NJ
Recruiting Supervisor

Education

Kean College of New Jersey
Degree Program: Psychology

PIRKKO LIISA KALENIUS
915 Lecara Lane
Atlanta, GA 47632
(404) 555-0085

UPSCALE RETAIL SALES

OVERVIEW:

Over nine years working for, and managing, fashionable boutiques and retail establishments on Atlanta's prestigious *Galt Avenue.* Recognized for delivering unexcelled customer service. A *verifiable* track record of success backed by impeccable references. Areas of expertise include:

- Sales - Exceptional Customer Service
- Merchandising & Display
- Employee Management
- New Location Start-Up Management
- Tri-Lingual (English/Swedish/Finnish)
- New Product Introduction
- Budgeting/Record Keeping
- Problem Solving
- Inventory & Pricing Controls
- Computer/POS Scanning Use

EMPLOYMENT:

Max Mara, USA Inc. on Galt, Atlanta, GA
SALES ASSOCIATE

The Village Shop on Galt Avenue, Atlanta, GA
STORE MANAGER / SALES

Gucci on Galt Avenue, Atlanta, GA
STORE MANAGER / SALES

Frances Brewster, Atlanta, GA
SALES ASSOCIATE

The Ritz Carlton Hotel, Atlanta, GA
BOUTIQUE MANAGER

EDUCATION:

Kuopion Teknillinen Opisto, Kuopio, Finland
Equivalency: Bachelor of Science in Land Planning & Surveying
- Drafting
- Land Surveying
- Blueprint Development

PERSONAL:

Enjoy & Active in:
- Studying Italian
- The Arts & Theater
- Classical Music, Opera
- Ice Skating
- Exercise

- References & Supporting Documentation Furnished Upon Request -

Michael Murado 52 Gerard Street ■ Bellport, NY 11713 ■ (516) 555-0074

Consultative High-End Retail Sales Professional

Career Profile

Highly experienced retail professional with extensive twenty-five year background in upscale home furnishings sales, business management, buying, and advertising.

Areas of Expertise

- Upholstery
- Bedding
- Case Goods
- Leather
- Broadloom
- Consumer Education
- Sales Training
- Customer Service
- Computer Use
- Advertising
- Buying
- Management

Summary of Qualifications

Over twenty years' experience in furniture and bedding as business owner, store manager, and furniture consultant. Impressive ten-year track record with furniture department of premier retailer.

Demonstrated track record of increasing revenues in declining markets. Contributed to high growth rate in sales and productivity of retail activities with personal leadership ability, analytical skills, and sales experience.

Excellent use of Summary of Qualifications to draw attention to the candidate's skills and not employment history

Extremely knowledgeable in all areas of furniture, bedding and broadloom design and construction as well as current trends and traditional styles.

Consistently requested by customers; have developed loyal customer base and referral network.

Train new hires in all systems and procedures, furniture and bedding knowledge and sales techniques. Often called upon to answer technical questions of fellow sales associates.

Employment History

Furniture Sales Consultant 1985 to 1995
Bloomingdale's, Garden City, NY

Sales and Advertising 1983 to 1985
Sunrise Sleep Shops, Lynbrook, NY

Store Manager 1980 to 1983
Sleepy's Bedding Centers, Syosset, NY

Store Manager 1978 to 1980
Suburban Colonial Shops, Jericho, NY

Operator of Family Business 1970 to 1978
Michael R. Murado Furniture Co., Bayside, NY

Education

Bachelor of Science Degree in Marketing
St. John's University, School of Business Administration, Jamaica, NY

Good visual of framed border
Good lead of Qualifications for any sales position
Good secondary lead of Education because medical sales can be technically oriented

WILLIAM B. SMITH
5555 Devon Court
Dallas, Texas 38702
(214) 555-1275

PROFESSIONAL OBJECTIVE: MEDICAL SALES

SUMMARY OF QUALIFICATIONS

- Member of **Top Performer's Club** three of past four years; consistently ranked #1 in Sales; National, Regional, and District Leader. Successful **negotiator.**
- Personally increased sales by approx. 200% within four years, from $1.4M to $4.6M.
- Expertise in **Sales, Marketing, Planning, Advertising, Promotions.**
- Thorough knowledge of medical devices; market PEG Procedures, PEJ Procedures, Laparoscopic Gastrostomy, Laparoscopic Jejunostomy. Medical terminology literacy.
- Computer literate: Windows, DOS, Lotus 1-2-3, Quicken, WordPerfect.
- Excellent communication and interpersonal skills; ability to establish positive rapport with medical professionals, peers, and superiors.
- Highly self-motivated, responsible, tenacious. Professional appearance and demeanor.

EDUCATION

THE UNIVERSITY OF TEXAS AT ARLINGTON - Arlington, Texas
Master of Business Administration (1989)
Emphasis in **Marketing** and **Management**

STEPHEN F. AUSTIN UNIVERSITY - Nacogdoches, Texas
Bachelor of Business Administration (1986)
Major: **General Business;** Minor: **Chemistry;** 24 Hours in **Biology** and **Physics**

PROFESSIONAL EXPERIENCE

STEPHENSON PHARMACEUTICALS — **Dallas, Texas**
Medical Nutritional Representative — **1990 - Present**

- Market medical nutritionals and enteral devices (PEG and PEJ Procedures, Laparoscopic Gastrostomies and Jejunostomies) to nursing homes, suppliers, physicians, hospitals, dieticians.
- Successfully negotiate and secure signed contracts with clients.

<u>**Significant Achievements/Awards**</u>

- Personally increased sales approx. 200% in four years; 1994, $4.6 million; 1990, $1.4 million.
- 1994 - Ranked #1 in entire division; increased sales by 50.54% and $1.15 million through September over previous year. Recognized as Number 1 in Region for 1994.
- 1992 - Regional dollar and percentage leader; increased sales by 30%, $725K.
- 1991 - Ranked #1 in Nation in all categories; increased nutritional sales by 47.95%, $841K; National Device Leader - increased sales by 101%, $225K; dollar percent nationally 39.43%.

WILLIAM B. SMITH   Page Two

JIFFY MART CONVENIENCE STORES - Dallas, Texas **1986 - 1988**

District Supervisor (1987-1988)

Oversaw operations of six retail convenience stores with annual sales in excess of $4.5 million; directed 26 employees.

Significant Achievements

- ♦ Established seasonal product line promotions; maintained gross margins in excess of 25%.
- ♦ Designed and implemented new Plan-O-Gram arrangements.
- ♦ Implemented formal company employee orientation program. Developed and directed employee job enrichment through employee participation.
- ♦ Developed innovative incentive program; stabilized turnovers.
- ♦ Instrumental in implementation of employee retention programs for store level operations.
- ♦ Established and executed weekly employee training programs; greatly improved productivity and efficiency.

Sales Manager (1986-1987)

- ♦ Supervised staff of five sales representatives.
- ♦ Increased sales by 20% during first year as Sales Manager with annual sales of $1 million.
- ♦ Conducted marketing research which resulted in increase in product category by 10%; significantly increased sales.

Night Sales Clerk (1986)

- ♦ Assisted customers with selections and purchases in 24-hour convenience store.
- ♦ Operated cash register; reconciled cash drawer.
- ♦ Promoted to Sales Manager within three months.

♦ ♦ References Furnished Upon Request ♦ ♦

JAMES R. PATTERSON

102 Lakeview Drive, Orchard Lake, MI 48000 (810) 555-3233

Qualifications

- Five years experience in sales, with a demonstrated track record of outstanding sales achievements.

Abilities

- Designing systems for prospecting and generating leads.
- Negotiating: Closing the deal on the "impossible" sale.
- Developing strategies that win customers from the competition.
- Leading: Motivating staff to excel by instilling confidence and creating incentives. Coaching staff on sales techniques.
- Introducing and promoting new product lines.

Experience

July, 1993 to Present

Furniture Gallery, Detroit, Michigan

Sales Manager (Promotion)
Sales Representative

Manage 25,000-square-foot bedroom furniture showroom and 5,000-square-foot warehouse with $110,000/month in sales (#1 showroom in the company). Oversee inside sales, staff of five, inventory, customer service, and bookkeeping.

- After assuming manager position, increased monthly sales from $85,000 to an average of $110,000—a 30% increase which has remained consistent since that time. Personally generate $35,000-$45,000 of that volume.
- Consistently #1 Sales Representative in the showroom, and within top two Sales Representatives corporate-wide (of eight stores in the Detroit Metro Area.)
- Excellent closing ratio: 80%-85%. Continually exceed sales targets.
- Introduced new prospecting system that has successfully increased sales corporate-wide.
- Changed the layout of the showroom by grouping together bedroom sets, which has increased sales of complete bedroom outfits.
- Introduced employee incentives that have decreased absenteeism and increased sales.
- Reorganized warehouse for easier access and inventory control.

Classic style of fonts and use of text in the margins
Each bullet in the Experience section tied to an accomplishment

May, 1990 to July, 1993

Superior Bedroom Company, Kalamazoo, Michigan

Sales Representative

- After first three months in sales, was #1 Sales Rep in the company (of two stores). Participated in numerous trade shows and conventions.

Education

Bachelor of Science-Organizational Communication (Expected June, 1997); Eastern Michigan University, Ypsilanti, Michigan (1993-Present)

Western Michigan University, Kalamazoo, Michigan (1990 - 1993)

Seminars: Tom Hopkins, "Competitive Edge Selling"
Anthony Robbins, "Unlimited Power"

Employment has been with the same company since college graduation.
Most of the writing is done in paragraph form that is easy to read and understand.
Provides good back-up for each skill listed.

SALES

JEANNE ROWLANDS

High-Technology Sales, Marketing & New Business Development

1632 112th Avenue SE, #A203, Bellevue, WA 98005
(206) 555-7150

SUMMARY

Aggressive, enthusiastic sales professional with proven talent for making new contacts, closing orders, and generating repeat business through effective account management. Leading-edge presentation skills. Experience managing unique marketing initiatives and programs. Mainframe and PC computer skills. B.A. degree.

1995 SALES ACCOMPLISHMENTS

- **Generated over $1 million in revenues** by landing key account with a major catalogue distributor, convincing them to switch their air shipping service away from our major competitor.
- **Increased average monthly sales volume by 32%** in less than 12 months by continuously strengthening relationships and building value with customers.
- **Played key role in team multimedia presentation** to top Boeing executives; created data show and assisted in delivery of a presentation that resulted in a new multi-year shipping contract worth over $3 million.

KEY SKILLS & AREAS OF EXPERIENCE

- **ACCOUNT MANAGEMENT:** Currently manage over 30 senior accounts in the Puget Sound region; consistently exceed revenue goals by actively prospecting for new customers, effectively prioritizing leads, and working with existing accounts to expand business and obtain valuable referrals.
- **RELATIONSHIP-BUILDING:** Selected to manage the UPS Associations Program, a unique marketing effort designed to sell shipping services through trade and professional associations. Closed $50,000 in new business in the first eight months, signing up five associations when none had been signed in over a year.
- **PRESENTATIONS:** Extensive experience designing customized proposals and sales presentations; skilled at listening to client needs and concerns, developing effective solutions, and persuading customers to take action; preference for presenting directly to senior executives and key decision makers.
- **TECHNICAL:** Excellent computer skills; strong experience using mainframe (AS/400) and PC-based systems, combined with working knowledge of multiple business software packages. Experience interacting with Logistics Services, Industrial Engineering, and Information Systems departments to clarify account needs, obtain resource commitments, and develop value-added solutions.
- **MARKET RESEARCH:** Familiar with modern data collection and statistical analysis techniques; compiled extensive research on shipping companies for inclusion in UPS 1993 Washington District Business Plan.

CAREER EXPERIENCE WITH UNITED PARCEL SERVICE (UPS)—1992-present

Within four years at UPS, demonstrated the skills and sales finesse necessary to move from internship to senior sales position for the Pacific Northwest region. Currently serve as **Senior Account Executive** (1994-Present); past positions include **Account Executive** (1993-1994), **Internship Coordinator** (1993), and **Marketing Intern** (1992).

EDUCATION

B.A. in Communications, University of Washington, 1992.
Currently pursuing M.B.A. degree (marketing emphasis) through Seattle University.
Completion of numerous professional sales, marketing, and technical training courses.

Good use of leading with achievements and accomplishments

SHIPPING

ROBERT G. THORESON

20 Locust Avenue • Smithtown, New York 11787 • (516) 555-9374

PROFILE

Hands-on manager experienced in effective operation of large shipping facility. Recognized for valuable systems contributions with positive P&L impact. Work effectively and independently in challenging environment. Computer literate with degree in data processing.

REPRESENTATIVE ACHIEVEMENTS

- **Broke ten year company volume record** while working with downsized trucking staff. **Increased shipping from 9 million square feet to 13½ million square feet** of corrugated per month.
- **Designed productivity analyzation program;** increased profitability and decreased overtime hours to under 24%.
- **Devised cost-effective systems** to track supplies, orders and stock; greatly improved warehouse efficiency. Procedure adopted company-wide.
- **Partnered with IBM to create quarterly report** to track non-returned freight pallets. Substantially enhanced retrieval rate and reduced lost revenue.

EMPLOYMENT

Southern Container, Deer Park, NY — **1991 to present**
Shipping Manager/Assistant to Plant Manager

Warehouse Management
Direct operations of delivery and support staff. Establish work plans, route outgoing shipments, direct loading and off-loading of all freight. Coordinate and calculate monthly inventory. Schedule driver off/on hours per ICC/DOT standards. Second in chain of command for warehouse safety program and evacuation decisions.

Computer systems usage and development
Design original programs. Utilize LOTUS SYMPHONY database/spreadsheet for routing, billing, cost accounting, production and personnel functions. Troubleshooter for shipping and computer system problems (24-hour call).

Personnel functions
Hire all transport and equipment operators. Conduct safety meetings and programs. Act as union/management liaison; formulate creative solutions to difficult shop issues.

White Rose Food, Inc., Farmingdale, NY — **1971 to 1991**
Commercial Transport Operator

First-level warehouse management responsibilities. Route and deliver wholesale foods and paper products to tristate New York area.

SKILLS

Computer/Data Processing
- Proficient in PC software and programming.
- Utilize IBM AS400 mainframe.

Transport operation
- Experienced driver of commercial freight vehicles.
- CDL / Class 1 NY license since 1986 / U.S. Government License 1991.

EDUCATION

A.A.S. Data Processing, 1985. Kingsborough Community College, NY
Graduation with honors. GPA 3.5/4.0 (earned while performing full-time job)

SCHOOL ADMINISTRATOR

Diana Reagan Collier
1778 Heritage Circle
Wilmington, North Carolina 28401
(910) 555-4567

Leads with academic credentials, important to the academic profession

Terse description of qualifications and responsibilities

Good back-up for each skill listed

SUMMARY

Experienced school administrator seeking a Principalship to apply my enthusiasm, focus on quality, and dedication to providing children with every educational opportunity possible. Effective motivator able to develop excellent rapport with staff and nurture individual strengths.

EDUCATION AND TRAINING

UNIVERSITY OF NORTH CAROLINA AT WILMINGTON
M.Ed. Educational Administration 1988
M.Ed. Educational Supervision
Curriculum Instructional Specialist

NORTH CAROLINA STATE UNIVERSITY
Bachelor of Science - Mathematics Education 1979

EAST CAROLINA UNIVERSITY
Accepted into Doctoral Program for Ed.D. Educational Leadership

Presented extensive in-service and workshops for County, Regional, and State conferences in areas that include Meeting At-Risk Needs, Manipulatives, and Probability and Statistics.

Trained in TESA, CHOTS, ETT, PAT, Total Quality Education, Mentoring Certification

EXPERIENCE

COLLIER COUNTY SCHOOLS — Collier County, NC
Assistant Principal — 1992-Present
South Lakes Middle School

- Curriculum/Instructional Supervision and Program Evaluation
- Data Analysis
- School Improvement Team Cochair
- Staff Development
- Testing Coordinator
- Textbooks
- Assistance Team Chairperson
- Staff Evaluations (Certified/Classified)
- Liaison with UNCW for Student Teachers/Teaching Fellows
- Southern Association Coordinator
- Substitute Teachers
- Discipline

Elementary Assistant Principal — 1987-1992
Creek Lane, Smith, Independence, Sharon Lakes, and Southwest Elementary

Middle Grades Summer School Principal — 1992 & 1994
Chestnut, Thomas Hill, and Myst Lane Middle

EXPERIENCE (CONTINUED)

COLLIER COUNTY SCHOOLS — Collier County, NC
Elementary Summer School Principal — 1988
Creek Lane

Interim Principal — Spring 1989
Smith Elementary

Mathematics Teacher/Department Chair — 1985-1987
Thomas Hill Middle School

Mathematics Teacher — 1981-1983
Myst Lane Middle School

Mathematics Teacher — 1979-1981
New Lakes High School

CHARLOTTE HIGH SCHOOL — Charlotte, NC
Mathematics Teacher — 1983-1985
Developed and instituted a restructuring of mathematics curriculum for system
Teacher of the Year - 1984

PROFESSIONAL AFFILIATIONS/COMMITTEES

Superintendent's Cabinet Member
State Math Committee Member
Local County Strategic Planning Committee
SAT Task Force Member
Substitute Review Committee Member
Alternative School Committee
Local County Principal/Assistant Principal Association
National Council of Teachers of Mathematics (NCTM)
North Carolina Council of Teachers of Mathematics (NCCTM)
National Middle School Association (NMSA)
Phi Delta Kappa - Graduate Educational Society
Delta Kappa Gamma - Women Educators' Fraternity, President 1992-1994
Sigma Kappa Alumni Chapter - Social Service Sorority

ADDITIONAL EXPERIENCE

UNIVERSITY OF NORTH CAROLINA AT WILMINGTON — Wilmington, NC
Lead summer programs in education as needed.

EAST CAROLINA UNIVERSITY — Greenville, NC
Teach college level mathematics courses at satellite campuses as needed.

BRIAN MAJESTY

1549 Northeast 128th Court
Pompano Beach, Florida 33064
(305) 555-9991

Unique use of font styling in title
Early focus on objective qualifications relevant to this profession
Second page details employment history while providing detailed information

PRIVATE SECURITY PROFESSIONAL

Executive Protection/Weapons Training/Domestic & Corporate Anti-Terrorism

OVERVIEW:

More than twenty years of solid security, military, and management experience with heavy emphasis on developing security strategies and programs for the private sector—conducting investigations, providing executive protection, and weapons training. A reputable and well-trained professional recognized for redefining and reshaping physical and protective security services in accordance with contemporary American needs.

SKILLS & CREDENTIALS:

- ☆ Florida Investigative License
- ☆ Florida Concealed Weapons Permit
- ☆ NRA Certified Firearms Instructor
- ☆ Proficient: Shaolin Kung Fu
- ☆ Florida Firearms Permit
- ☆ NAUI Scuba Qualified
- ☆ Anti-Terrorism Training
- ☆ Member A.S.I.S.

MILITARY:

United States Marine Corps, 1964 - 1970
Communications / Intelligence, Top Secret Clearance
Foreign Service: Vietnam, (1965 - 1968)

RECOGNITIONS (Partial Listing):

- ☆ Bronze Star Medal
- ☆ Purple Heart
- ☆ 2 Presidential Unit Commendations
- ☆ Navy Unit Commendation
- ☆ Cross of Gallantry w/Palm
- ☆ USMC Rifle Expert

EDUCATION:

NORTHEASTERN UNIVERSITY, Boston, MA
Bachelor of Arts Degree, Criminal Justice - Corporate Anti-Terrorism

* Federal Law Enforcement Institute, Atlanta, Georgia
Cultural Resource Protection and Investigative Techniques, 1987
* National Rifle Association, Miami, Florida
Firearm Instructor's Course (Pistol, Rifle, Shotgun)
Certified Instructor, Personal Protection, Home Safety, 1991
* NRA, Law Enforcement Firearms Instructor's Development School,
Weapons Training Battalion, USMC Headquarters, Quantico, Virginia, 1992

PROFESSIONAL EXPERIENCE:

1990 - Present

Wells Fargo Investigative Services, Inc., Miami, Florida
DIRECTOR: EXECUTIVE PROTECTION SERVICES - Manage Executive Protection for individuals / corporate clients in accordance with the protective concepts used by the United States Secret Service. Evaluate risk situations, both domestically and abroad, providing personalized executive protection programs structured around individual needs. Work closely and in conjunction with local law enforcement agencies.

Facets of executive protection services include: Advance, Route & Site Surveys, Security Sweeps (Explosive Detection / Disposal and Technical Surveillance Counter Measures), Physical Security, Site and Residential Protection, Office Area Security, Personal Escort Details, Motorcade Route Security, Vehicle Escort, Intelligence, Protective Threat Assessment, and Law Enforcement Liaison and Coordination.

1984 - 1991

Commercial Security Services, Miami, Florida
CHIEF INVESTIGATOR - Supervised undercover surveillance and internal investigations. Directed Security for the PHAR-MOR L.P.G.A. Women's Classic Golf Tournament, Inverrary, Florida, 1991. Provided executive protection to CEO and Board of Directors for Pan American Airlines during their 1990 shareholders' meeting. Provided protective services to top executives of Eastern Airlines and their families, supervising a team of 60 officers (1989-90).

1980 - 1984

Shell Oil Exploration Division, Livingston, Texas
CULTURAL PROTECTION INVESTIGATOR - Represented the Florida Department of Natural Resources while accompanying survey team cutting a petroleum exploration line through the Florida Everglades. Supervised the safe handling and placement of high-explosives used in seismic testing.

1970 - 1980

Special Projects In Conjunction With U.S. Department of Defense
WEAPONS & LOGISTICAL CONSULTANT TO U.S. GOVERNMENT - Contracted by U.S. Department of Defense to work on Top Secret weapons and logistics projects. Specific information available upon request.

- References & Supplemental Information Furnished Upon Request -

Devon

18 Elm Street
Anna, Texas 75000
(214) 555-2008—Pager (214) 555-0695

Data

Height: 5'1"
Weight: 105

Hair: Red
Eyes: Blue

Age: 16
Birthday: 5/19/79

Vocal Profile

- ★ Powerful, wide-range contralto; comfortable in high and low registers.
- ★ Varied musical styles including Country, Blues, Rock, Top 40, and Classics.
- ★ Strong live performer, singing with passion and energy in vocal styles ranging from graceful ballads to power-driven blues-rock and hard core honky-tonk.
- ★ Captures audience with lyric-focused phrasing and emotion that comes from the heart.
- ★ Has looks, personality, and style for video.

Vocal Performances

Audiences' Reactions:
Shouts, Cheers, Standing Ovations, Requests to Disc Jockey for Encores.

"I've never heard singin' like that!" ***"You ought to be recording."****—Audience*
(A large group of cowboys stood, holding their hats over their hearts in appreciation.)

"Boy folks, SHE can sing!"*—Disc Jockey*
"Why aren't you in Nashville?"*—Disc Jockey*
"You made me cry, little lady."*—Audience*
"What a show!"*—Disck Jockey*
"Tremendous power!"*—Audience*
"Fantastic voice!"*—Disc Jockey*

1995

Sparky's, Commerce, Texas—***Talent Night***
Songs:
IF YOU'RE NOT IN IT FOR LOVE (artist: Shania Twain)
TOTAL ECLIPSE OF THE HEART (artist: Bonnie Tyler)

Brass Rail, Greenville, Texas—***Karaoke Night***
Songs:
ANY MAN OF MINE (artist: Shania Twain)
DOWN ON MY KNEES (artist: Trisha Yearwood)
JUST AROUND THE EYES (artist: Faith Hill)
IF YOU'RE NOT IN IT FOR LOVE (artist: Shania Twain)

Very creative styling, appropriate for a singer or someone in the arts
Good use of different fonts
Excellent inclusion of the "Audience Reactions" sections

Addendum

Prior to 1995

Lou Hamilton Center, San Antonio, Texas—***Our Part of Town Talent Show—Winner 3rd Place***
McCreeles Mall, San Antonio, Texas—***Our Part of Town Talent Show—Featured Singer***
YWCA, San Antonio, Texas—***Fund Raiser—Featured Singer***
Carlos Kelly's Restaurant, San Antonio, Texas—***Special Guest Singer***

Additional solo performances in San Antonio and Houston.

Professional Associations

Member: **Metroplex Country Music Association (MCMA)**

SOCIAL WORKER

Marlene K. Rivers, MSW

988 Knight Street
Monroe, MI 48161
Home: (313) 555-9087

Well presented—a neat and clean, one-page resume

Areas of Specialty

- Domestic Violence
- Sexual Abuse
- Runaway Teenagers
- Depression
- Substance Abuse
- ADHD

Education

Master of Social Work
Wayne State University, Detroit, Michigan — August, 1993 - May, 1995

Bachelor of Arts in Human Services *(Minors: Psychology & Sociology)*
Carson-Newman College, Jefferson City, Tennessee — August, 1988 - May, 1991

Experience

COUNTY SOCIAL SERVICES, Taylor, Michigan — January, 1992 - Present

Parents United Therapist

- Provide therapeutic intervention services to children, adolescents, and adults using individual, family, and group treatment. Included were adult and teen survivors and perpetrators of sexual abuse and incest.
- Qualified as expert witness in child and adolescent therapy; testified in court on the issue of sexual abuse.

Substance Abuse Counselor

- Coordinated and provided community-based substance abuse prevention counseling to teenagers, including the BABES puppet program for elementary school children and the PRIDE parent program.

Runaway Services Counselor

- Coordinated runaway services program for teenagers in Wayne and Monroe counties in Michigan.
- Counseled individuals, families, and groups. Provided 24-hour crisis intervention.
- Placed children in foster care.
- Advocated at the state and local levels for runaway program funding.
- Spoke to schools and community organizations about parenting and adolescent issues.
- Supervised three bachelor-level students from Adrian College, Adrian, Michigan.

Community Service Activities

Michigan Network For Runaway and Homeless Youth Member
(Advocated politically at the state level)
Wayne County Child Advocacy Network Member
Wayne County Child Sexual Abuse Task Force Member
Presenter on Child Abuse & Parenting, Monroe County Parenting Conference, 1993

STOCKBROKER

JONATHAN W. MOORSE

1862 Hamscott Circle
Jupiter, Florida 33458 (407) 555-6676

TOP PRODUCING INVESTMENT BROKER

Specializing in High Volume, High Commission Sales

OVERVIEW: A consistent, *verifiable* record of sales achievement in highly competitive and volatile environments. Recognized for developing strong networks, expert salesmanship, and attaining above-industry-standard closing ratios.

ACHIEVEMENTS:

▲ Top 12% in nation for: *New Accounts Opened*
▲ Top 16% in nation for: *Production*
▲ Top 14% in nation for: *Assets Under Management*
(Out of 11,000 Merrill Lynch Brokers)

STRENGTHS: Excellent sales record in both tangible and intangible products and services, in *fast-track* industries. A *peak-performance professional* with a reputation for selling to high net-worth individuals, as well as corporate accounts. Known for integrity, relationship selling, and providing outstanding quality service.

EMPLOYMENT:

Raymond James — Stuart, Florida
Senior V.P. of Investments — 1992 - Present

High focus on title and achievements, important to the sales profession
Simple, easy-to-read format that is totally results-oriented

Within 18 months, developed an upscale clientele base of 134 and ranked in the top 18% nationally for assets under management (and 20% for production and new account development). Extremely successful in *New Product Development.*

Merrill Lynch — Lake Worth, Florida
Financial Consultant — 1985 - 1992

Managed territorial growth, achieving top 20% ranking in all sales-related categories. Hired, trained, and supervised a support staff of seven. Recognized as a *team-spirited professional,* training and motivating new brokers and elevating Jupiter office to one of the *Top Producing Offices in the Nation.* Member of the Executive Club and the President's Club.

EMPLOYMENT (Other): Between 1982 and 1985, sold copiers and financial products and services.

EDUCATION: Western Connecticut University, Danbury, Connecticut
Bachelor of Business Administration: Marketing, 1982

- References & Supplemental Information Furnished Upon Request -

Good use of testimonials
Leading with quantitative achievements—necessary in the academic profession
Easy-to-read layout

Maria Loscalzo

192-42 35th Avenue
Flushing, NY 11358
(718) 555-6804

"... exceptionally energetic and enthusiastic teacher ... projects a charisma that captures the imagination of students ... demonstrated excellent classroom management skills ..."

Robert G. Pisido
former administrator

"... business background in technology was supportive to the use of videos and computers in the class ... She volunteered for cooperative opportunities in the media center and helped teachers to accommodate computers ... I recommend her with the highest regard ..."

Tom Delaney
2nd Grade Teacher
New York City Schools

Professional Profile

Eager to bring elementary students into the twenty-first century using a unique combination of education experience coupled with ten years' business background in computer systems management.

- Hold Masters Degree in Elementary Education and Bachelors Degree in Computer Science.
- Experienced in use of the Internet and educational software.
- Dedicated to enthusiastic and dynamic teaching as a means of creating and nurturing a lifelong love of knowledge in children.

Education, Honors, & Certifications

M.S. Elementary Education
Queens College, Flushing, NY. 1995

Bachelor of Science Computer Science
Hofstra University, Hempstead, NY. 1984

Kappa Delta Pi Honor Society Member

Provisional Certifications
NY State Elementary Education. 1995
NY State Business Education. 1995

Key Qualifications

Certified in Elementary (K-6) and Business Education

Plan and instruct each subject area using wide variety of teaching aids, motivational and implementation strategies to engage students in active learning.

Incorporate learning modality principles into classroom and individual instruction. Develop and conduct intergrade activities. Utilize Heath automated math management system.

Implement technological approaches to subject material. Research educational resources on the Internet. Assist with information retrieval.

Experienced Computer Educator

Designed and conducted various faculty and student workshops for training in word processing and spreadsheet software. Instructed corporate personnel in use of word processing, desktop publishing, and drafting programs for conversion from manual typesetting and drafting to computer assisted methods.

"... deeply involved in learning about the educational state-of-the-art, investigating research and designing instructional materials.... I look forward to the time when Diane will bring her love of children, enthusiasm, initiative, and intelligence into her own classroom."

Jennifer T. Brown Ed.D.

"My ability to motivate students and share a love of learning fosters a successful classroom environment. ... I would welcome becoming part of 'the village that raises the child' in your district."

Maria Loscalzo

Computer Skills

- **Software (IBM and MAC environments):** Windows and DOS, WordPerfect, Lotus123, Microsoft Word, Pagemaker, AutoCad, Books in Print, Baker & Taylor Links, Bibbase
- Working knowledge of the **Internet**
- **System installations and debugging;** terminal/printer operations

Employment

Professional Development in Education

- **Substitute Teacher,** K thru High School, April 1995 to present
- **Graduate Advisor, Education Dept.,** October 1995 to present
  Queens College, Flushing, NY
- **Workshop Presenter,** November 1995
  First combined International Reading Association Regional Conference, Nashville, TN
- **Information Services Assistant,** May 1994 to August 1995
  Queens College, Flushing, NY
- **Student Teacher,** September to December 1994
  P.S. 32, Flushing, NY

Computer Related Training Positions

- **Workshop Presenter,** February, 1995
  East Islip High School, East Islip, NY
- **Graduate Assistant,** August 1993 to May 1994
  Queens College, Flushing, NY
- **Software Engineer,** 1989 to 1991
  Craftsman Corporation, Smithtown, NY

Corporate Computer Systems Management

- **Systems Manager,** 1987 to 1989
  Metricase Corporation, Bohemia, NY
- **Software Quality Assurance Engineer,** 1986 to 1987
  Gull, Inc., Smithtown, NY
- **Staff Administrator, Executive Department,** 1984 to 1986
  Brooklyn Union Gas Co., Brooklyn, NY
- **Student Director/Assistant, Computer Science Lab,** 1981 to 1984
  Hofstra University, Hempstead, NY

Professional Affiliations

International Reading Association
Association for Supervision and Curriculum Development

STUDENT

RICHARD M. SUTTON

912-555-9892

RÉSUMÉ OF QUALIFICATIONS
328 PRINCETON PLACE
SAVANNAH, GEORGIA 31401

SUMMARY OF QUALIFICATIONS

> *Lead of Education for a student resume*
> *A lot of detail of educational experience in Summary*
> *A full look for a student resume*

EDUCATION

Master of Arts in English (expected 1996)
Georgia State University, Atlanta, Georgia
GPA 4.0/4.0

Bachelor of Arts in English, *Summa Cum Laude,* 1988
Minors in French and Education
Armstrong State College, Savannah, Georgia
GPA 3.963/4.0

HONORS/AWARDS

♦HIGH SCHOOL VALEDICTORIAN.
♦Won citywide Essay Competition senior year in high school.
♦Won "Best Freshman Essay" Contest out of 800 students at Armstrong State College.
♦Invited to statewide Academic Recognition Ceremony at State Capitol.
♦Awarded distinguished *Silver A* award from Armstrong State College.

FELLOWSHIPS AND LITERARY DISTINCTIONS

♦Awarded fellowship through UCAL at Berkeley for National Writing Project.
♦Reviewed, edited, and revised a 100-page historical documentary.
♦Wrote three critical articles for publication.

SKILLS/STRENGTHS

♦Proficient in all facets of French communication.
♦Creative storywriter, with solid copywriting skills.
♦Highly skilled in delivering formal presentations to large groups of up to 300.
♦Proven tact and diplomacy in handling interpersonal relationships.
♦Computer skills using WordPerfect, Letter Perfect.

PROFESSIONAL EXPERIENCE

1990 to Present

SAVANNAH CHRISTIAN PREPARATORY SCHOOL, Savannah, Georgia
English and French Instructor/Chairman Foreign Language Department
Responsibilities include curriculum development and instruction of English, French, Journalism, Speech, and Drama. Supplementary activities include managing all facets of yearbook production, including layout and design, copywriting and editing, and negotiating with publishers. *1991 School Yearbook distributed nationally by Publisher for marketing purposes. Built curricula for French I through IV and two advanced English courses.*

1987 to 1990

ARMSTRONG STATE COLLEGE WRITING CENTER, Savannah, Georgia
Assisted college students through all phases of the writing process to enhance writing proficiency and facilitate self-expression.

1984 to 1989

AUSTIN'S/LAUREN'S BOOKSTORE, Savannah, Georgia
Promoted to Assistant Manager with responsibility for purchasing decisions and coordinating autograph signings, in addition to supervising daily operations.

AFFILIATIONS

National Trust for Historic Preservation
Historic Savannah Foundation

References, writing samples, and publications are available upon request.

STUDENT

TODD S. RICHARDSON

Permanent Address:
930 Archibald Terrace
Cherry Hill, NJ 08002
(609) 555-1210

University Address:
105 Main Street
Springfield, MA 01102
(413) 555-3476

"... I have rarely, in my ten years in the hospitality industry, encountered an individual, in the dawn of his career, that has shown as much promise as Todd Richardson."
—Former Supervisor

Unique use of shaded box of testimonial, an excellent touch for a student resume from a former professor
Leads with Education, a general rule for students.

HIGHLIGHTS

- Expect to graduate in June 1995 from well-respected HRTA program
- Proven self-starter who does what needs to be done without being asked
- Team player with track record of establishing productive work relationships
- Friendly, outgoing, excellent customer relations abilities
- Computer skills: WordPerfect, Lotus 1-2-3, Q&A, Delphi space management software

EDUCATION

Western New England College, Springfield, MA
Bachelor of Science, Hotel, Restaurant, and Travel Administration (expected May 1995)
Area of Concentration: **Food Service Management**

HOSPITALITY EXPERIENCE

CENTER CITY HILTON HOTEL, Philadelphia, PA
Intern (Summer 1994)
Received a highly complimentary, ***unsolicited*** letter of recommendation from the Director of Conference Services specifically praising my initiative and interpersonal skills.
CONFERENCE SERVICES (7 weeks): Responsible for preparation of meeting rooms, audiovisual equipment, internal accounting documents, distribution of reports concerning incoming conference groups, and coordination with group representatives.
FOOD AND BEVERAGE DEPARTMENT (5 weeks): Management of dining room, including hospitality, guest check reconciliation, floor plan preparation, beverage control, and waitstaff supervision.

PIZZA HUT, Cherry Hill, NJ
Cook (Summer 1993)
Responsible for daily setup of kitchen before opening and food preparation for lunch. Waited and bussed tables. Operated computerized cash register and serviced credit card receipts.

VOLUNTEER ACTIVITIES

SIGMA ALPHA MU FRATERNITY, Western New England College, Springfield, MA
Caterer (Fall 1992, 1993, and 1994)
Sole responsibility for planning, purchasing, cooking, and serving food for the fraternity's Alumni Weekend (twice) and Parents Weekend (twice). Average attendance was roughly 125 at these events. Made all burgers, salads, etc., from scratch.

SIGMA ALPHA MU FRATERNITY, Western New England College, Springfield, MA
Kitchen Steward (January to December 1992)
Established kitchen procedures, many still in use, for newly chartered chapter of this fraternity. Responsible for food budget, purchasing food and supplies, interviewing and hiring kitchen personnel, supervising kitchen and dining room operations, and preparing food. Also held positions of Scholarship Chairman and Fundraising Chairman.

OTHER EXPERIENCE

FIRST AID UNIT, WESTERN NEW ENGLAND COLLEGE, Springfield, MA
EMT/CPR Coordinator (1993 to Present)
Responsible for first aid at all athletic events, concerts, and Fine Arts Center activities. Coordinated and instructed CPR program sponsored by the College's Environmental Health and Safety Office.

Other positions include Head Instructor and Lifeguard (Summers 1989, 1990, 1991, 1992).

SPECIAL ACHIEVEMENTS

NRA Certificate in Sanitation, Certificate in Basic Mixology, Emergency Medical Technician, New Jersey, American Red Cross CPR and First Aid Instructor, Member of Cherry Hill Volunteer Rescue Squad, Certified Water Safety Instructor.

STEVEN TINE

705 E. Smokey Court
Boynton Beach, FL 33426

(407) 555-9876

TECHNICIAN / INSTALLER / TROUBLESHOOTER

Specializing in ... Telephone, Cable TV, and Stereo System Installation & Repair
- Utilizing Strong Electrical Background -

SUMMARY: An experienced, hands-on technical professional with a *verifiable* record of achievement in low voltage electrical installation/service of customized systems including telephone, stereo, & cable TV for upscale residences.

WORK HISTORY:

Mellon Vacuum and Sound Systems, Inc., Lantana, Florida **1984 - 1996**
SERVICE TECHNICIAN - Professional installation/service of custom electronic systems for private upscale residences (5K-48K sq. ft. homes - $250K - $5 million). Skills include:

Good look, especially for technical/trades discipline
Interesting closing with "Last But Not Least" section.

- **Extensive Knowledge of Audio and Related Equipment**
- **Solid Equipment Programming Experience; Layout & Design Experience**
- **Expert in Troubleshooting/Installing Via Complex Instruction Manuals**
- **Strong Problem-Solving/Troubleshooting Abilities**
- **A Professional Demeanor/Polished Customer Service Skills**

Equipment Knowledge includes:

* Custom Audio Systems - AM/FM tuners, CD, cassettes, laser disc, infrared, speaker selector, & low-level switching systems. (Boston, Acoustic, Bose, Pioneer, Sony, Niles, Adcom, Yamaha).
* Intercoms (Nutone, Music and Sound Aiphone)
* Central Vacuums (Beam, M & S, Electrolux, Fastco, Airvac)

Perform service on all **phone systems** and **cable TV, low-voltage gate release systems, security camera systems** and **1&2 electronic key systems** (Panasonic, Southwestern Bell, Merlin and Viking electronic equipment). Program all equipment.

Patrick Power, Inc., Fort Lauderdale, Florida **1982 - 1984**
COMMERCIAL ELECTRICIAN - Installed all low- and high-voltage lighting in the Cosmetic Departments for both Bloomingdale's and Burdines (Boca Raton).

Gulfstream Harbor Apartments, Boynton Beach, Florida **1980 - 1982**
MAINTENANCE MECHANIC - Repaired/maintained all central A/C and heating units. Responsible for all electrical, plumbing, and appliance repairs.

EDUCATION: Graduate: H.L. Morse Technical School, Hollywood, FL, 1977

LAST BUT NOT LEAST: Can read blueprints, schematics, and diagrams, in addition to service repairs for appliances, A/C, heating, electrical, and plumbing. Built and reside in my home with my wife and 2 children. I am highly dependable, loyal, and committed to pursuing and achieving company objectives.

BARBARA WILLIAMS

10 Wishbone Lane • Las Vegas, NV 78142• (702) 555-4799

Proper listing of Objective because it is clearly defined
Good inclusion of Areas of Strength section
Good use of Other section

PROFESSIONAL TELEMARKETER
... Home-based

OBJECTIVE: A part- or full-time, home-based position with a highly reputable telemarketing organization sponsoring and representing solid products and services.

AREAS OF STRENGTH:
- Powerful telephone skills, able to establish immediate trust and confidence
- Dale Carnegie trained—highly professional and effective closer
- Persistent, patient, and sensitive to customer's needs and apprehensions
- Effectively overcome objections to sales in a calming and convincing manner

HIGHLIGHTS OF EXPERIENCE:
- Awarded *Diamond Award* (Time-Life Publications) for consistently exceeding quota
- Maintained strong 64% closing ratio (Haverhill) and 59% closing ratio (Glasser)
- A Top Producer, consistently in the top 10% nationally
- Had lowest return rate in SW region - 4.8% (Time-Life)

EXPERIENCE:

The Gallup Companies, New York, NY — 1994 - 1996
Home-Based Telephone Surveys - (20 hours/week)

Time-Life Publications, New York, NY — 1990 - 1994
Home-Based Telephone Sales - (20 hours/week)

Haverhill Promotional Products, Portland, ME — 1987 - 1990
Home-Based Telephone Sales - (25 hours/week)

Daniel Glasser Fashions, Baltimore, MD — 1987 - 1990
Home-Based Telephone Sales - (25 hours/week)

EDUCATION: Dannon-Phillips Junior College, Cleveland, OH
Associates Degree: Secretarial Administration

OTHER ...

Dale Carnegie	*Effective Telephone Communications*	1995
	How to Win Friends and Influence People	1994
	Public Speaking and Overcoming the Fear	1993
Anthony Robbins	*Turning Fear Into Power Seminar*	1993
Dr. Stephen Covey	*Seven Habits of Highly Effective People Seminar*	1995

INTERESTS: Tennis, golf, hiking, celebrity autograph collecting, theater, personal development

- References Furnished Upon Request -

LEN TORKANIAN

Written with scanning capability in mind
Key use of the Selected Accomplishments section

25 Lehigh Drive
Wamstead, Illinois 62327
(618) 555-4446
E-mail: torkyl@opscom.safb.af.mil

KEY WORDS

Senior Transportation Manager. 20 years' experience. Global and domestic operations. Multimodal air, motor, rail, and water transportation activities. Strategic human and material resource planning. Budgets in excess of $2.5 million. Cost reductions. ITV management. Quality controls. Customer service. Training. Security. Communications. Productivity. Line-haul transportation. Asset utilization. Capacity planning. Fuel and dry cargo capability. Wheel cargo vehicles. Maintenance. Tractor trailers. Masters Degree in Logistics Management.

PROFESSIONAL EXPERIENCE

United States Army, 1976-Present
Current rank: Lieutenant Colonel, U.S. Transportation Command
JOINT MOBILITY OPERATIONS MANAGER

Selected Accomplishments:

- Served as Executive and Operations Officer of the only Army line-haul transportation battalion in Korea consisting of headquarters, two medium truck companies, four trailer transfer points, and a trailer maintenance center. The 450 vehicles and trailers accumulated more than three million miles annually hauling government cargo along a 350-mile line of communication.
- Directed the movement of more than 1,000 commercial containers during a Korean trucker's strike while simultaneously downsizing the organization.
- Managed all air and surface transportation assets for an 11-country, 3,500-member peacekeeping force in the Middle East. Planned and coordinated the effective utilization of all aircraft and wheel cargo vehicles.
- Supervised an administrative-use vehicle fleet, motor pool operations, and maintenance shops consisting of more than 200 personnel and 550 vehicles.
- Managed a 196-man transportation unit responsible for the maintenance and operation of 111 vehicles including tractor-trailer combinations with both bulk fuel and dry cargo capability and 5-ton cargo trucks.
- Developed and improved internal procedures for the movement of cargo and passengers across international boundaries.
- Referred to by superiors as "a recognized master at developing and conducting challenging, realistic and productive training" for a transportation assistance unit. Evaluated the logistics of simulated military operations; provided corrective input via after-action reports.

EDUCATION AND SPECIALIZED TRAINING

- M.S. Degree, Logistics Management, Florida Institute of Technology, Melbourne, FL
- B.A. Degree, History, Midwestern State University, Wichita Falls, TX
- Logistics Executive Development Course

AFFILIATIONS

National Defense Transportation Organization

REFERENCES AVAILABLE UPON REQUEST

TRAVEL INDUSTRY

SARAH CLAUSEY

238 Henderson Mill Road
Atlanta, Georgia 30301
(770) 555-6402

Good use of graphic image
Clean look for a one-page resume

Million Dollar Plus Corporate Agent ...
with strong customer service skills, ability to thrive under pressure, detail oriented, low agent error, and experience in both domestic and international ticketing. Proficient with Prism, System 1, and Windows.

Experience

BUSINESS TRAVEL, Norcross, Georgia **1991 - Present**
Corporate Agent
Lead agent with $3 million accounts. Converse with customers to determine destination, mode of transportation, travel dates, financial considerations, and accommodations required. Determine which specific facilities would best service clients' style, budget, and needs. Comprehensive knowledge of rules and restrictions of fares and various types of upgrades. Experience as on-site agent and in domestic/international reservations. Extensive use of System I, Prism, and Windows environments.

BONADVENTURE TRAVEL, Atlanta, Georgia **1989 - 1991**
Corporate Agent
Planned itineraries and arranged accommodations as well as other travel services for corporate and leisure clients. Expertise in arranging large packages and meetings. Searched for lowest air price and coordinated hotel, car, seating, and specialty arrangements. Utilized System 1 to obtain and reserve travel and flight information. Ability to successfully resolve problems to customers' satisfaction.

TRAVEL AGENTS INTERNATIONAL, Atlanta, Georgia **1986 - 1989**
Corporate & Leisure Agent
Coordinated transportation arrangements for corporate and leisure travel. Planned, arranged, and sold itinerary tour packages utilizing knowledge of available travel services. Advised on available activities or special events occurring at corresponding locations. Computed and collected payments for travel and accommodations. Utilized System I to purchase tickets.

COUNTY SEAT, Atlanta, Georgia **1973 - 1986**
Store Manager
Managed three retail apparel stores simultaneously. Administered all phases of personnel hiring, training, and scheduling. Oversaw inventory control, markdowns, ordering, and merchandising of stores. Reconciled cash with sales receipts and prepared daily operation records. Increased sales and reduced shrinkage through providing quality product and service.

Education

OMNI SCHOOL OF TRAVEL, Atlanta, Georgia **1986**
Travel Industry, System 1

DEKALB COMMUNITY COLLEGE, Atlanta, Georgia **1972**
Fashion Merchandising

Associations

- Austrian Society Club of Atlanta
- Atlanta Ski Club

Example of a resume for a business
Excellent use of graphics

D'Scribe

RÉSUMÉS

112 Preston Road, Dallas, TX 75000
Metro 214-555-4000

Darby Deihl

OBJECTIVE:
EMPOWER
THE
JOB SEEKER

Professional Credentials:

CERTIFIED PROFESSIONAL
RÉSUMÉ WRITER

Certified Word Processor

Professional Associations:

A member of

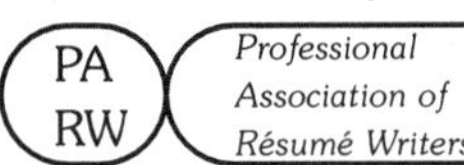

Highlights Of Qualifications

◇ 15 years administrative support in single staff and supervisory positions.

◇ Experienced professional employment counselor.

◇ Intuitive interviewer; employs genuine enthusiasm to discover client's full marketing potential.

◇ Committed to helping clients get the results they want.

Technical Skills

◇ Type 90 wpm.

◇ Packard Bell 486DX2.

◇ Microsoft Word, Microsoft Publisher.

Abilities

◇ Style traditional and nontraditional formats including scannable and theatrical résumés.

◇ Enhance documents with graphics; craft presentations including brochure layouts.

Professional Experience

Résumés

◇ Design successful résumés—for individuals with diverse career situations—that capture employer interest, generate interviews, increase job offers.

◇ Create impressive cover letters and thank-you letters that promote client throughout hiring process.

Additional Writing & Editing

◇ Originated sales reports, performance reports, and correspondence in the capacity of regional office manager, division office secretary, and executive secretary.

◇ Authored detailed training manual for executive secretaries that became the company standard.

◇ Edited, typeset, and proofed manuscripts and book proposals.

Graphic Design & Layout

◇ Develop information and promotional materials for D'Scribe Résumés that prompt compliments and appreciative comments from printers and clients.

◇ Designed fliers, brochures, door signs, and other promotional materials for Made By Hand craft store chain; endorsed by company vice president.

◇ Created property listing fliers for Spradley Real Estate; endorsed by owner.

Good explanation of experience in summary
Proper lead of Education for this profession
Good description of disciplines

WRITER

VICTORIA L. ROTHCHILDS

7194 N. Washoe • Berkeley, CA • 415/555-8018

CAREER FOCUS: Writer/Editorial responsibilities with a magazine, PR firm, book publisher or newspaper.

EXPERIENCE SUMMARY

- Experienced in writing feature articles, short stories, biographies, essays, editorial pieces, press releases, research reports, and creative print/radio ad copy.
- Well versed in copyediting, transcription/editing of interviews, and proofreading, most recently as assistant editor for a business periodical.
- Strong technical command of the English language … familiar with virtually all writing styles ... serious commitment to excellence in the printed and published word.
- Competent researcher, interviewer, and reporter.

EDUCATION

M.A., Journalism — News Editorial Option, University of California, Berkeley 1992
B.A., English, University of California, Los Angeles 1989

PROFESSIONAL EXPERIENCE

Assistant Editor — *Business & Industry News,* San Francisco, CA 6/93-Present
Edit, rewrite, and proofread all articles for southern California's leading business periodical, a biweekly publication targeting executives and entrepreneurs. Work with guest writers (many of whom have no formal training in writing) to organize and refine articles. Assist with copywriting and advertising layout.

Writer, Newsroom — *KTED Radio,* San Ramon, CA 9/92-6/93
Wrote newscasts as intern with #1 rated station and 5th most listened to station in the U.S. Developed contacts with city officials, congressmen, and business leaders. Monitored news wire for national ground-breaking stories and developed local angles. Accompanied reporters on assignments. Fielded calls from listeners on news line. Operated equipment (reel-to-reel, tape, switchboard).

Editorial Staff — *Music Mania Magazine,* Los Angeles, CA 4/92-8/92
Completed editorial internship with international music publication. Exposure included various aspects associated with publication. Developed contacts with record companies and PR firms. Worked with magazine during its transition from black and white to full color.

Reporter — *The Collegian,* Long Beach, CA 2/92-5/92
Authored several front page articles and covered a variety of writing assignments. Additionally assisted with editorial functions including final editing.

Public Relations Assistant — *KQED Channel 5,* Long Beach, CA 1/89-2/92
Assisted in the writing and production of public relations materials for southern California public television station.

COMPUTER SKILLS

WordPerfect • Microsoft Word • Pagemaker • Ventura Publisher • IBM and Macintosh Systems

Writing Samples & References Available

COMMERCIAL DESIGN/SPACE PLANNING

DIANA TABACOPOULOS

*12466 Sawmill Court * Wellington, FL 33419 * (407) 555-5192*

A nationally recognized *DESIGN MANAGEMENT CONSULTANT* specializing in Interior Design Planning, Marketing and Project Management. A successful/verifiable record of achievement directing projects ranging from $2,000 to over $6 million. Experienced working with a diversification of client industries including ...

- **Healthcare**
- **Financial**
- **Publishing**
- **Education**
- **Government**
- **Aviation**

OVERVIEW:

A highly motivated and creative *Design Management Consultant* with 26 years of successful experience. A results-oriented, solution-focused professional with strengths in the follow areas:

Easy-to-read formatting
Comprehensive listing of personal strengths
Notice one date for all jobs

Identifying/meeting client needs	Functionally creative
Compliance with ADA/regulatory codes	Move logistics
Personnel management	Project organization
Technical skills/aptitude	Budgeting skills
Directing small to large projects	Strategic planning

HIGHLIGHTS OF EXPERIENCE:

Hired to manage the start-up of The Goldberg Design Group, Inc., from $0 in gross sales to more than $1.8 million in less than five years.

A nationally acclaimed Design Consultant for the *publishing industry.* Have directed major projects for the *Palm Beach Post,* the *Stewart News* (Florida), and the *County Telegram Tribune* (San Luis Obispo, CA).

Coordinated the Nise East Engineering Center Project (Charleston, SC), a 256,000 sq. ft. construction project for a military base command center (1,200 work stations).

Developed a design department for Corporate Design Interiors, which became a profit center for an office furniture dealership. Secured Barnett Banks as a key, ongoing client.

Developed a prototype business center for high traffic areas for Abramson Vereen Associates, Inc., providing design schematics, budgets, interior selections, and working documents that interfaced with architect's structurals. Supervised design teams for major projects for financial institutions.

SPECIFIC AREAS OF EXPERTISE **• Design concept • Space planning • Installation supervision • Growth projections • Refining/detailing space plan • Ordering/scheduling furniture, fixtures, equipment • Telecommunications & MIS installations, conversions/moves**

PROFESSIONAL EXPERIENCE: (1977 - Present)

Corporate Design Interiors, Riviera Beach, FL
DESIGN DIRECTOR

Abramson Vereen Associates, Inc., Boca Raton, FL
SENIOR PROJECT DESIGNER

The Office Mart, Santa Barbara, CA
DESIGN DIRECTOR

CSA, Inc., (a div. of Carlson Companies), Minneapolis, MN
SENIOR PROJECT DESIGNER

The Goldberg Design Group, Inc., West Palm Beach, FL
PRINCIPLE / DESIGN MANAGEMENT CONSULTANT

The Pavlow Company, Miami, FL
DESIGN COORDINATOR

James Wineglow & Partners, Architects, Millburn, NJ
INTERIOR DESIGN MANAGER

Max Blau & Sons Company, Inc., Newark, NJ
DESIGN COORDINATOR

EDUCATION & ACTIVITIES:

New York School of Interior Design, New York, NY
B.A. Interior Design, 1977

Member: BOMA Florida, 1979
Lecturer: University of Miami - *Practice Management*
Lecturer: Steelcase Seminars - *Facilities Planning*
Participant: Production/Publication of Steelcase Design Management Manual
Member: National Association of Women Business Owners
License: Licensed Designer, State of Florida, Registration No. ID 0000652
Certified: Women's Business Enterprise

- References & Supporting Documentation Furnished Upon Request -

11

Tips to Get You Hired

25 RESUME-WRITING TIPS

1. Absolutely no spelling, grammar, punctuation, or typographical errors.
2. Know your audience before you begin to prepare the document. Then write the resume for your defined audience.
3. The resume must match your skills and abilities to a potential employer's needs.
4. A resume must address your *market value* and, in 20 seconds or less, answer the question, "Why should I hire you?"
5. Key in on accomplishments, credentials, or qualifications.
6. *Sell features and benefits.* What skills do you possess and how will they contribute to the organization's goals and objectives?
7. Avoid fluff. Ambiguities and generalities represent fluff; they render a resume inept.
8. Be different, courageous, and exciting. Boring resumes lead to boring jobs.
9. Package the resume in an exciting way.
10. Be sure the resume is well organized.
11. The resume must be professionally presented, consistent with the industry you are pursuing.
12. Your resume can have a distinct personality to it. Choose your language carefully; it can make a world of difference.
13. A chronological resume format emphasizes employment in reverse chronological order. Begin with your most recent job and work back, keying in on responsibilities and specific achievements. Use this format when you have a strong employment history.
14. A functional format hones in on specific accomplishments and highlights of qualifications at the beginning of the resume, but does not correlate these attributes to any specific employer. Use this format when you are changing careers, have employment gaps, or have challenges to employing the chronological format.
15. A combination format is part functional and part chronological and is a powerful presentation format. At the beginning of the resume you'll address your value, credentials, and qualifications (functional aspect), followed by supporting documentation in your employment section (chronological component).
16. A curriculum vitae is a resume format used mostly by professions and vocations in which a mere listing of credentials describes the value of a candidate. Examples include actors, singers or musicians, physicians, and possibly attorneys or CPAs.
17. The five major sections of a resume are: 1) Heading, 2) Introduction, 3) Employment, 4) Education, and 5) Miscellaneous sections.
18. Miscellaneous sections can include Military, Publications, Speaking Engagements, Memberships in Associations, Awards and Recognition, Computer Skills, Patents, Languages, Licenses and Certification, or Interests.
19. Write the resume in the third person and avoid using the pronoun "I."
20. Salary history or compensation requirements should not appear in the resume. The cover letter is made for this purpose if it needs to be addressed at all.
21. Always include a cover letter with your resume.
22. If you are a graduating student or have been out of the workforce for a while, you must make a special effort at displaying high emotion, potential, motivation, and energy. Stress qualitative factors and leadership roles in the community, on campus, or elsewhere. By employing a degree of creativity and innovation in your career design campaign, you are communicating to a hiring authority that you can be resourceful, innovative, and a contributing team member.
23. Employment gaps, job-hopping, and educational deficiencies can be effectively handled by using the combination format (or functional format).
24. The resume should be a positive document. It must tell the truth, but not necessarily the whole truth. Don't lie, but you need not tell all, either. Keep negative thoughts and concepts out of your resume.
25. The shorter the better—one to two pages in most cases.

25 TIPS FOR WRITING COVER LETTERS

1. Use customized stationery with your name, address, and phone number on top. Match your stationery to that of your resume—it shows class and professionalism.
2. Customize the cover letter. Address it to a specific individual. Be sure you have the proper spelling of the person's name, his or her title, and the company name.
3. If you don't wish to customize each letter and prefer to use a form letter, use the salutation "Dear Hiring Manager." (Do not use "Dear Sir." The hiring manager may be a woman.)
4. The cover letter is more informal than the resume and must begin to build rapport. Be enthusiastic, energetic, and motivating.
5. The cover letter must introduce you and your value to a potential employer.
6. Be sure to date the cover letter.
7. An effective cover letter should be easy to read, have larger typeface than the resume (12 point type is a good size), and be kept short—4 to 5 short paragraphs will usually do the job.
8. Keep the cover letter to one page. If you are compelled to use two pages, be sure your name appears on the second page.
9. The first paragraph should ignite interest in your candidacy and spark enthusiasm from the reader. Why is the reader reading this letter? What can you do for him/her?
10. The second paragraph must promote your value. What are your skills, abilities, qualifications, and credentials that would meet the reader's needs and job requirements?
11. The third paragraph notes specific accomplishments, achievements, and educational experience that would expressly support the second paragraph. Quantify these accomplishments if possible.
12. The fourth paragraph must generate future action. Ask for an interview or tell the reader that you will be calling in a week or so to follow up.
13. The fifth paragraph should be a short one, closing the letter and showing appreciation.
14. Demonstrate specific problem-solving skills in the letter, supported by specific examples.
15. Unless asked to do so, don't discuss salary in a cover letter.
16. If salary history or requirements are asked for, provide a modest window (low to mid thirties, for example) and mention that it is negotiable (if it is).
17. Be sure the letter has a professional appearance.
18. Be sure there are no spelling, typographical, or grammatical errors.
19. Be sure to keep the letter short and to the point. Don't ramble on and on.
20. Do not lie or exaggerate. Everything you say in a cover letter and resume must be supported in the eventual interview.
21. Be careful not to use the pronoun "I" excessively. Tie together what the company is doing and what their needs might be. To come full circle, explain how you fit into their strategy and can close potential gaps in meeting their objectives.
22. Avoid negative and controversial subject matter. The purpose of a cover letter and resume is to put your best foot forward. This material (job hopping, prior termination, etc.) can be tactfully addressed in the interview.
23. If you are faxing the cover letter and resume, you need not send a fax transmittal form so long as your fax number is included in the heading along with your telephone number.
24. To close the letter, use Sincerely, Sincerely yours, Respectfully, or Very truly yours.
25. Be sure to sign the letter.

25 INTERVIEWING TIPS

1. Relax. The employment interview is just a meeting. And although you should not treat this meeting lightly, don't forget that the organization interviewing you is in need of your services as much as, or perhaps more than, you are of theirs.
2. The key to successful interviewing is rapport building. Most people spend their time preparing for interviews by memorizing canned responses to anticipated questions. Successful interviewers spend most of their time practicing the art of rapport building through the use of powerfully effective communicating techniques.
3. Prepare a manila folder that you will bring to the interview. Include in the folder:
   * company information (annual reports, sales material, etc.)
   * extra resumes (6–12) and your letters of reference
   * 15 questions you've prepared based on your research and analysis of the company
   * a blank legal pad, pen, and anything else you consider helpful (e.g., college transcripts)
4. Dress appropriately. Determine the dress code and meet it. If their dress is business casual, you still need to be dressed in business professional. Practice proper grooming and hygiene.
5. Shoes, of course, must be polished.
6. Wear limited jewelry.
7. Call the day before and confirm the appointment—it will set you apart.
8. Be certain that you know exactly where you're going. Arrive in plenty of time. You should be at the receptionist's desk 10–12 minutes before the scheduled interview.
9. Prior to meeting the receptionist, check your appearance. Check your hair, clothing, and general image. Test your smile.
10. Secretaries, administrative assistants, and receptionists often have a say in the hiring process. Make a strong first impression with them.
11. Look around the office and search for artifacts that disclose the personality and culture of the company—and possibly the interviewer. This information will be helpful in initially breaking the ice, when you first begin discussions.
12. Be aware of your body language. Sit erect, with confidence. When standing and walking, move with confidence!
13. Your handshake should be firm, made with a wide-open hand, fingers stretched wide apart. Women should feel comfortable offering their hand and a firm and friendly handshake. A power handshake and great smile will get you off to a great start.
14. Eye contact is one of the most powerful forms of communicating. It demonstrates confidence, trust, and power.
15. During the interview, lean forward toward the interviewer. Show enthusiasm and sincere interest.
16. Take notes during the interview. You may want to refer to them later in the interview. If you are uncomfortable with this, ask permission first.
17. Be prepared for all questions, especially uncomfortable ones. Before the interview, script out a one-page response for each question that poses a problem for you, and practice repeating it until you're comfortable with it.
18. Communicate your skills, qualifications, and credentials to the hiring manager. Describe your market value and the benefits you offer. *Demonstrate how you will contribute to the bottom line.* Show how you can 1) improve sales, 2) reduce costs, 3) improve productivity, or 4) solve organizational problems.
19. Key in on *specific accomplishments*. Accomplishments determine hireability. They separate the winners from the runners-up.

20. Listening skills are priceless! Job offers are made to those who listen well, find hidden meanings, and answer questions in a brief but effective manner.
21. Let the interviewer bring up salary first. The purpose of an interview is to determine whether there is a match. Once that is determined, salary should then be negotiated.
22. There is no substitute for planning and preparation, practice and rehearsing—*absolutely none.*
23. Practice interviewing techniques using video technology. A minimum of five hours of video practice, preferably more, guarantees a stellar performance.
24. Close the sale. If you find you want the position, ask for it. Ask directly, "Is there anything that would prevent you from offering me this position now?" or "Do you have any reservations or concerns?" (if you sense that). At the very least, this should flush out any objections and give you the opportunity to turn them into positives.
25. Always send a thank-you note within 24 hours of every employment meeting.

25 SALARY NEGOTIATING TIPS

1. From the moment you make initial contact with any company or organization you wish to work with, you are in negotiation. You may not be discussing money openly, but you are making a permanent imprint on the mind of the hiring authorities.
2. Delay all discussions of salary until there is an offer on the table.
3. You are in the strongest negotiating position as soon as the offer is made.
4. Know your value. You must know how you can contribute to the organization. Establish this in the mind of the hiring manager.
5. Get employers enthusiastic about your candidacy, and they will become more generous.
6. There is no substitute for preparation. If you are well prepared, you'll be confident, self-assured, and poised for success.
7. Prior to going into employment negotiations, you must know the average salary paid for similar positions with other organizations in your geographical area.
8. Prior to going into employment negotiations you must know, as best you can, the salary range the company you're interviewing with will pay, or what former employees were earning.
9. Prior to going into employment negotiations you must know your personal needs and requirements, and how they relate to numbers 7 and 8 above.
10. Remember, fringes and perks, such as vacation time, flex time, health benefits, pension plans, and so on have value. Consider the "total" salary package.
11. Salary negotiations must be win-win negotiations. If they're not, everybody loses in the end.
12. Be flexible; don't get hung up on trivial issues, and always seek compromise when possible.
13. Listen carefully and pay close attention. Your goals will most likely be different from the goals of the employer. For instance, the firm's main focus might be "base salary." Yours might be "total earning potential." So a win-win solution might be to negotiate a lower base salary but a higher commission or bonus structure.
14. Anticipate objections and prepare effective answers to these objections.
15. Try to understand the employer's point of view. Then plan a strategy to meet both the employer's concerns and your needs.
16. Don't be afraid to negotiate out of fear of losing the offer. Most employers *expect* you to negotiate as long as you negotiate in a fair and reasonable manner.
17. Always negotiate in a way that reflects your personality, character, and work ethic. Remain within your comfort zone.
18. Never lose control. Remain enthusiastic and upbeat even if the negotiations get a little hot. This might be your first test under fire.
19. Play hardball only if you're willing to walk away from, or lose, the deal.
20. What you lose in the negotiations will most likely never be recouped. Don't be careless in preparing for or conducting the negotiation.
21. Be sure to get the offer and final agreement in writing.
22. You should feel comfortable asking the employer for 24 to 48 hours to think about the deal if you need time to think it over.
23. Never link salary to personal needs or problems. Compensation should always be linked to your value.
24. Understand your leverage. Know if you are in a position of strength or weakness and negotiate intelligently based on your personal situation.
25. End salary negotiations on a friendly and cheerful note.

25 NETWORKING TIPS

1. Two-thirds of all jobs are secured via the networking process. Networking is a systematic approach to cultivating formal and informal contacts for the purpose of gaining information, enhancing visibility in the market, and obtaining referrals.
2. Effective networking requires self-confidence, poise, and personal conviction.
3. You must first know the companies and organizations you wish to work for. That will determine the type of network you will develop and nurture.
4. Focus on meeting the "right people." This takes planning and preparation.
5. Target close friends, family members, neighbors, social acquaintances, social and religious group members, business contacts, teachers, and community leaders.
6. Include employment professionals as an important part of your network. This includes headhunters and personnel agency executives. They have a wealth of knowledge about job and market conditions.
7. Remember, networking is a numbers game. Once you have a network of people in place, prioritize the listing so you have separated top priority contacts from lower priority ones.
8. Sometimes you may have to pay for advice and information. Paying consultants or professionals or investing in Internet services is part of the job search process today, as long as it's legal and ethical.
9. Know what you want from your contacts. If you don't know what you want, neither will your network of people. Specific questions will get specific answers.
10. Ask for advice, not for a job. You cannot contact someone asking if they know of any job openings. The answer will invariably be no, especially at higher levels. You need to ask for things like industry advice, advice on geographic areas, etc. The job insights will follow but will be almost incidental. This positioning will build value for you and make the contact person more comfortable about helping you.
11. Watch your attitude and demeanor at all times. Everyone you come in contact with is a potential member of your network. Demonstrate enthusiasm and professionalism at all times.
12. Keep a file on each member of your network and maintain good records at all times. A well-organized network filing system or database will yield superior results.
13. Get comfortable on the telephone. Good telephone communication skills are critical.
14. Travel the "information highway." Networking is more effective if you have E-mail, fax, and computer capabilities.
15. Be well prepared for your conversation, whether in person or over the phone. You should have a script in your mind of how to answer questions, what to ask, and what you're trying to accomplish.
16. Do not fear rejection. If a contact cannot help you, move on to the next contact. Do not take rejection personally—it's just part of the process.
17. Flatter the people in your network. It's been said that the only two types of people who can be flattered are men and women. Use tact, courtesy, and flattery.
18. If a person in your network cannot personally help, advise, or direct you, ask for referrals.
19. Keep in touch with the major contacts in your network on a monthly basis. Remember, out of sight, out of mind.
20. Don't abuse the process. Networking is a two-way street. Be honest and brief and offer your contacts something in return for their time, advice, and information. This can be as simple as a lunch or offering your professional services in return for their cooperation.
21. Show an interest in your contacts. Cavette Robert, one of the founders of the National Speakers Association, said, "People don't care how much you know, until they know how much you care." Show how much you care. It will get you anywhere.

22. Send thank-you notes following each networking contact.
23. Seek out key networking contacts in professional and trade associations.
24. Carry calling cards with you at all times to hand out to anyone and everyone you come in contact with. Include your name, address, phone number, areas of expertise, and/or specific skill areas.
25. Socialize and get out more than ever before. Networking requires dedication and massive amounts of energy. Consistently work on expanding your network.

25 TIPS FOR DEVELOPING EFFECTIVE REFERENCES

1. Turn your references into testimonials that promote you to the marketplace.
2. The majority of employers check references. Do no treat this portion of the job search lightly.
3. Use professional references only. Professional references provide all the information an employer needs to make a hiring decision.
4. Academic references can be used if you are a recent graduate.
5. Think of five or six strong references. A good mix would be:

   —2 superiors —1 subordinate

   —1 peer —2 major clients/vendors

   Superiors attest to your value—your ability contribute to the bottom line. Peers endorse your ability to work as a team member/leader. Subordinates will vouch for your training and coaching skills, and customers and vendors will endorse your high-quality customer service and professional integrity.
6. If you have difficulty meeting the mix above (in number 5), carefully select the five or six people who can best endorse your credentials and value.
7. *All references should be in writing* in the form of reference letters. Before you formally begin your job search, you should have five or six current reference letters.
8. When you are terminating your employment (for whatever reason), be sure that a condition of termination is that the company or organization provides you with a favorable reference letter in writing.
9. If you have left a job on less than stellar terms, make every effort to mend the fences. Solid references are critical to getting the best positions. Most fallouts can be repaired if there is a genuine effort, *on your part,* to patch things up.
10. Once you have determined who you want your references to be, contact them. Ask them to support your job search by providing a favorable reference.
11. Upon an affirmative response, *you should write the reference letter.* There are roughly 750,000 words in the English language. The words you would want in the reference letter will, in all likelihood, not be the same provided by your reference.
12. When writing the reference letter, be sure to support the critical information contained on your resume. In other words, link the reference letter to the resume.
13. If your references would rather write the letters themselves, that's OK, but coach them. Review the main subjects you'd like them to mention in the letter. Guide them so they will address the information you want emphasized.
14. Regardless of who writes the reference letter, *the finished letter must appear on company letterhead.*
15. If a company or organization, as company policy, won't provide references except to verify dates of employment, write a reference letter anyway—one that would be safe for the company to sign. Then go to the company and tell them how vital this is to your future. Use charisma and charm to get that elusive reference letter.
16. If that fails, try to get your reference to provide a letter, personally.
17. The reference letter should not be long. Do not exceed one page.
18. Dates on the reference letters should be current, if possible. In most cases, the more current the reference letter, the more credible.
19. Information on the reference letters should be specific. The letters should address specific achievements and contributions you made.
20. If you write the reference letters, be sure to use a different style of writing for each one.

21. Write a cover sheet with the names, titles, company names, addresses, and phone numbers of all your references (like a traditional reference sheet). Then, place your reference letters behind the cover sheet, in a bound folder. This is your reference portfolio.
22. Send thank-you notes back to your references along with a copy of your resume and the reference letter. Ask that they keep it handy in the event a phone reference is made.
23. Keep in touch with all your references and be sure to contact them after each interview.
24. Consider distributing your reference portfolio with your resume. You'll have five or six additional salespeople making the call along with you.
25. Be sure you have six sets of reference portfolios with you at every interview.

25 TIPS FOR WORKING WITH EXECUTIVE RECRUITERS

1. Find a comprehensive listing of executive recruiters, those in your geographic region and those national firms that specialize in your industry. The best source of this information is *The Guide to Executive Recruiters* by Michael Betrus (McGraw-Hill).
2. Retained search firms are paid in advance or on an ongoing basis for a search, usually for higher level positions or unique, hard-to-fill positions. Retained searches would be for positions such as a pulp and paper expert for Scott Paper or a senior level corporate officer.
3. Contingency firms are paid when the client company hires the candidate. Typical contingency searches are for positions such as a sales representative or a business manager.
4. Recruiters are paid by the client company, not by you. So don't misinterpret their motivation or loyalty.
5. Executive search firms never charge prospective candidates.
6. Prior to speaking to a recruiter, have a description of your background well thought out and rehearsed.
7. Make sure that background description addresses your education, number of years of experience in your industry, your primary professional discipline, and several key accomplishments.
8. When the recruiter asks you what you want to do, do not appear indecisive or say anything like "I don't really know."
9. Contact every recruiter in your preferred geographic region, whether they specialize in your industry/discipline or not. They will know what is going on in your region.
10. Contact every recruiter in the country that specializes in your specific industry/discipline. If your area of expertise is finance, accounting, or sales, you may limit it to your region of the country first.
11. Get the recruiter to like you. If they like you, they will help you. Also, in order to stay in contact with recruiters who currently have nothing that suits you, try to call with information or leads for *them* as a result of your own research. You'll be giving them something, and they'll be more apt to take your calls and help you network.
12. If the recruiter cannot help you immediately, probe further for a networking contact. This is an extremely valuable approach to use with executive recruiters.
13. Have a good resume prepared to send them. Unless you have a specific reason not to, always send them a resume and cover letter rather than a broadcast letter. They're going to need it anyway, so don't slow down the process.
14. Extend the recruiters the same respect you would a hiring manager with whom you are interviewing.
15. If you're targeting a large company that only works with recruiters, find out the name of the recruiting firm from the company. In many cases they will refer you.
16. Do not feel hesitant to ask the recruiters for advice. This is their business and they deal with employment every day. If you develop a good rapport, invite them to lunch, your treat.
17. You are more attractive employed than unemployed because you appear to be a lower risk. However, in today's business climate recruiters understand that many good people are looking for work. A strong reference from your previous employer will help.
18. Many recruiters have a tougher time finding qualified candidates than finding job orders from companies. Use this to your advantage and try to present yourself as someone of value to the recruiter.
19. Call the recruiter first as opposed to sending an unsolicited letter. This way you can use the letter to reflect a prior phone conversation. Though it builds more work for them, recruiters we interviewed said it is to the candidates' advantage to call first.
20. Try to bring other business or company information to the recruiter. That will help your relationship.

21. Keep in mind that when negotiating your salary through a recruiter, he's playing both sides to come to terms. It's usually an easier process on a personal level to negotiate through a recruiter because of the buffer. Just don't forget that the recruiter is trying to get you hired, not necessarily get you the highest salary.
22. Though there are many large national firms, don't overlook smaller operations. A small firm may be dedicated to one client company that could be your next home.
23. Contact every recruiter described as a generalist. A generalist will take on a variety of searches, one of which may fit your background.
24. Don't be shy about asking recruiters what you should expect while working with them. If they're a quality firm, they'll be happy to walk you through the process.
25. Stay away from any firm that tries to prevent you from contacting other search firms. No legitimate recruiter will try to work with you on an exclusive basis.

25 "WHAT DO I DO NOW THAT I HAVE MY RESUME?" TIPS

1. Develop a team of people who will be your board of directors, advisors, and mentors. The quality of the people you surround yourself with will determine the quality of your results.
2. Plan a marketing strategy. Determine how many hours a week you will work, how you'll divide your time, and how you'll measure your progress. Job search is a business in itself—and a marketing strategy is your business plan.
3. Identify 25 (50 would be better) companies or organizations that you would like to work for.
4. Contact the companies, or do some research, to identify hiring authorities.
5. Define your network (see Networking Tips). Make a list of everyone you know including relatives, friends, acquaintances, family doctors, attorneys, and CPAs, the cleaning person, and the mail carrier. Virtually everyone is a possible networking contact.
6. Prioritize your list of contacts into three categories: 1) Strong, approachable contacts, 2) good contacts or those who must be approached more formally, and 3) those who you'd like to contact but can't without an introduction by another party.
7. Set up a filing system or database to organize and manage your contacts.
8. Develop a script or letter for the purpose of contacting the key people in your network, asking for advice, information, and assistance. Then start contacting them.
9. Attempt to find a person, or persons, in your network who can make an introduction into one of the 25 or 50 companies you've noted in #3.
10. Spend 65 to 70 percent of your time, energy, and resources networking because 65 to 70 percent of all jobs are secured by this method.
11. Consider contacting executive recruiters or employment agencies to assist in your job search.
12. If you are a recent college graduate, seek out assistance from the campus career center.
13. Scout the classified advertisements every Sunday. Respond to ads that interest you, and look at other ads as well. A company may be advertising for a position that does not fit your background, but say in the ad they are "expanding in the area," etc. You have just identified a growing company.
14. Seek out advertisements and job opportunities in specific trade journals and magazines.
15. Attend as many social and professional functions as you can. The more people you meet, the better your chances of securing a position quickly.
16. Send out resumes with customized cover letters to targeted companies or organizations. Address the cover letter to a specific person. Then follow up.
17. Target small to medium-sized companies. Most of the opportunities are coming from these organizations, not large corporations.
18. Consider contacting temporary agencies. Almost 40 percent of all temporary personnel are offered permanent positions. Today, a greater percentage of middle and upper management, as well as professionals, are working in temporary positions.
19. Use online services. America Online, Prodigy, and CompuServe have career services, employment data bases, bulletin boards, and online discussion and support groups, as well as access to the Internet. This is the wave of the future.
20. If you are working from home, be sure the room you are working from is inspiring, organized, and private. This is your space and it must motivate you!
21. If your plan is not working, meet with members of your support team and change the plan. You must remain flexible and adaptable to change.
22. Read and observe. Read magazines and newspapers and listen to CNBC, CNN, and so on. Notice which companies/organizations are on the move and contact them.

23. Set small, attainable weekly goals. Keep a weekly progress report on all your activities. Try to do a little more each week than the week before.

24. Stay active. Exercise and practice good nutrition. A job search requires energy. You must remain in superior physical and mental condition.

25. Volunteer. Help those less fortunate than you. What goes around comes around.

Index